One Day I'll See You

The remarkable autobiography of

Peter Jackson

Published by BIBLE MATTERS, 50 St Lawrence Avenue,
Worthing, West Sussex, BN14 7JG England.

Designed by Steve Carroll

Manufactured in India

ISBN 1-904636-06-3

Contents

AN APPRECIATION

WHEN I WAS ASKED TO WRITE an appreciation of Peter Jackson for his new book, words of the apostle Paul came immediately to mind. Speaking of his close friend and colleague Timothy, Paul said, "I have no one like him." Philippians 2:20 NIV

The apostle Paul had a wide circle of friends and co-workers, yet to Timothy he gave this remarkable accolade. Changing the phrasing slightly, I would apply the words to Peter Jackson, "I know of no one like him."

The story of Peter Jackson is a fascinating one. Blind before he was two, brought up in difficult circumstances and with more than his share of hard and sad issues to face, it is remarkable how such a positive and joyful character has emerged.

For many people, it is Peter's unique musical gift, which they appreciate the most. The range and creativity he displays on the piano is truly amazing, some would say awesome. I have witnessed firsthand people of all ages, with no particular interest in piano music; left lost for words after hearing him play.

On one occasion in the home of an accomplished pianist who owned his own classic grand piano, Peter was asked to play pieces by Beethoven, the Beatles, Charles Wesley and Fats Waller. After hearing these pieces played individually and blended together the host said, "Peter, you are a genius."

Of course, Peter does not think so but many are left struggling for adjectives to describe his playing and the effect it has on them. The most colourful and enthusiastic introduction I have ever heard of Peter's piano playing came from an Assistant Head, teaching in Larkhall Academy. Having been to a concert and hosted a previous visit and having bought tapes for his parents, he introduced Peter as "Simply the greatest piano player on the planet!" Well maybe that's going a bit too far, but you can see where he was coming from.

Others would identify Peter's irrepressible sense of humour as what they remember and appreciate about him. His vast stock of jokes, puns, limericks and quick wit brighten up any occasion. Yes, he is great fun to be with and his warm personality and broad beaming smile are remembered by many as leaving a powerful impression.

Those who have worked with Peter often refer to his capacity for work and his zeal for ministry, which are striking and incredible. Now past retirement age, he still travels the length and breadth of the country, usually alone and on public transport in a tireless, enthusiastic manner. Peter seems to thrive on ministry and in what he calls, "giving the enemy trouble." Having arranged several exhaustive programmes for him in Scotland his attitude is, "Let's get stuck in with all guns blazing." How he sustains his workload and maintains his motivation is something of a wonder and mystery. Yet there is still time for his family, his local church, and writing, composing and recording. It is also notable that the time Peter gives in each place must be quality time as he makes good friends wherever he goes.

All the above is wholly true and only a glimpse of the man, but the most significant feature and the key to Peter and his ministry is his spirituality; his personal relationship with Christ. To quote the apostle Paul again he said of himself,

"For me to live is Christ." Philippians 1:21 NIV

Although Peter would not compare himself to the apostle Paul, this attitude and ambition would accurately reflect Peter's own attitude and ambition. It is his own relationship with Christ, which I believe, is the secret of Peter's character and successful ministry.

Peter's ministry and character spill over out of who he is, rather than being the creation of a public persona. He is the same genuine Christ-centred person in private as on the public platform. Spirituality, like humility is never recognised by the possessor. It is in the nature of true spirituality to be more conscious of weakness and shortcomings.

Peter has a phenomenal memory and his well-stocked mind of Biblical truths not only equips him for his preaching ministry but also has helped to shape him into the person he is; a person most of us could learn from, as we can from any man or woman who walks closely with God.

I am sure you will find this book interesting; I know you will find it moving and I believe you will find it enriching to your soul. It is a joy and a privilege to commend this book and its author to you. If you know the man you will want to read the book, for it is true, "I know of no one else like him."

Stuart Wadsworth
Minister, Larkhall Baptist Church, Scotland
November 2002

Acknowledgments

I wish to express my sincere thanks to the following organizations for the invaluable help I have received in the writing of this book:

The Royal National Institute for the Blind, the Guide Dogs for the Blind Association, and the National Library for the Blind.

I am immensely grateful, too, to Mr. Clarence Brown of Birmingham who, due to his phenomenal memory corrected certain chronological details that were somewhat amiss in the first edition. Clarence was contemporary with me at school, and we were able to compare notes for the writing of this book.

Finally, to my great friend, Mrs. Helena Rogers who ghosted the original 'One day I'll see you'. Hers was the brilliant idea for the title, and she very kindly undertook the proof-reading of this edition. I shall always feel indebted to her for her literary ability, advice, and her unstinting support over many years.

Peter Jackson

Chapter One

Sounds of Loneliness

THE SHOCK, WHEN IT CAME, was essentially my mother's. The consultant looked gravely across his imposing desk and stated flatly: "I'm afraid this child will be blind for life."

At the age of sixteen months, I had been admitted to hospital for surgery on what was described as a 'tubercular gland' in my neck. The operation was successful, but an epidemic of measles broke out actually in the hospital, and in my weakened state I was a ready victim. The infection attacked and ravaged my optic nerves causing inflammation and swelling. The specialist explained to my mother that the measles had atrophied my optic nerves to the point of uselessness: my eyes would have to be removed.

Mum was at her wits' end. She was not only horrified at the tragedy of the situation, she had four children under seven years of age, and was four months pregnant with number five. How could she possibly manage the colossal added problem of a blind toddler?

To begin with there was never enough money. In 1933 jobs were scarce; however, my father was relatively fortunate. He had an interesting and unusual job. He was a goldbeater – that is – beating out gold leaf for books and other specialist items – but it hardly provided a wage to support a large family and his fairly frequent pint of beer.

My mother was obliged to work in order to help feed the family, and she somehow managed to look after babies at the same time. This new calamity, however, was just too much to bear. It was not only a disaster for me, but for my whole family.

Social welfare advised her.

"There is a solution, Mrs. Jackson," my distraught Mum was told. "The National Institute for the Blind has a home for blind babies at Leamington Spa. When Peter is two years old in a few months' time, he could leave home and go to live there. In this way he will receive the expert help which he needs to enable him to cope adequately in a sighted world."

It was not an easy decision for Mum. On the one hand she would seem to be abandoning her little boy into the hands of strangers. On the other, she had no idea how to teach me, let alone earn a living and look after the other children at the same time. She really had no choice, and with a heavy heart, my Mum and Dad agreed that I should go to Leamington: after all, it would only be some eighteen miles away.

My admission to 'Sunshine House' and institutional living, with the benefit of those who could teach me what I needed to know, did not impress me at the age of two. Being catapulted into blindness left me desperate for familiar sounds. I wanted to hear the voices of my brother and two sisters; the noise of my mother preparing food in the kitchen; the sound of horses' hooves and traffic on the Birmingham streets, and even my Dad's sometimes irritable shouts.

Instead, everything changed. I was taken to a strange place with unfamiliar sounds and new smells; there were unknown voices and different echoes in the rooms. Nothing was the same, and I was desolate.

Now and again my Mum came to visit me, and although my memories of this early part of my life are practically non-existent, I must have detected a change in our relationship that filled me with uneasiness as I clung to her. All I wanted was to be taken home to all the old sounds and familiar things. But she never came to take me home. Although she hugged me, my eager fingers felt the tears on her face, and I knew she would leave me again.

I could not judge the times between her visits – they were simply unexpected surprises. But the surprises became fewer and further between until they ceased when the authorities decreed that the home at Leamington Spa should undergo certain changes.

Much later I found out that a decision had been made that the more precocious babies, the 'brighter' ones should be moved to another 'Sunshine Home' at East Grinstead, Sussex.

My new home was a kind of rehabilitation centre, hundreds of miles from Birmingham, which made it virtually impossible for my parents to visit me.

The nurses at East Grinstead were so important to us. They supervised our washing every morning and evening; bathed us; cut our nails, taught us to undress and dress ourselves. They treated our cuts and bruises. Every evening they would remove our shell-like artificial eyes, and re-installed them each morning – in other words, they took the place of our mothers.

There was a rigid routine. We got up and went to bed at the same times; we ate together at the same time and always in the same place. We played in the playroom with the same toys, and walked or played outside on the same grass.

There were notable consistencies: for instance, on waking in the morning, there would be a rich tea biscuit lying beside our heads on the pillow – not a digestive or a shortbread – a rich tea – always a rich tea. It was unfailingly there, and we knew, when we awoke, that we could stretch out a hand and touch it. When we were dressed we would go to breakfast in the dining room. We learned how to eat properly, how to hold a cup, and eventually how to hold a spoon so that the food didn't slide off!

Correct eating habits were impressed upon us:

"No, Peter. You must hold your bread in your other hand – your left hand," the nurse insisted, "And your cup always stands on the right." She would grip the appropriate hand as she spoke.

Much of our day was spent in the playroom where there was a seesaw, a rocking horse, and a slide, which was known as the chute, as well as smaller toys. I remember a cylindrically shaped music box that fascinated me. I turned the handle, enthralled by the changing notes. There was a little birdcage with a toy canary inside. When it was wound up, it would trill a brilliant song. Other toys didn't mean as much to me – they were shapes to be felt, or fitted into each other they had nothing to 'say' to me!

On fine days, we could play out on the soft grass, and smell spring and summer flowers; feel the warm sunshine, and find cooling shade beneath big trees. I loved the smell of the wood, and liked to feel the rough texture of the bark and breathe in its scent.

There was one tree, however, which smelled better than any other – and this one was not outside, but actually indoors!

At Christmas-time a tree was put up in the playroom. What excitement there was on the day when the door was opened! We crowded into the playroom to be met by that pungent smell! It seemed to embody happiness, excitement, fun and an indefinable togetherness, for this was the time when Father Christmas had come to visit us.

We were all taught to believe strongly in Father Christmas. Hardly any of us really knew our real fathers, and if we did, they were by this time dim and misty figures.

Women were the dominant factors in our lives, men hardly figuring at all. So Father Christmas was a loving father of the kind none of us had known. He visited us rarely, of course, but when he came he always brought a present. We looked forward to his coming with a mixture of awe, fascination and love.

As each year passed by, Christmas took on an increasing significance, which could shatter our happiness if anything occurred to alter our expectations.

The days and months seemed to pass by slowly and somewhat monotonously, until the summer returned once again. This time of year brought a different kind of treat – a day at the seaside.

It was not only the new surroundings with its irresistible sounds and smells that made us almost delirious with delight. It began from the very moment we set out, because the journey was usually made in cars or a small bus.

Like all little boys, I loved cars. I liked to hear the noise of the engine; the way it changed pitch as it got up speed. I loved the seats with their leathery feel and smell, their interesting creases and shiny patches. The smell of petrol became synonymous with joyful anticipation. Whenever we could, we squashed together on the back seat, savouring every moment to the full.

The seaside was full of new scents and sounds. The fishy smell of the ozone, the sound of the breeze as it made the windbreaks flap, and sometimes nearly took our breath away. There were such a variety of sounds – children laughing and shouting to one another; the 'thwack' of a ball hit by a bat or caught in the hand. Even the ever-present coming and going of the traffic on the nearby road somehow seemed gloriously different from the sound it made at home.

But best of all, we loved to listen to the sound we could not hear anywhere else – the noise of the sea. Sometimes the waves were small, and we could paddle about with the water splashing to our knees. But sometimes the waves came crashing on to the sand so that it felt as though we might be pushed over if an unexpectedly big wave came. This was all part of the excitement! We would listen to the sand being dragged back into the sea, and hear a coming wave as it seemed to hover for a moment before crashing on to the beach. We would try to get out of its way, loving the fear of being caught by it with screams, laughter and shouts to each other!

Tired out, we would sit on the sand with our bucket and spade making sand pies. How we loved the feel of the sand! On one part of the beach it would be warm and dry. We ran the smooth grains from one hand to the other; but nearer the sea it was damp, and we made rows of pies, which we could smash down with our feet, screaming with delight and sheer pleasure.

Even the rain couldn't dampen our spirits on one of these rare days out. So long as we could be kept dry, we could listen to the raindrops pattering on the road, or even more loudly on the umbrella over our heads. But if there should be a storm with thunder...! How I loved the thunder! The distant rumbling that built up, sometimes slowly, then to recede disappointingly to nothing: Then to begin a few minutes later. But there were times when it went on and on more urgently until it gave way to a rolling crash, which made me gasp with wonder! It was a glorious, awesome noise, and I clapped my hands joyfully every time!

One day, when I was four years old, we had an outing, which was unique, and must have been one of those times when the staff were more nervous than we were.

Representatives from East Grinstead Sunshine Home were invited to the Mansion House in London to have tea with the Lord Mayor. We could not have understood then that it was to include a presentation to the National Institute for the Blind in recognition of their work. (This was before it had its 'Royal' patronage).

We were to be on our best behaviour. Excitement was mixed with apprehension as we were threatened with dire punishments if we forgot our manners.

"Sit still!" Said the nurses. "Keep quiet, and do as you are told!"

The journey was undertaken with suppressed exhilaration, which gradually gave way to nervousness as the lower, more intense roar of the London traffic met our ears. By the time we reached our destination, we were struck dumb with the enormity of the occasion, and our good behaviour was assured.

We climbed the steps of the Mansion House, conscious of the many people rushing past us who all seemed to be going to important appointments like us. We were ushered into a large hall where we were to have tea. I could tell that there were a lot of people present, all talking in hushed excitement. I had never been in a room as large as this one, and I could not fully understand the vastness of the place until I put the memories into context as I grew older.

Even the food was different. As this was tea, I could confidently and delicately explore the contents of my plate as I had been taught. This was not the bread and jam that we were used to. It was certainly bread – I could tell that by its texture, of course. The sandwiches were neatly cut into an unusual shape. Much later I was able to define it as having been triangular in form. At the time, however, I was overcome by the novelty of such a thing! It was all very wonderful and completely overwhelming!

On the return journey to East Grinstead, most of us were overtaken by tiredness and sleep, but there cannot have been one child who would forget the wonder of the day that we spent at the Mansion House with the Lord Mayor of London!

Back in our usual routine I had to be content with more mundane pleasures, although there was always one thing that attracted my attention. I seem to remember that in one of the corridors upstairs an extension speaker had been placed through which we could hear the radio. In those days it was called 'the wireless'. It was a source of delight to all of us. Many wonderful sounds came from it, but some stirred my imagination more than others.

It was a box of crackles, voices, and music – totally fascinating! At that time, one sound attracted me more than any other. Between programmes there would occasionally be an interlude during which the sound of Bow bells were played. This was no simple affair like the gong at Leamington Sunshine Home of my earliest musical memory. No, this was a glorious cacophony of interwoven sounds, which held me spellbound until it finally died away, and the next programme began. I would shut out the unwelcome new sound, trying to hold onto the beautiful melody of the bells for as long as possible. How I wished that they would play them more often!

The world of a toddler revolves largely around himself. This is particularly true of the blind toddler who is unable to interact with his peers by sight. Add to this the fact that we were at first too small to talk very much to one another, and the world becomes a limited, rather introverted circle, punctuated by the necessary directions from the staff. Discipline was seen as necessary to a child's upbringing, and was rigorously applied. Occasionally we would fall out with one another, and I did resort once in frustration to smacking one of the other children. The smack was soundly returned by the nurse, and I responded to the injustice by sitting on the floor and screaming uncontrollably.

My memory of those days, and of the other children is extremely hazy. As I later came up through school and college, I was surprised to meet some of them who remembered me. We were too immature to form binding and meaningful friendships at East Grinstead – probably we were too intent on personal survival in what then sometimes seemed a hostile world.

Even my memories of the staff are vague, but there were those who stood out among the rest. Miss Clark was one of them. Her dedicated attention to her charges was never forgotten by any of them.

Another much loved member of staff was Matron Johnson; she was devoted to us children. Her gentle touch and caring manner left lasting memories in all our minds.

One day – shortly after our memorable visit to the Mansion House – she tried to prepare me for the inevitable. With her hand placed lightly on my head, in a sign of warmth that would be achieved by sighted people with a look, she said gently:

"You're going to leave us soon, Peter."

I didn't understand straight away, but instinctively sensed a feeling of dismay.

"You're going to the big school."

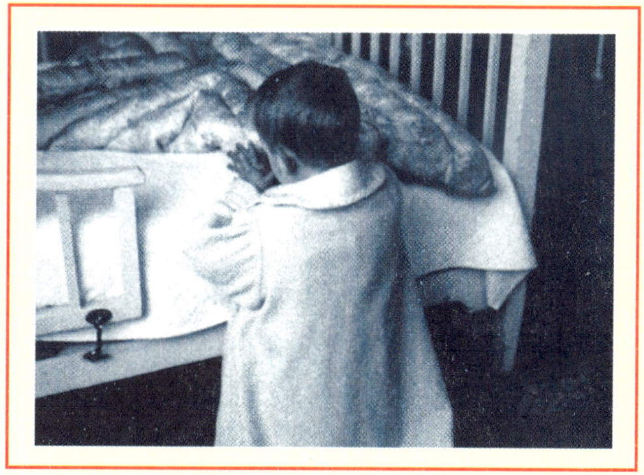

My dismay now turned to fear: I was to move again! I didn't want to leave Sunshine Home, the nurses, matron, everything that had belonged to my early, formative years. Surely my nurses wouldn't abandon me – I thought that they loved me...My Mum and Dad had virtually abandoned me – I rarely saw Mum now, and I couldn't bear to leave my replacement family and begin all over again.

"I don't want to go!" I protested in desperation.

"I'm afraid that you must," replied Matron firmly, but kindly.

But my mother made that long, arduous journey from Birmingham, and was with me on the dreaded day of my departure. She was by now almost a stranger, yet I was glad to have her with me even though I was filled with foreboding. I clung to her hand as the goodbyes were said. I felt that I was being let down once more by those I loved most.

In recounting this episode to me much later, my mother told me that Matron had tears in her eyes as she stood at the door to wave farewell.

At five years old there was to be a whole new hurdle to overcome in my young life.

Chapter Two

A Harsh World

On Thursday, 3rd September 1936, I left the 'Sunshine Home' at East Grinstead for 'The Big School'. In the company of one of the nurses, and my mum, we began the long journey to the Birmingham Royal Institute for the Blind at Harborne – or 'The BRIB' as it came to be called.

Conversation was limited as we went to London by car, boarded a train to Birmingham, resuming the journey by taxi to Harborne. I was sullen; past tears. At almost five years old I was learning that life never seemed to stay happy. Just when you thought it was turning out right, something happened to change it all again.

My heart thumped in fear as I clung to my mum's hand. We got out of the taxi and stepped onto the gravel drive. Our feet crunched their way reluctantly to the front door of the school...we were admitted.

My mother and I were asked to wait a few moments in a kind of vestibule. We sat on a polished wooden bench, and my nurse left us for a few minutes.

By now I knew that the resonant sounds of feet and voices meant that the place was very large. I leaned closer to my mum. There was a strange smell that pervaded the air that I later came to understand to be a combination of carbolic, floor polish and stale stew! It was not the smell of 'Sunshine Home'.

My nurse returned, and I was conscious of so much rushing about. Urgent footsteps told me that everyone was in a hurry. People pushed by us, or we had to move out of the way to let them pass as we were ushered to the office to be introduced to the Matron.

When the formalities were over, my nurse said "Goodbye"; my mother gave me a hug and a kiss and said: "You'll be all right now!" They left in the taxi, which was still waiting on the drive. Once more I felt abandoned.

Here, maids and teachers comprised the staff, and I was taken by a maid to the dining room, given food and drink, and then whisked to the bathroom upstairs where I was bathed and put to bed. The maid tried to comfort me as she saw my distress, but to no avail. I lay awake for what seemed to be hours, listening to the sounds outside the window. "Would the taxi come to take me back to East Grinstead?" I desperately willed it to come, listening in vain to the sound of its wheels on the drive.

Other children came into the dormitory, chattering amongst themselves, and were being supervised by a maid as they undressed and got into bed. They didn't notice me as I tried to check my tears with my head beneath the bedclothes.

As the other boys settled down and the night drew on, I heard strange and frightening sounds in this place. Even the wind seemed to be trying to get away as it whistled through the ventilators. I lay there listening to its two–toned howl, eerie and ghostly in the silence of the night, and the breathing of the other boys. The ventilators tried to stop the wind's escape. I noticed a 'click' and a low moan as the wind tried to force its way through. Then, as it tried harder, the pitch rose up in an agonizing wail until there was another 'click' and the wind gave up in order to build strength for another try. It seemed to voice all the desolation and abandonment I was feeling.

I began to imagine it as a friend sympathising and putting into sound what I could not vocalise myself. As time went by, I was to build up a strong picture of what I thought the sky was like, and what was going on outside. I used to dream that I had friends in the sky who would look down on me and share in my desolation. I charted a mental picture of the rise and fall of the wind. In September it began to sound more urgent, but in the spring it would be more capricious. The impressions grew and became very vivid and real.

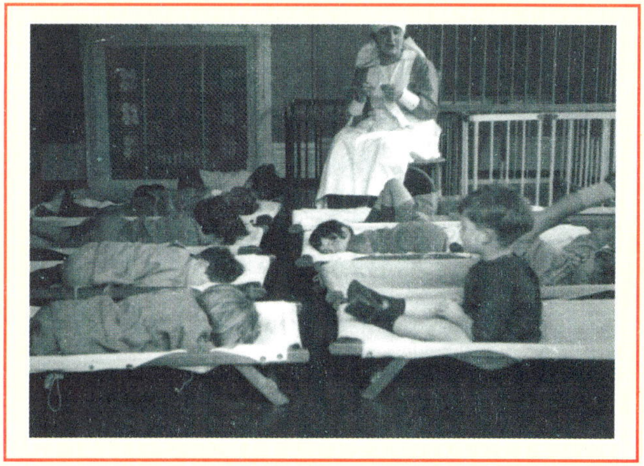

Now and again on that first night I heard another strange noise in the dormitory. There would be a scuffling sound, followed by a careful scraping noise. It happened several times, and eventually I realised that it was the sound of the children getting out of bed and pulling their chamber pots out from under the beds!

In the morning I was to discover that our clothes were kept in a basket alongside the chamber pot. Each night we were expected to fold our clothes neatly, place them in the basket, ready for the morning.

A maid got us up, supervised our dressing, and then escorted us downstairs to the washroom. Here there was a long, trough-like sink with swinging bowls. After washing, you simply tipped the bowl of water into the trough for disposal. We all had our own number, which we were taught to read. We used the same bowl each morning and evening, and we knew which bowl was ours by our number on the shelf above. My number was 22, and was taped to all my clothes. The boys had even numbers, the girls odd numbers.

After breakfast, it was time to make my bed. It had to be done precisely. A maid instructed me: "You must put this sheet on first," she said, and then she directed my hands to the bottom of the bed.

"It has to tuck in like this." She yanked my small frame to feel the smart, mitred corners. I could hardly lift the mattress to force the sheet underneath. It was a very complicated feat to produce those impeccable 'hospital' corners. I could not understand why they were so important.

"Now here are two blankets," said the maid: "They are grey, and go on to your top sheet." These blankets had a smooth feel, and after this little lesson, I mentally joined 'grey' with 'smooth'. The difficult mitred corners were insisted on, once more. Then she made me feel another blanket. It was much rougher in texture.

"This brown one must go on top of the others."

I thought 'brown' must be a horrid colour to feel like that. Lastly, a counterpane covered everything else.

This was the beginning of my 'tactile' understanding of colour. 'brown' signified a rough feel, with 'grey' meaning Smooth. Ever afterwards, colours began to take on different 'feels'.

I associated red with hot, because – when I had done something wrong and was found out – I was told by the sighted children: "Oo, you haven't half gone red!"

When I was eventually to get to know my family again, my mum would instruct me not to touch the red-hot poker in the fireplace, so it became synonymous with danger.

There was also a box on the hearth containing coal for the fire. I was told not to touch the coal either, because it would make my hands black and dirty. So black became a forbidding colour. This was reinforced because the night was black, and I suffered my worst fears at night.

Blue had two different aspects. When someone was pinched with cold, they were said to look 'blue with cold'. It could also be a 'happy' colour, because when the sun was shining, the sky was blue. I heard people say that the day might turn out fine "If there was enough blue to make a sailor a pair of trousers!"

I began to wish I knew what made the weather fine and the sky blue; or what caused my friend the wind to blow.

Most of the time I liked green. It was the colour of the grass where, at East Grinstead we played in good weather. I thought of green, therefore, as restful. But it did have its sinister side too. The mould on bad food was apparently green, so it could not be entirely trusted as a colour.

There wasn't to be much sitting on grass here – only the girls had grass to play on, the boys were restricted to the tarmac area. A line of vertical railings, with a gate that was normally kept locked, separated the playgrounds.

There were, however, some large playthings available to us. A pedal train on lines went round the entire perimeter of the school grounds. We liked to see how fast we could make it go.

At the bottom of the boys' playground was the toy shed, with a scooter, a pedal car, tricycles, and a flat-bottomed conveyance known as the coaster.

At the time of my arrival at the school, the finishing touches were being made to what was known as the 'new part'. This was an extension to the playground, with a new innovation – a sand pit. I was not surprised when I learned that this popular playing place had been the idea of my favourite teacher, Miss Richardson. She seemed to have a better understanding of our needs than some of the other staff. I came to depend upon her a great deal.

At East Grinstead the staff had tried to make up to us for the lack of home life and parental love. Now, I began to realise that things were going to be different. I was going to have to learn to be more independent, more self-sufficient.

Breakfast was regulated and varied very little. Porridge and bread and hot milk alternated from day to day throughout the week. Maids would lay the breakfast table the night before with basins. When it was to be bread and milk tomorrow, the bread would be broken up in the basins, to be left overnight. When Grace had been said, maids would come round with jugs of hot milk to be poured on the bread – no sugar – just plain crusts in milk! In order to get the last dregs of milk out of the basin, we were actually encouraged to put down our spoons on the table, take hold of the basin and drink! (It's something I'm tempted to do even now when

I'm finishing my cereal, but only when I'm strictly at home.)

Following this, there might be a half slice of bread with marmite or virol. Sometimes on Sundays, there would be cornflakes with warm milk, which we used to call 'post toastiest' for no apparent reason!

I soon got to know the maids that were there to help us at the table. One whom I remember well was named Dora. Her first task was to tie on our bibs, or feeders as they were called. Even now I remember her cold fingers on the back of my neck as she tied the little bow.

At the end of the meal, monitors would collect up all the feeders, and any that were too soiled to be used again would be sent to the laundry. The rest remained to be handed out at the next meal – not necessarily to the same child!

Dinner in the middle of the day was the meal I came to hate most of all. It usually consisted of meat, potatoes and vegetables, but to my undeveloped taste it was a most uninviting, uninspiring meal. I loathed onions, turnips, swedes, and just about tolerated cabbage. School stew was worst of all! It might have been just as well that most of us couldn't see what it looked like. The trouble was, you didn't know what you were picking up with your spoon until the wretched stuff was virtually in your mouth!

Puddings were not much better. The range of puddings consisted of rice – sometimes with sultanas – tapioca, sago, macaroni, and steamed suet puddings, sometimes with marmalade, jam, or currants to make 'spotted dick'. The suet puddings were my favourite, and served to fill me up somewhat.

Tea consisted of one half slice of brown bread-and-butter which was already on our plates. When we wanted more bread, we would have to put up our hand; then a maid would come and provide half a slice of white bread, but we could only do this twice. There seemed to be an absolute limit of three half slices. Sometimes there would be honey or jam, but only on Sundays would there be any cake.

Some children received food parcels from home, but they were not allowed to keep the food to themselves. It had to be shared out with everyone – one cake would be divided between fifty-six children!

We were obliged to eat everything we were given. Most of the time we did – no matter how much we disliked it, because there was not usually enough to fill us. Should any child refuse to eat, apart from being genuinely unwell, they would be punished.

Punishments were handed out for a variety of misdemeanours. A common punishment was to be 'off extras' for a week or more, depending on the seriousness of the misdemeanour. This meant that a child could be denied something sent from home – even a birthday cake! This was a major catastrophe; home was our link with love, and to be denied that slender, almost tangible bond, was a severing of a vital lifeline.

Corporal punishment was adhered to strongly by some of the staff as a necessary part of a child's upbringing. (As someone put it: "The board of education was applied to the seat of learning!") It would be meted out to boys and girls alike either with a large hairbrush, or we could be whipped with a strip of wood kept for the purpose. All of this would, of course, be applied to bare bottoms.

It was not only offences like rudeness to staff, or fights with other children that brought retribution. We could incur punishments for not drying our hands or behind our ears properly, and jumping up and down on beds was also considered cause for a beating.

There were also mistakes, which we were unable to anticipate. One of these I learned one day when I was walking behind Matron in the school grounds. I misjudged the distance that was between us, and stepped on her heel. She turned on me angrily:

"You stupid child!" she shouted, "You need to learn to be more careful! Go straight to bed!"

In terror, I knew what this would mean. I would have to put on my nightgown, (we were not allowed to wear pyjamas), and I would wait, shaking in fear for the inevitable. Some time later, at a convenient time for the supervisor involved, she would be heard coming step by step up the stairs, nearer and nearer. She would march to the bed, rip down the bedclothes, and grab the offender by the ankles, thus holding him or her almost upside down so that the night-gown fell down over the head, exposing a bare bottom. Then we would be beaten with the hairbrush, finally to be left sobbing and bruised.

Another occasion when I incurred a beating was the result of a piece of mischief in the playground. In a foolish moment, I saw that some fun could be had by placing a stone in a strategic place on the train track. I thought it would be great to hear the train topple over when it hit the stone.

In mounting excitement, I listened to the rumbling sound as the train moved closer, bringing the unsuspecting driver towards where I had placed the stone. I giggled in delight as it went over, but my laughter vanished instantly when I was grabbed roughly by my teacher, Miss Richardson. With mounting dread I realised that I was going to get a whipping. My teacher dragged me into the boys' boot room and ordered:

"Take your trousers down." I heard the sound of the whipping wood being picked up; my heart stopped with fear.

"I don't want to," I murmured desperately, but she forced me to comply. The whipping was mercilessly applied.

The combination of loneliness, fear and desolation took its toll. We had to do as we were told during the day, but at night, after we had gone to sleep, our minds could not be ordered. Mine signalled its disturbance by causing my body to sleep walk. Many times I was found wandering about the school fast asleep. At that time, too, I was afflicted with fantasies and nightmares: I dreaded the night time.

There was to be a pleasant change coming into my life, however. Whilst I was being bathed by one of the maids, she told me about it.

"There's a new boy coming to school," she said as she wrapped me in the bath towel.

This was interesting news. It would be nice to meet someone different.

"What's his name?" I asked.

"Joseph," the maid replied kindly, rubbing my legs.

Miss Richardson had told us Bible stories, and the name rang a bell.

"Has he got a coat of many colours?" I ventured, half in question and half thoughtfully.

"No", she said, "Not that one; this boy is called Joseph Hayward," as she helped me into my nightgown.

We became inseparable. Joseph was partially sighted, and became one of my first real friends. Since he was very insecure, he was glad to have a companion too. It was to be the start of a life-long friendship.

I began to develop other friendships, of course. Leslie Hall came to sit by me at table on his first day at school. I knew how he was feeling; it was a lost, uncomprehending feeling. Leslie's home was way out in the country, near the Welsh border.

There was Michael Lloyd from Bromsgrove whose birthday coincided with mine. He was mad about tractors! Every Saturday, he would receive a parcel from home with a Farmhouse cake: it came unfailingly for years!

But Joe (as he was later to be called) is the friend that has stuck closer to me than a brother!

Chapter Three

Shaping the Future

As well as maids and supervisors, the staff comprised four teachers at Harborne. There was averagely some fifty-six children, with classes never too big, and dependent on the learning needs of the children. Miss Morley and Miss Williams mainly looked after the partially sighted boys and girls; Miss Janus taught the 'Advanced' braillists. Miss Richardson's responsibility was to get the blind children started on learning Braille. I found myself, therefore, in her class.

Miss Morley had the unhappy knack of instilling fear in us children. I can only think in retrospect that she did not seem to be able to identify with what it meant for us young children to be blind.

Although there was very little which stopped us from doing what we wanted to do, we were all rather obliged to take a little care when moving about. Part of our training consisted in learning to be reasonably cautious.

Miss Morley, however, was a stranger to caution. She had a deep, sonorous voice, charging from place to place like a hurricane: chivvying and bellowing at everyone, pushing those who did not move fast enough.

I didn't really get to know Miss Janus very well. But – like Miss Williams – she was kind and caring. It's strange how memory seems to retain the more dramatic impressions like those of Miss Morley.

I had a good deal more contact with Miss Williams later on in my childhood. She was from North Wales, and was keen to teach us how to count to ten in Welsh. She would read stories to us, and at the end of term would ask us what favourite story we would like her to read as a treat. Unanimously we chanted: "Bedd Gelert! Bedd Gelert!"

"Why," she would ask, "You cry every time you hear it."

This was the legend of the hunter in Snowdonia who left his faithful dog Gelert in charge of the cottage and baby. There were wolves in that part of Wales hundreds of years ago, but the hunter was confident in his dog's ability to look after things successfully.

A hungry wolf came to the cottage; managed to gain entrance, and Gelert fought with the beast, eventually overcoming him. After blood had been shed, the injured wolf slunk away into the forest. In the struggle the baby's cradle had been tipped over, but the baby was hidden safely underneath the fallen cradle.

The hunter came back, and found the blood-strewn floor of the cottage, and no baby. Gelert was, as usual, so pleased to welcome his master home: but he suspected the worst, and in a frenzied panic rent vengeance on poor Gelert, plunging a knife into his heart.

Gelert sank to the ground, licking his master's hand, and then died.

His master then noticed the upturned cradle, picked it up, and there was the baby, safe and unharmed. It was only then that the hunter realised that Gelert had been faithful, and that he – by his own hand – had killed him

We loved that story, and we loved Miss Williams for recounting it again and again.

But Miss Richardson was my favourite teacher in spite of the fact that she was the principle exponent of corporal punishment. My earliest experiences of a whipping were at her hands. It seems difficult to equate this violent behaviour with the gentle, caring side of her character, which, thankfully, we experienced more often. Someone once said, "Anger is the reverse side of the coin of love". This perhaps describes – or to some degree explains – the anomaly.

Most of the time she was the soul of consideration, fully understanding the problems we faced both as children and in our sightlessness. She referred affectionately to us, the youngest children in the school, as "little ones".

"Forward, little ones!" she would say as we filed out of Assembly in our straight, orderly line. "Come along, little ones", as we came back in from play.

Whenever we went for supervised walks outside the school, it had to be in crocodile formation – two by two, and holding hands. Joseph and I would always try to stay together, and before long we had established a routine, which was broken only on Sundays, when we had to go to church. Church, therefore, became doubly trying. It was not only incredibly boring, but it separated me from Joseph. He did not have to go like most of us, because apparently he was something called a 'Catholic', and that meant he escaped our weekly ritual. I wished I were a 'Catholic' too: mind you, I hadn't realised, then, that 'Catholic' went to church – Joseph just didn't talk about that.

I didn't enjoy the services, which were dull and unintelligible to us children. The vicar droned on and on, oblivious to the fact that none of us understood, and indeed he never ever referred to our existence. As far as I remember, there was never a children's story or a song that we could sing and understand. We might as well not have been there.

Miss Richardson did her best to make up for the gap in our Christian education. She played the piano, and her morning assemblies were times that I looked forward to most. She taught us the songs we loved to sing, and were to remember ever afterwards. We sang with gusto:

Wide, wide as the ocean,
High as the heavens above;
Deep, deep as the deepest sea
Is my Saviour's love!

Then there was "In my heart there rings a melody", and "He did not come to judge the world, He did not come to blame".

One of my favourites was the less grammatical, but very beautiful:

Jesus, the Saviour is of boys and girls –
None other ever could save boys and girls.

I think this was my first emotional experience brought about by pure melody. I felt a surge of joy every time we sang it.

They were all lovely, and we built up a veritable wealth of choruses and hymns that would never be forgotten, even though many children might not be churchgoers when they grew up.

But the learning and singing of the songs was not my only enjoyment during these times of assembly. I was just as interested in the way Miss Richardson played the piano. It began from the moment we went into the new hall, which also served as a gym and playroom. She would get the key and turn it in the lock to open up the piano. I listened to the 'Click' of the turning lock and the 'tap' as the lid came into contact with the front of the piano. I waited in eager anticipation.

Lovely sounds would come from the instrument, which I longed to try to imitate. But I had a long time to wait before that could happen.

My friend Joseph was a very insecure little boy. He had suffered the removal from his family like the rest of us. Such insecurity affected us all in different ways. I had nightmares, and sleep walked; Joseph was a bed-wetter. There was only one way to deal with bed-wetters in our school. In anguish for Joseph, I knew what would happen when the maid came in one morning to get us all up. Having inspected his bed, she reported the incident to the supervisor on duty. What happened then is almost unbelievable!

She shouted at him angrily: "You dirty boy! How many times

must I tell you not to do that?" She caught hold of his arm with one hand, and the large hard-backed hairbrush with the other. We were all ushered out of the dormitory, and had to leave Joseph to his fate.

Later that day, he told me how he had been beaten yet again. This seemed to be the routine way of supposedly curing insecurity problems. It would be Joseph's turn to sympathize with me some time later.

After tea, one evening, most of the boys and girls were in the new playroom. I was about to join them. I came along the corridor, which sloped down to the playroom; on the left of the entrance stood a foam fire extinguisher which we were frequently told to "Leave alone". I was fascinated by this strange object and wondered how it worked.

On this occasion I was overcome by investigative desire: I was gingerly feeling its round wheel-like thing at the top; its dangling hose and fat cylinder.

"Leave that alone – what have I told you!" shouted the supervisor peremptorily. To implement her command, she pulled me sharply away. At that time of the year, all the boys wore jerseys, and the sleeve of mine caught round the top of the extinguisher, bringing it crashing to the floor! It was at that moment that I discovered what effect the extinguisher would have in the event of a fire!

The pent-up foam suddenly and dramatically realised its full potential. It suddenly went off, showering children and playroom with a strong force of spreading foam reaching right to the limits of the room! Mayhem followed. Children screamed and gasped as the foam covered them from head to foot. People came rushing in to see what had happened. The whole episode was so confusing – the rushing sound of escaping foam, the screams, and even laughter, of some of the children; the shouts of the staff that desperately tried to stop the flow. The extinguisher, however, could not be checked, but continued remorselessly until it was empty. The devastation was complete – and I was the cause!

I was dragged away, sent to bed to await a beating which I remember to this day. I was 'off extras' for a fortnight!

Our lessons consisted mainly of three subjects. Learning Braille formed the majority of the day's work; arithmetic came next, and as a close third, Scripture. After the other classes had left the hall, we heard Miss Richardson say, "Forward, little ones!" We knew it was our turn, then, to follow each other in a single line, through the door and up the sloping corridor, and into our classroom. We made our way to our desks, and stood quietly behind our chairs.

"Quiet now! Hand together and close your eyes!" We did so, obediently, and the irony of the situation didn't occur to me until many years later. What was the point in commanding blind children to close their eyes? But thinking about it now, I imagine it was all part of engendering an attitude and atmosphere of quiet reverence in God's presence. Our hands were not allowed to wander, and even the act of a blind person keeping their eyes closed demands a certain amount of concentration.

Then she would pray reverently to her Heavenly Father, talking to him as though she knew him intimately. Many of us had a very hazy recollection of our fathers; some of us had no recollection at all, so we listened to her words with fascination. She prayed for the boys and girls who were in sick bay; for our parents and loved ones, and then she would pray for the lessons of the day.

Years later when I was to recount this memory, I would add that – in my case – I felt that particular prayer was much needed: my arithmetic was always 'mental', my fractions 'vulgar', and my decimals 'pointless'!...

Literacy was regarded as being of the utmost importance. Braille is a method of reading which uses raised dots in groups of up to six to form different patterns. Each letter is a different permutation of the dots, and so we had to learn the shape of each letter.

Later we were to learn that whole words could be formed by setting the patterns side by side, or that the process could be abbreviated by using one pattern for a whole word. There are sixty-three possible permutations, so that means there are twenty-six for the letters of the alphabet, and thirty-seven for punctuation and word contractions.

First we were introduced to a wooden board with holes in it, into which pegs could be placed in the appropriate patterns. It took most of us about three years to become reasonably fluent. I grew to love reading, and particularly enjoyed Aesop's Fables and Enid Blighton stories.

We were encouraged to read aloud in Scripture lessons, passing the volume to our neighbour with a finger held on the spot to show where we had got to. Miss Richardson, however, would sometimes tell us the Bible stories, keeping us interested with her vivid descriptions of the amazing adventures from its pages. She also encouraged us to memorize verses from the Bible, giving prizes to those who learned the most. I became the proud possessor of Braille copies of the Gospels of Matthew and Luke, which I treasured for years.

Many of us came from poor families, and some of the boys and girls didn't know their families at all. During the holidays, whilst most of us went home, these other children were fostered out. None of us had very much in the way of possessions, and if our birthday happened to fall in the school term, we were anxious to know if the folks at home had remembered. In my case, sometimes they did, and other times they couldn't afford to send a present.

On my seventh birthday, my mum sent me a bar of Lux soap as a present! I was allowed to unwrap the parcel, and press the sweet-scented soap to my nose. It was so different from the square lumps of carbolic soap we had to wash with, or the medicated soap with which our hair was washed. I was not permitted to keep my soap: Matron decided there was a better use for it elsewhere.

But my teacher did what little she could to make us happy. She could not openly give us presents, but as I got dressed on that birthday morning, I discovered something hidden amongst the clothes in the basket under my bed. I felt the unexpected shape and realised that it was a little mouth organ. Mouth organs were familiar playthings to us, but this one was for me, personally, and I knew it must have come from Miss Richardson. I was overjoyed, and soon learned to play it tolerably well. It became a source of delight to me for a long time.

Good class work was rewarded by her too. She always kept a jar of Dolly Mixture sweets to hand. If we did well, off would come the lid of the jar, and she would put a sweet or two into our open hand. Those little treats were highly prized, and we worked hard – not only for the reward – but because we had respect and affection for our teacher.

We learned our arithmetic by means of an ingenious device called a 'Taylor frame', but which we knew as a 'type board'. It was constructed in such a way to enable us to do all kinds of arithmetical calculations in 'Maths code'.

It was a metal frame with a number of octagonal holes in it set on a wooden backing board. A tray on the right hand side held the 'type': these were small blocks of metal which had a bar projection at one end, and two points at the other. They were inserted into the octagonal holes, the numbers being represented depending upon the positioning of the 'type'. It had to be turned clockwise – the bar end rotating to produce numbers around the compass points starting with 1,

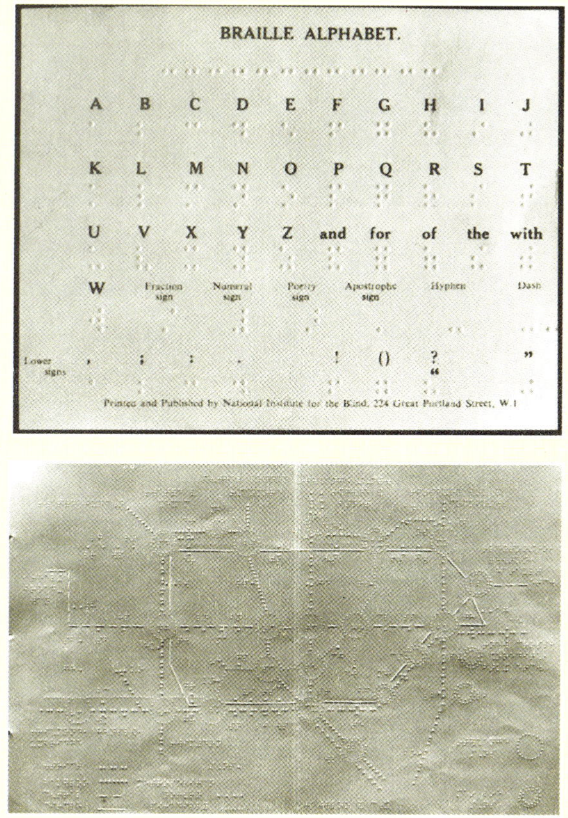

The Braille alphabet above, with a Braille map of the London Underground below.

(South–West) 2, (West) 3, (North–West) 4, (North) and so on until we got to 8, (South). The figure 9 was represented by lifting the type out of the hole and replacing it with the two points uppermost at the Southwest point of the compass. 0 was West, and other mathematical symbols were obtained by rotating at different angles.

The nine and the nought, together with the arithmetical signs, were produced by turning the 'type' over so that the two points could be placed into the octagonal holes, and the process repeated.

This method of teaching was eventually replaced because the type was made of lead and the children would absent-mindedly suck it! Teachers and pupils were quite unaware of the dangers in those days of lead poisoning, and we shall probably never know what problems might well have been caused.

The advent of the age of seven was a big year for us. For one thing, we were allowed to join the 'second lot' in terms of our going to bed. Another was the prospect of being admitted to the 'Cubs' pack. Even at this young age we were conscious of the prestige and honour of belonging to this youngest section of the Boy Scout Movement. We wore our special jerseys with pride.

Each week we would go to the meeting in the nearby Scout hut, (known as headquarters) and take part in as many of the activities as possible.

A rare and special treat was to be able to play, under careful supervision, with the model railway that ran around the walls of the hut. There was always a great rivalry for a turn.

A highlight of the time we spent in the Cubs occurred when the 78th Birmingham troop to which we belonged was singled out for a particular honour. As far as we knew, we were the only troop in the country – and perhaps the world – specifically for blind boys, and we learned with delight that the leader and founder of the Boy Scout Movement Lord Baden-Powell was coming in person to visit us.

It was a day to be remembered! We waited, and listened in awe as the great man himself arrived by car, and was met by local dignitaries. We boys were meticulously smart in our uniforms: neckerchiefs in place, woggles positioned correctly, polished shoes, etc.

Speeches were made, explanations given, but when they were over, the fun was really to begin. Lord Baden-Powell undoubtedly had a gift for knowing what boys would enjoy, for instead of 'standing on ceremony', he got down amongst us all and played the games we loved. He laughed and joked, joined in everything, and even allowed us to ride on his back! I'm not sure we altogether realised that this man was a world figure, but he gave us a truly wonderful day of fun.

I have very fond memories of one of the members of staff who was not one of the teachers; Miss Penny was a supervisor who was more involved in out-of-school time and activities. She was a favourite with the children, and had special 'pet names' for a number of us. Mine was 'Peterkin'. (Much later in reading of books, I came across 'Peterkin' in R. M. Ballantyne's Coral Island.) I was never afraid to hear her calling me, since she did not have the hard, formal tone which some of the others had. She was kind and thoughtful, and made little caring gestures like slipping a fluffy toy dog or bunny rabbit into our beds with us at night. To children who were deprived of a loving parent, and regimented in most of what they did, small touches such as this meant a great deal to us.

I remember at this time having a fascination to know the ages of grown–ups. I don't think I was unique in this, but I remember asking Miss Penny how old she was. "As old as my tongue," she said, "and a little bit older than my teeth."

By now, we had shortened Joseph's name to Joe, and even at times, Joey. He was for the most part in Miss Williams' class, and was developing rapidly into being a good reader.

But as before mentioned, I had other friends too, and Les Hall was one of these. Les had cataracts, but had retained a fair measure of sight. I well remember haring around the place like a couple of mad things. I would hang on to his shoulder as a necessary safety precaution.

There were, in the toy cupboard in the playroom two donkeys on wheels. Whenever we could, we would commandeer them and race each other across the room, trying to avoid obstacles and children.

I gave names to the donkeys, Marley, who was very worn and actually developing bald patches; and Hygiene, who felt soft and clean – obviously a much newer toy. Les and I spent many a happy hour together, and our friendship lasted right into adolescence before our careers took us in different directions.

The toys in the playroom were given to the 'BRIB' by friends and well-wishers. There were a variety of toys there: building bricks, at least one humming-top, Meccano, furry animals and dolls for the girls.

We would play with these toys when the weather wasn't suitable for playing in the playground with the bigger toys after dinner.

Once each year the playroom was the scene of a special get-together. It was called 'Dolls and mouth organs' day, – dolls for a girl – or a mouth organ for a boy. During a three-year stay at the school, it would be possible, if you were careful, to acquire a set of three dolls or three mouth organs! No one seemed to know why this day had come about, and no one knew either why only dolls and mouth organs were given. It was simply the done thing, and there was no more to be said!

Another treat I well remember was an outing to Dudley zoo. The partially sighted children like Joe had lots to see, and he would describe the animals that I could only hear – but I loved it all! The chattering monkeys, the queer cough of the sea lions, and the grunts of other animals made it a special day. Memory forbids me to be clear as to whether I won as a prize, or was given as a present a kazoo. Singing into this tiny instrument, which contained a film of thin paper made a kind of rasping noise.

I'm not sure whether it was because of the lack of home comforts, or even an attempt to establish one's own identity in the larger school family; either way, I became acquisitive, and to a degree, still am. But I have noticed this tendency with others, my fellow blind people. Even as a child, I loved new things: especially new shoes with their leathery smell and extra shiny surface. The only thing I now possess that was given to me as a child is a wooden Braille writing-frame given to me by Elsie Olive Richardson. I still use it to make notes, especially during long rail journeys. I often wish she could know that I still treasure this tangible link with her.

The annual Harborne Carnival was another time that could be guaranteed to take our minds off our work for a few days in anticipation of the fun and excitement to be had.

We could hardly wait for the afternoon to come when we would be allowed to stand at the roadside and be part of the noisy, chattering crowd as the procession passed by. We shouted and cheered, clapping our hands with all the rest as the floats went by.

But even after it had all gone, our fun was not entirely over. We knew that the Carnival procession would return along the same route later, and we would hear it when we were in bed. It would be very late before we slept that night.

The bedtimes for the different age groups were six o'clock, six-thirty, and seven o'clock. Normally we would all have been well asleep by eight o'clock, but we endeavoured to keep each other awake until we began to hear the distant beat and throb of drums. Our excitement mounted as the band got nearer and nearer; soon the other sounds would become clear until they were passing at the closest point. We would hold our breath in excitement until it all gradually died away again. It was so much the more wonderful because it seemed to us that it was all happening in the middle of the night!

My seventh birthday occurred near the beginning of the autumn term of 1938. A momentous event, which was to eclipse all others. Although I didn't realise it at the time, it was to set me up for life.

The day it happened was ordinary enough. It had begun in the usual way – washing, breakfast, bed making, and lessons – the rigid routine which we had always followed. I had no reason to suppose this day would be any different.

It was usual on Friday afternoons for us to be able to choose an educational toy from the toy cupboard in our classroom. This particular afternoon I chose the rubber bricks, and began to build quietly by myself. Suddenly, to my surprise, Miss Richardson interrupted my endeavours.

"Peter," she called, "You must leave that now, you are going to learn to play the piano this afternoon."

I hesitated, a brick still in my hand, trying to take in what she had said. "Learn to play the piano this afternoon." I repeated it in my mind. Could she really mean that? It was the thing I had most longed to do ever since I had heard the first notes Miss Richardson had played to us each morning, and Miss Jones in our singing lessons.

But we were never allowed to touch the piano – after all – how could fifty-six pairs of piano-bent hands be controlled? Surely she couldn't mean that I was to be allowed to turn the key, lift the lid and make those lovely sounds?

"Come along now," she continued, "Mr. Clark is going to teach you this afternoon."

It was true! I really was going to learn how to play the piano – this afternoon…this was wonderful! Mr. Clark was actually going to show me how to play this afternoon! Perhaps on Monday morning, I would be allowed to play for the hymns and choruses! At the end of the lesson, I was rather disappointed. I had learned very little in my opinion, and wished that grown-ups meant what they said!

Mr. Clark, who was himself blind, began by teaching me the names of the notes and how to find them. We played 'Find the note' games, which were fun, but I could see that the whole job was going to take longer than I thought.

My first exercise was called 'Very sedate', a simple little piece consisting of a solo in the right hand, a solo in the left hand, and then co-ordination of the two in contrary motion. I was taught from the Walter Carroll book, and I was soon playing 'Jolly Farmer', 'On the lake', 'Milkmaid's song' and 'In the quiet wood'. (The way I played this last piece would have been more appropriately called 'A herd of elephants'!

I was keen to learn and practise; savouring every moment I spent at the beloved piano. Although I could never have been described as a genius, my technique began to develop fairly rapidly, and I knew that I was on the way to being able to play well.

When the holidays came round I would be able to tell my mum and dad about the piano. I had an even greater reason for longing to go home.

Chapter Four

Family Performances

WE ONLY WENT HOME three times a year. At the beginning of each term, we knew how many weeks it would be to 'Going home day'. As the time came round, we would almost be beside ourselves with anticipation, and could hardly wait to go to the homes and families, which had become so distant to us.

On 'Going home day' morning the chatter in the washroom would be more animated than usual as we would try to tell one another about what we hoped we would do during the holidays.

My real home was a very different world from school. I had to get used to confined space instead of the lengthy corridors, hard stairs and large rooms such as dormitories. My brother Harry and I had to share a double bed. He was some five years my senior, so that when I was nine years old, he had left school, and had to be up early for work. I would be left in bed, listening to the ticking clock on the mantelpiece, and hearing my three sisters in the other bedroom chattering away – it was all so very different.

There was one similarity however. I still had to go downstairs to wash, since we had no facilities upstairs. I would wash in the kitchen, and have an occasional bath in the bathroom that was off the kitchen. Our toilet was an outside one.

There were not many toys to play with, and there were times when I had to be looked after by a neighbour when mum was at work. Quite often I would have my dinner by courtesy of the day school my sisters went to.

I was treated well, and remember being quite fond of Miss Damby, a primary teacher who gave me a ball to play with which inevitably got lost, much to my frustration. Thinking about that now, it was really a most unsuitable present for a blind child, but I knew she meant it as a very kind gesture.

It's true to say that during my holidays, I missed my school friends. Much later on, Joe and Les Hall, together with others, would spend time with our family.

I had been away for about five years by now, apart from the occasional holidays, and during these times I realised that I was really the stranger in a family of established children. By this time, Harry was twelve; my sister Lily ten, and Marjorie was nine. They weren't very interested in playing with me – I was so different – but my younger sister Betty was quite another matter. She was only five, and was delighted to have someone to play with. She wasn't allowed out on her own any more than I was, and so we became great friends in the short times we had together. I was so glad to have someone to relate to at home.

There were always two standard questions asked at the beginning of holidays. The first one was almost impossible to answer; the second one I didn't even want to answer. "What have you been doing this last term?" And, "When are you going back to school?"

But now I was seven, I was ready to answer the first question: "I'm learning to play the piano," I declared confidently.

My parents were, indeed, thrilled by that statement. Unfortunately, we didn't own a piano, and as the holiday progressed, I realised how much I missed having one available to me. But all was not lost. My maternal grandparents had a piano, which was invariably out of tune. Nevertheless I was able to practise my pieces, though not often enough. My parents were concerned about the situation too, and they decided to do something about it.

Whilst I was away at school, it was discovered that Mr. And Mrs. Dale who lived opposite had a piano for sale. It was probably not advertised as such, but it was known that they were always in need of money, and they were delighted to have something that was saleable. My parents didn't have much money either, and I can only imagine the careful bargaining that went on before the piano became resident in our home. It was a secret kept for my next holiday, and my joy knew no bounds when I 'discovered' it.

It did not score very highly in the good piano ratings, but I loved it. It became my refuge when the going was tough; my Confidante when I had no one to talk to, and my companion in joy.

The other members of my family could 'knock out a tune', but lessons were too expensive and so progress was non-existent. This is where I scored, for my ability to play grew rapidly. The sacrifice made by my parents to acquire that old piano must have been considerable. Life in the late 1930's was not easy for most people; work was scarce, and my parents had known nothing but struggle.

My father's parents had been forced to go to great lengths in order to live. Grandma Jackson (as we called her) had been left with several young children when her husband died, and she was obliged to consign them to Marston Green 'Cottage Homes'. We always felt that dad was reluctant to talk about this period of his life. There was a kind of shame in having been placed in care, and – understandably – he had scant respect for his mother. Dad's brothers were George, Herbert, and Leslie. George played the piano well, even though he didn't have any tuition. Herbert had a very sunny disposition, and was always my favourite Uncle. Uncle Les probably would be described today as having 'learning difficulties'. Having been at the 'Cottage Homes' with his brothers, he was then sent to a mental institution for the rest of his life.

He was allowed out for specific Saturdays, and would visit us from time to time. I remember how much he enjoyed coming to us, having to catch two buses to reach us, and of course, two buses to get back. Looking back on that now, I can't think he was entirely irresponsible.

When the time came for him to go back, he would become noticeably anxious not to be detained. In his Brummy accent he would say, "I've gorra go now else I shall gerra towlin'". How readily I sympathised with him, fully understanding his apprehension.

My mother belonged to a big family too. In all, there had been eleven children, but two died in infancy. I loved and respected my grandparents. George Middleton had been active in the Boer war, and the 1914-18 war. He had, as I well remember, a rasping cough that seemed to tear at his very vitals. He would explain breathlessly, "That's the gas!" Apparently the Germans had used gas as a weapon in the First World War, and many troops were poisoned, whilst others were left with physical or nervous debilities.

I always enjoyed going to Gran's. For one thing, it was so different from the house we lived in. As well as the living room, it had what was always referred to as 'the front room', with largely unworn furniture, and the piano with the creaky right pedal. There were four bedrooms upstairs, and a bathroom!

Mum's youngest sister Edna and brother Fred weren't then married, so Edna was put in charge of my getting up and going to bed at Grandma's.

Fred, I remember, was never good at getting up in the morning. Gran would come to the bottom of the stairs calling his name: "Fred! When are you going to get up?" Eventually she would have to come right into his bedroom and virtually drag the bedclothes off him. Nevertheless, he was a family celebrity.

He played a piano accordion very well, and would sing to his own accompaniment. I knew he was a big, tall fellow, and must have been quite handsome. I used to love standing and listening to him perform, and wished I could play an accordion. His 120-bass was far too heavy for me.

Fred was seventeen years old when war broke out in 1939, and he wanted to join up there and then. At that time, lads were not permitted to enlist until they were eighteen. However Fred, being Fred, managed it, and in 1940 went over to France – with his companion, the piano accordion!

He became involved in the famous Dunkirk episode. France had surrendered to the Germans, and British troops had to make a dramatic retreat to the Dunkirk beaches. Uncle Fred was wounded, but managed – with his accordion – to get on a boat back to England. He spent some months in Chatham hospital, before being discharged from the army.

For us, he was a hero. I happened to be home when he arrived at Gran's, and we all gathered round him, to listen to what he had to say about his experiences.

We were spellbound at what he was telling us:

"We were under orders to retreat to Dunkirk," he said. "It was all pretty chaotic, and our platoon was quite near the advancing German lines. We were cut off, and surrounded by Germans who would have taken us as prisoners-of-war. It looked all up with us, so I got my accordion out of its case, strapped it on, and started playing and singing German songs that I had picked up. The surrounding Germans listened in amazement, and before I had finished, another platoon of British soldiers put the Germans under fire, and they scattered. We were saved!"

Perhaps we were gullible; but after all, this was war, and here was our own courageous soldier back in one piece. Perhaps he romanced a bit, but I'm sure that somewhere between our gullibility and his exaggeration, some truth lurked. At any rate, I still love to believe it all!

Uncle Fred wasn't going to find Civvy Street to his liking. Having been discharged from the army, he then joined the Bomb Disposal Service!

He eventually married a girl from Manchester, moved there, but could only find work in nightclubs and dives, and died in reduced circumstances having left his wife and children. My hero had fallen!

My grandparents kept the family united in those days by means of parties. These would occur at Christmas, New Year, Bank holidays, and birthdays. Enough drink was brought in to keep things going, and Uncle George – my dad's brother – would officiate at the piano. Most of the parties were held in our house, because we had the one largish room.

When I was about eight years old, I acquired a small, eight-bass accordion, and I sort to emulate my Uncle Fred, to the encouragement of my family.

As my ability on the piano increased, so did my interest in music. My holidays became times of release when I could listen to any kind of music I liked. At school we were not encouraged to listen to 'dance music', only 'good' music. We only heard the former when we pressed our ear against the staff room door!

At home we had a Cossor valve wireless, which I listened to avidly. I would sit in my favourite armchair, turn the switch on the side of the set, and wait for it to warm up. Then I would turn the dial, looking for a station that happened to be transmitting music. I loved the songs of the day. I would listen to Victor Sylvester's' 'Dancing Club' on a Wednesday evening, the pianist Carol Gibbons and his orchestra. His signature tune was one of his own compositions called 'On the air', and he would introduce each orchestra number or piano solo in a very slow, dreamy voice, plus his American accent. Another favourite pianist with his own distinctive style was Charlie Kunz. The best way I can describe it is that of a soft-loud left-hand accompaniment. Carol Gibbons, on the other hand (no pun intended) played with a number of little chromatic runs in his left-hand. I noticed these different styles, and tried to imitate them.

Twice each day there would be a thirty-minute block of continuous music on the wireless called 'Music while you work', the signature tune having been specially composed: 'Calling all workers'. I would play along with it, in this way learning this very popular music. My dad encouraged me too. He recognised a talent, which might reap substantial financial reward at some future time.

Dad was the secretary of the local dominoes and darts team at 'The Dog and Partridge' – an establishment which was always described as being 'Round the corner'. Whenever he was heard to say, "I'm just going for a walk round the corner", we knew wither his steps were bent. (They were a little more bent upon his return journey!)

I was into my eleventh year when dad hit upon an idea. He invited the visiting darts team to come and hear me play the piano. It was wartime by now, and meat was severely rationed. However, the resident team included the local butcher, and it was arranged that enough ham be provided, my mum supplying the pickles.

I remember being called, and hauled from sleep late at night, coming downstairs in my night attire, and 'requested' to play the piano. A dining chair would be placed at the piano for me to sit on – we couldn't afford a piano stool – and I would wonder what to play.

"Give 'em your pieces," commanded my dad. I would give a recital of what I'd learned at school. Then my dad would say, "Let's have some of the old songs now." The assembled company would sing whatever I played: 'If you were the only girl in the world'; 'I'll be your sweetheart if you will be mine'; 'Pack Up Your Troubles'; 'It's a Long Way to Tipperary', and 'I'll Take You Home Again, Kathleen'. (Just how many times that girl had been taken home is anybody's guess!)

I had learned many of these older songs from a record collection we'd been given along with a wind-up cabinet gramophone. Frank Davis, an amateur boxer was our benefactor, and we felt we were in no position to refuse even an amateur!

Dad managed the whole production. He saw to it that the folks were sufficiently entertained, and then he would bring on the Finale. There was usually a tenor – often in the form of my Uncle Stan from Bridgend – to whom my dad would signal at the appropriate moment. He would step forward, place an affectionate hand on my shoulder, and render – in more ways than one – the song: 'He was only a poor blind boy!' As the hankies were brought out, and sniffs suppressed, a suitable collecting vessel would be passed round.

This particular evening saw a good collection. My dad was my manager, on 95% commission. Having amassed the sum of nine shillings and sixpence, dad paid himself what was due: I went back to school with fourpence!

But my desire to entertain had been kindled.

I hated going back to school after the holidays. Just as I had got used to the relaxation of home, of listening to the shows on the wireless – Tommy Handley, 'ITMA'; 'The Happydrome' with Ramsbottom, Enoch and Harry Lovejoy; and of course, 'Henry Hall's Guest-night', and Uncle Mac's 'Children's Hour' – and my special friendship with Betty. I had to give all that up and go back to the rigidity of school routine.

On the eve of 'Going back day' the signs were ominous. There was quite a procedure really. School clothes were produced; my hair was combed with a solution of Detol to make sure there were no bugs. My bath was prepared, before I went to bed in the big double bed.

The BRIB and the local authority found most of the cost for our education and clothing. Sooner or later, however, a bill would arrive at home for the parental contribution. My parents could never manage it, and it was a continual embarrassment to them. The authorities persisted, and my father was called upon to pay the ultimate price – a night in Winson Green prison for debt. The money was still not forthcoming, and in the end, the BRIB footed the entire bill.

In my earlier years, I remember begging my mum not to let me go back to school.

"Please don't make me go back," I pleaded. "I promise I'll be good – I'll do anything you say – please don't send me away again!"

But it was no use. When the day came for my return, I cried bitterly, and clung to my mum. By way of consolation she gave me a bag of raisins to eat on the way. They tasted so good, and seemed to be such a lifeline to home that I hardly dared to eat them. But they provided no lasting diversion – they were no substitute for a loving family.

In the summer term of 1939, a new sound met our inquisitive ears. Our school was situated near a barracks; and we began to hear the sound of soldiers being prepared for war.

The soldiers drilled most of the time, and at night we would lie awake and listen to the tramp of their feet as they marched about the parade ground. We noticed the way the shouted orders changed the pattern of the marching. It seemed urgent and foreboding. We would fall into an uneasy sleep.

'Going home day' was at the end of July that year, and I recall listening to conversations between grown-ups about what had happened the previous summer in Czechoslovakia, and what might be about to happen to Poland.

It was almost as if my parents knew what was to happen: they planned a family holiday to Barry Island. It's the only time I remember our family going to the seaside. For me, even the train journey had overtones of the threatening international situation. As the train took us into Wales, I imitated its rhythmic pattern by saying: "Czechoslovak, Czechoslovak!"

The weather was unsettled too. Auntie Emily came with us, my mum's youngest but one sister, and although I didn't find the holiday particularly memorable, one event stands out. We were on the pebble beach at Cold Nap. Suddenly a heavy squall with drenching rain soaked us through. We hastily picked up our things, and ran as fast as we could back to our landlady Mrs. Lewis. Such was my Auntie Emily's panic that she actually wet herself! Some remark was passed to the effect that it hadn't made much difference: we were all wet through!

Normally, by early September we should have been back at school, however, my parents were notified that plans were afoot to evacuate city children if war was declared.

After we'd returned from our Barry Island holiday, people were discussing openly the possibility of Germany invading Poland. "If ever they do," people were saying, "Mr. Chamberlain will definitely declare war."

On Friday, 1st September, the invasion of Poland took place, and as if by magic, a big furniture van drew up outside our door, and in a matter of half an hour, with my few belongings around me, I was on board, being whisked away, picking up various children on the way: some to go to Worcester College for the Blind, and the younger ones like me to Herefordshire. To me it felt like a big adventure, yet there was, I remember, a feeling of nervous apprehension all around, and by Sunday of that weekend we were at war with Germany.

All this meant that I was parted from friends, notably Joe, who lived between Wolverhampton and Cannock Chase, and Les Hall, who lived well out in the country.

There were nine of us from the Birmingham area taken to a safe haven which was a large house called Bockleton Court near

Tenbury Wells, not far from the Herefordshire and Worcestershire border. The senior girls from the school in Edgbaston were already in residence, but all the other children from Harborne were to have a nice long holiday.

To our surprise the change proved to be very much for the better, for here began a completely unexpected time of fun and relaxation.

To start with, we were 'adopted' by some of the girls to be fussed over and indulged in everything. Mr. Myers, the principal, put the more senior girls in charge of us. They were supposed to be our supervisors – making sure that we made our beds correctly etc. But they spoiled us dreadfully, and waited on us hand and foot. One of their tasks was to cut our bread and butter thinly, explaining that this was part of the 'saving' for the war effort. Perhaps it was because they themselves had known shortages in the past that they knew how hungry little boys were. They didn't try very hard at 'saving', and so made everything a bit of a game!

As far as we were concerned, the war had been pushed into the background for the time being. (Later on chroniclers would describe this period as the 'phoney war'.) There were no guns firing, no bombs falling – not here or anywhere – so we all relaxed in our new and friendly surroundings.

It was only the staff that showed any signs of nervousness. They seemed to be waiting for something to happen before they could organise any lessons. We, therefore, had nothing to spoil those idyllic autumn days. We laughed, played, rolling down the big grassy bank; picnicked, and ate rosy, juicy apples from the orchard. Mr. Myers, who was both kind and understanding, saw to it that there was a basket of apples placed by the entrance of the dining–room from which we were free to help ourselves when we came down to breakfast each morning.

The older girls were not my only friends, however. I was soon to make a special friend of 'the Colonel' who was the owner of Bockleton Court. Colonel Prescott lived nearby and often dropped in to see the youngsters who were occupying his old family home. He seemed to enjoy our company, and we certainly looked forward to seeing him.

"Come on then," he would say jovially, patting his knee, and I would willingly climb onto the large lap.

"I know what you would like," he would laugh. Then he would allow my hands to go straight for his waistcoat and the chain that dangled across it. I would follow the chain through until I reached the pocket, and then feel for the watch inside. I was really fascinated by that watch. I loved to feel its smooth shape, and feel the weight of it in my hand. Then, of course, I would put it to my ear so that I could listen to its wonderful, rhythmic tick.

One day the Colonel sought me out especially. "Here," he said, "I've got something for you. I thought you might like this." He took my hand and placed something in it. I felt it all over with rising excitement – and I knew what it was straight away.

"It's only an old one, you know", added the Colonel, "But you can have it to play with if you like."

I held the watch lovingly in my hands, wondering that it was actually mine! I held it to my ear, but it wasn't ticking. I gave it a cautious shake, and then, to my delight, the ticking began! It went on for a while before stopping again, but a little shake would set it off every time. I was overjoyed with it, and kept it as a special treasure.

Now and again one of the girls' teachers, Mrs. Ennis, would take some of us to the little village school in Bockleton. There were just fifteen children in the school, and we were greeted with enthusiasm. We showed the children how we read Braille, and they were fascinated. Looking back now over the length of all those years, I still sense the affection of those children, and it was another lovely touch to that happy autumn.

But this was only an interlude; it couldn't last long. We were told that Miss Richardson had found a large house in the village of Wolverley, near Kidderminster. The time had come when we had to leave our many new friends at Bockleton. There were tears and hugs, and promises to keep in touch: but for the most part, that would be the end of our contact with the girls at Bockleton Court. But for one of the girls in particular, Gwen, it was going to be some thirty–two years later that we would actually meet – in Belfast!

The same nine children were the first to take up residence in Sion Hill House on 30th September. A local farmer, Mr. Wyre, owned it. That first evening, when we were taken upstairs to wash, I remember being intrigued by the low-flush lavatory! The position and feel of the cold, smooth porcelain cistern with the handle – I was totally fascinated!

We tried to resume the idyllic lifestyle that we had come to enjoy at Bockleton. For a time we were not disappointed: there were still no organised lessons, and no overt signs of war. Food, however, was not abundant, and we settled back into the routine of porridge one day, bread and milk the next. As we came into the dining room each morning, we could smell the phosphorus of the matches, and hear the 'bump' as the gas fire burst into life.

We were gradually joined by some of the other children as they were evacuated to the 'safe' school in the country. Joe Hayward, Les Hall, Kenneth Howarth, Ron Staton; Dorothy Stone, (who had a beautiful singing voice) Rene Langford, Betty Compson, and little Vera Sykes – to mention but a few.

There were some changes in staff too. Miss Morley had left, and Matron – I learned much later on – had been expelled for cruelty. The Misses Janus and Williams came with Miss Richardson: and now we had a new Matron. There was something mysterious about her. At a time when we were learning that all foreigners could be suspect, and that strangers could be 'Fifth Columnists' – or spies – we were instantly on our guard when we realised that Matron Berry could speak German! She made no attempt to hide the fact, and openly greeted us with "Guten Morgen!" or "Dankerschoen", if we held a door open for her.

In retrospect, perhaps we were looking for a bit of excitement, but she proved to be just as much a tough disciplinarian as the previous Matron, and that seemed to fit the bill as a "German!"

As the school routine settled down, another disaster was to affect me perhaps more than some of the others. My favourite teacher, Miss Richardson left to take up a position at Worcester College for the Blind where the older boys were temporarily accommodated. (Later in 1940 they would take up more permanent residence at Kinlet Hall, near Bewdley.)

It's possible that I leaned on her too much. She had been incredibly kind to me. I remember that once, when my mother couldn't come to take me home for my holidays, Miss Richardson took it upon herself to escort me home all the way from Harborne to Yardley Wood.

Eventually, she would leave Worcester College when the boys moved to Kinlet Hall, and take up a post at a sighted school near Chelmsford, Essex.

I missed her positive Christian influence, but she had sown good seed, which was to produce fruit in my later life.

Chapter Five

Shattered Illusions

WITH ALL THE UPHEAVAL brought about by the declaration of war, I lost my first music teacher, Mr. Clark. He took up duties with the boys at Worcester College, and would later transfer with them to Kinlet Hall. My new piano teacher was to be Miss Monica Colquhoun who came to Wolverley in the snowy winter of 1940.

She lived in Birmingham, and was herself blind, and yet managed to come for three consecutive days each week. I can only conjecture, as I write, that she must have stayed locally, rather than make that formidable trip each day.

So by 1940 our resident teachers were Miss Williams and Miss Janus who had come from the Kindergarten at Harborne, and Miss Francis who mainly looked after the boys and girls with sight. (Perhaps Miss Francis was a bit more 'modern' in her outlook, for I managed to find out her age relatively easily – she was just twenty-one when she joined the staff.)

There were just two pianos at Wolverley: the Riley & Son in the conservatory, (a Birmingham made piano) and a Spencer in Miss Francis's classroom. Most of us young pianists were already discerning enough to know that the piano in the conservatory was inferior to the one in the classroom. Yet it was on the inferior piano

, in the conservatory, that the teaching was done. (I wonder whether we were more discerning than the staff!)

I remember Miss Francis's room particularly for its crackly sounding floor. It must have been the way the floor was laid, and its sound impinged itself on my memory.

Although Miss Colquhoun was assigned to teach the earlier stages of playing the piano, she soon recognised in me not only the ability to learn, but also to extemporize and actually compose little pieces of my own. Two of these pieces I still remember, and occasionally play to children in school to demonstrate my development as a musician: 'Merry march', and 'Swing-boat song'. (The latter sounds a bit like a Barcarolle.)

To her credit, Miss Colquhoun encouraged this potential in me, for she, too, was a composer in her own right. To this day, I can't understand why she took to me as she did. I was a wild, moody child, and perhaps that's why she wrote a piece called 'Rain and Sunshine'. It depicted in its style change and variableness, like the weather – like me!

I could only have been nine years old when Miss Colquhoun gave me the challenge of accompanying the sung grace at table. It was a challenge, because there not being a piano in the dining-room meant that I had to accompany the boys and girls from Miss Francis' classroom which was across the hall. To start them off, I had to play one cord and the first note of the tune in the key of F. That's when my leading congregations in song began!

It was during this time that I began to tackle the difficulties of Braille music notation. Some of the boys and girls mastered it much better than others, and it was a constant struggle for me.

It's based on the domino principle using Braille symbols: the top four of the six dots denoting the name of the notes, the remaining bottom two dots determining the value of the notes. Instead of treble and bass clefs, a little sign was placed before the first note of a bar indicating the octave on the keyboard. Everything has to be learned by memorising each section of left – and right-hand until the piece is thoroughly learned. Although I had to learn for examination purposes, I never really came to terms with learning Braille music.

On the other hand, as a Gospel pianist now, there is no music of that kind in Braille, so I really don't lose out after all.

The bond between my teacher and me grew stronger, and we were to remain friends for many years to come. One day she actually gave me a little wind-up gramophone and a few records from her own collection. There was a record of 'Jesu, joy of man's desiring' on one side, and the last movement from Bach's B minor suite for flute and strings on the other side. This was generous indeed!

Music figured prominently at Wolverley as Miss Colquhoun developed a percussion band in addition to her piano teaching. This drew most of the children together in music making. I had to play a tambourine, but I didn't like it much. I tried the triangle, and some tiny hand-bells, but nothing satisfied me – it had to be the piano.

I suppose that, because of the shortage of available teaching staff, no other wind or stringed instrument featured in our school. Apart from the percussion band, if you didn't play the piano, you didn't play anything.

By now, there were more ominous signs of war. The single up and down wail of the air raid siren was to be heard as it was being tested. One day, the siren sounded continuously, which meant that there was an imminent air raid threatening. We had practised for just such an occasion.

Beneath the building was a large cellar, which accommodated a dynamo, which generated electricity for the house. We were not on mains electricity here in Wolverley village. The cellar now became not only our refuge, but also the single dormitory for boys and girls alike. It was equipped with mattresses, but it was cold, damp, fumy, and not very comfortable. It took some time, too, to get used to the continual hum of the dynamo and the smell of the paraffin that fuelled it. Still, we felt ourselves to be safer there, so no one complained.

Mr. Whitton – who was to become one of the major influences in my life – used to come at least once a week to teach us singing. When Kinlet Hall became available for the older boys, he would operate between the two schools. He had a lovely tenor singing voice, and taught and played the piano really well. (Later on, he was to become my piano-tuning instructor.)

We always knew when he arrived because the smell of his cigarette smoke pervaded the whole building. Strangely enough, that would remind me of my home, and dad's woodbines.

Mr. Whitton was a cheerful character, and we all looked forward to singing to his accompaniment and encouragement. We learned many songs with him and Miss Colquhoun. One afternoon we were singing 'Dashing away with the smoothing iron' lustily, when the continuous sound broke through our singing; the gong sounded, and we had to break off and form up in an orderly fashion as we had practised on a number of occasions, ready to descend the steep stone steps down to the subterranean regions! As we talked excitedly to each other, there was the sound of a prolonged, deep rumble. We all wondered what it was. Later we learned that a bomb had fallen and exploded scarcely a mile away, just outside the Land Oak pub in Kidderminster. That was the only bomb we heard at Wolverley, but from that moment, it began to feel like war. Previously, I had gone on record as complaining that: "This isn't much of a war; there are no guns!"

It was considered important that we got plenty of fresh air and exercise. To this end we were required to take frequent walks. We would sometimes go towards Kidderminster, which meant going down Sion Hill, past Broadwaters garage. This was the way to the local paper mill, which we visited once. Wood was unloaded there from the river Severn to be pulped and made into paper. We were given a conducted tour, and it was all very fascinating: the smells, the noise of machinery, the feel of the pulp, and then – at the end – the feel of the finished paper.

Then again, we would go the other way, turning left out of the drive towards the canal and Cookley village. At Wolverley, we were no less hungry than at Harborne, and I remember walking to Cookley and smelling the new bread which was being baked in the village bakery. It was torture to growing children who never got enough food, and I remember the fainting feeling in the pit of my stomach – it was no good – we just had to keep on walking.

The war could not be entirely blamed for our lack of food. I knew hunger before the war – but here at Wolverley we were desperately hungry all the time. We would get up from the meal table always wishing there was more, and our walks only served to fuel an appetite that was never satisfied.

It was on one of these walks that we met Miss Richardson for the last time. She seemed to materialise from nowhere – totally unexpectedly to bid her 'farewell'. This must have been when she was leaving Worcester College to take up new responsibilities in Essex. As a parting gesture, she did a strange thing to my mind: she gave to each one of us a packet of popcorns! Although we must have been hungry, we hastily put them in our pockets, and this was to be the nearest we would aspire to the 'midnight feast' – we saved them up to eat in bed that night in the gloomy cellar! That was the last memory of one whose influence would permeate my future.

I don't ever remember meeting Mr. Wyre – the farmer who had lent Sion Hill House to us as an evacuated school. He must have been a very kind man, for in the spring of 1940 he gave us the opportunity to 'adopt' a lamb. Miss Janus thought that it would be good for us to take a hand in caring for the little creature, and we entered into the project with a great deal of excitement and enthusiasm.

We called the lamb 'Frisky', and there was a good deal of rivalry as to who was to do the feeding. We clamoured to stroke it, and threatened to overwhelm the poor little thing. Its living quarters were in the conservatory, which was situated between two class-rooms, and we could hear him bleating for his milk, which greatly disturbed concentration on lessons. We were given turns to feed him from a bottle, and I remember how we were all surprised at the strength of his sucking. He simply guzzled his milk, and we were delighted, and we cared for him tenderly.

Each day Frisky would be put on a lead and taken for a walk – just like a pet dog, causing quite a stir in the neighbourhood. Sadly, however, there were those who seemed to begrudge us children our pet. During the Easter holidays, the unbelievable happened! Some boys from the village saw little Frisky walking with Miss Janus. One of the boys had a powerful airgun, and for no apparent reason, shot the lamb, fatally wounding him.

We returned from our holidays fully expecting to resume our caring of Frisky, and were completely devastated by this awful news. No one could understand such a senseless, cruel act. It left us feeling bereft and desolate, and many of the children cried inconsolably. We had all lavished our pent-up love and emotions on the little lamb, and once again we had been thwarted. This event was to become indelibly etched on all our memories forever afterwards.

Years later, when I studied the Scriptures, I felt an acute sympathy with Jewish children in the sacrificing of the Passover

Lamb each year. I reasoned that the lamb would have been taken into the home to become the family pet. How fond the children would become of this gentle, submissive creature. But the time would surely come when it would have to be killed, supposedly by the father of the family, to the distraction of little Hebrew boys and girls. Protestations would be made; tears would flow, and worst of all, they would all have to eat of their 'Frisky'!

Thus the lesson would be taught each year that the blood of the lamb had been Israel's protection from the destroying angel in Egypt. And then, one day, when the young man Jesus was walking near Jordan, his cousin John suddenly exclaimed in a moment of divine revelation: "Look! The Lamb of God who takes away the sin of the world!"

It seemed strange that having taken so much trouble to protect us from the main threat of air raids, we were still sent home for holidays. Add to that the fact that in the summer of 1940 Great Britain was under the very real threat of invasion.

As for me, I was glad to be home for my summer holidays, even though talk of invasion was palpable. Earlier that year, two of my sisters, Marjorie and Betty had been evacuated to the rural parts of Staffordshire, but they were so unhappy and homesick that I went on the train with my mother to 'rescue' them. When they saw us, they cried, clinging to us, and begging us not to leave them. I understood only too well how they felt.

Shortly after war had been declared, the goldbeating workshop closed, and my father got a job with I.C.I.'s 'Imperial Metals Industry'. This work was totally different to that which he had been used to. Now he was dealing with hot, smoking furnaces and molten metal in steaming vats that had to be carried from the furnaces to cool in another part of the huge workshop. Sometimes the hot metal would splash, and I remember my dad showing me the holes in his shirt and socks, which had been burned.

In looking back, I now realise that none of us really understood the working conditions for those gallant men. This, together with my dad's Spartan upbringing, not to mention his smoking and drinking habits would lead to an early grave. Although he was born too young for the First World War, and was deemed too old for the second, he – like everybody else at that time was avidly interested in news bulletins. He sparked my interest too, even though I was still only eight years old. He would read to me from the Birmingham Mail, and we rejoiced together when the R.A.F. shot down Nazi aircraft by the score at the beginning of what was to be known as 'The Battle of Britain'.

My mother kept a scrupulously clean home, making sure that we bathed regularly; yet in spite of all her efforts, my brother Harry, Marjorie and Betty began to feel unwell, and by Friday, 16th August, the doctor ordered the ambulance to ferry us to Little Bromwich Isolation Hospital.

We arrived at six o'clock in the evening, and Harry and I were put in the same ward. After the usual formalities, we were put to bed and given a bowl of soup and a slice of dry bread. Then a big, horrible rough blanket was thrown across each of us to give us some protection from flying glass caused by bombs; we tried to relax into an uneasy sleep.

Through the delirium of illness I could hear the 'Bleep-bleep' of crickets caught in the heating system; the drone of aircraft in the sky above, and the ever-increasing anti-aircraft fire punctuated by the heart-stopping crash of bombs falling nearby.

As I began to recover, I became aware of the other patients in the ward – all men who spent their time listening to the wireless, keeping up with the fortunes of the war. Each night they would tune in to Germany, from where the sinister voice of William Joyce could be heard broadcasting propaganda aimed at demoralising his British compatriots. He came to be called 'Lord Haw-Haw', and his nasal sounding voice chanting "Germany calling, Germany calling" haunted my dreams.

Little Bromwich Hospital was in a vulnerable and dangerous part of East Birmingham. Not far away were the railway marshalling yards in Small Heath, and the B.S.A. factory, world famous for its motorbikes, but now mobilised for the production of munitions. These were, of course, prime targets for the enemy, with the not-too-far distant 'attraction' of industrial Coventry that would eventually suffer the blitz.

In silent fear we lay listening to the wail of the air-raid sirens, the approaching throbbing of the two-stroke engines of the German planes. Anti-aircraft guns, exploding bombs shook our isolation ward, and then there came the more heartening sound of what we were soon to recognise as Spitfires that seemed to rip across the sky to engage with German Messersmidts, Junkers, and Heinkels. The sickening thud of bombs seemed to come nearer and nearer, buildings were being destroyed, people killed all around us. We waited for it to happen to us.

One night, fifteen bombs fell in the hospital grounds. One hit the nurses' Home killing two nurses. All through the days I lived in fearful dread of what might happen once night came. The hospital staff could see my distress so they put me in the same bed as Harry, my brother. He was a big thirteen-year-old, and I took comfort from his strength. As we lay there, the ward was suddenly shaken to its foundations by a thud, which seemed to reverberate inside my head. A time bomb was dropped, and it fell right outside the door of our ward. The significance of our perilous situation was not lost on any of us: we knew that, had it not been a delayed action bomb, we would surely have been killed. A bomb disposal team was rushed in, and the work of dismantling the heinous device went ahead. We waited breathlessly until the word was given that all was now safe: it had been a narrow escape.

By now, my brother and I were up patients, and he took me for a walk round the grounds of the hospital, showing me the bomb craters, and gathering shrapnel for me to play with! I was still in a fairly weak state, and remember falling over, cutting my right elbow quite badly. I was glad to have had Harry with me during those days. It's probably the time when we were closest to each other. During the years to come, we would find that we had less and less in common with one another.

Being brought up in residential school doesn't, to my mind, foster family relationships. One tends to be closer to those with whom one spends a good deal of time with. An understanding grows between us, and an almost desperate willingness to hang together whatever the consequences. A school has many contemporaries from which to choose one's friends: a family is limited by its very nature. If you don't get on with a particular boy at school, you simply look for somebody else – the choice is both wide and varied.

I suppose it's a truism to say that in any given situation there are advantages and disadvantages. Although my education lacked in so many ways, especially in later years, I still think that I got a generally better education than my brother and sisters. All his childhood, Harry had longed to learn to play the piano, but my parents couldn't afford his tuition. My piano lessons were part and parcel of the school curriculum, and made learning music just as important a subject as maths, history, geography, etc.

When the day came for Harry and me to be discharged from hospital, I was returned straight away to school. I was immediately placed in strict quarantine for another two weeks. It was considered too dangerous for me to be kept in sick bay: it had to be Matron Berry's room. A bed was set up for me there.

It was almost like being sentenced to solitary confinement in prison. I could not mix with any of the other children, of course, so I had no one to talk to. I wasn't even given any schoolwork to do. There was only the occasional visit of one of the maids who came to clean and tidy the room: I was bored almost to distraction. My imagination started working overtime, working on the generally held assumption that Miss Berry was, in truth, a German spy!

There was nothing to do except wait for the next meal, which was not worth waiting for. Even the hospital food was much more to be desired than this subsistence. I spent ten hours a day, sitting, or walking around the lonely room, and fourteen hours in bed. Eventually, I plucked up courage, and dared to send a message via Mary Morris, one of the maids, to my teacher Miss Williams. "Could I please have some books to read?" This was to be my salvation, and the beginning of my love affair with books. I read copiously, and at these times at least, actually began to enjoy myself.

When morning came, my empty tummy would long for the meagre breakfast of unsweetened porridge or bread and milk, and I tried to make my poor fare last as long as I could. Then followed the usual slice of bread and marmite, or Virol, and a mug of tea.

Having completed my breakfast, I became conscious of a delicious smell wafting up from the kitchen below. This was a smell that reminded me of home, although at that period of the war, it was an infrequent smell. It got stronger and stronger until my tummy began to rumble again, and my mouth water. It was unmistakably the smell of bacon cooking! I could hardly believe it. Bacon! Was it possible that I could be having extra breakfast because I had been ill? I heard footsteps coming nearer, and my heart began to beat faster. I heard the door handle turn, and Matron walked into the room. Without so much as a word, she walked over to the table and sat down. Almost immediately a maid followed her into the room: the tantalizing smell becoming almost intoxicating. I turned instinctively and eagerly towards her but she did not come in my direction. Instead, she went straight to the table and I heard the sound of the tray being set down.

"Thank you," said Matron, "that will be all." She picked up her cutlery, and I heard the sound of the knife slicing through fried bread and bacon and egg, to be followed by what I imagined was toast and marmalade.

I was crushingly disappointed. I was so desperately hungry. I sat there, my senses trying to shut out the sounds and smells of the delicious meal denied to me, and I felt unspeakably lonely: and that's the way I spent my ninth birthday.

But at last, my 'sentence' was over, and I was released from this ennui to take my place in school. But it was then that I discovered that a number of my friends had left to go to Kinlet Hall, among whom was my good friend Joe.

Boys went to Kinlet at the age of ten, so I would join them sometime during the autumn of 1941.

At the beginning of every term, we would calculate just how many weeks there were to 'going home day'. The term drifted on through leaf-strewn October and foggy November, into December when Christmas activities would begin.

The first 'Christmas feeling' began when we started to learn and practise carols and plays for the school concert. Once December came, we were into Christmas in a big way: Christmas dinner – the best meal of the whole year, with crackers, and diminutive Christmas trees decorating the tables. There were table coverings made of pretty Christmas paper, which felt strange to the touch. (This was the nearest we ever got to table cloths.)

The Christmas concert with songs, percussion band items, recitations – all conspired to increase our animated excitement. The school play followed by the final climactic party to which

Father Christmas came! Our names were called, and we were given presents, which we treasured and triumphed over – it was all so very exciting! This was followed by a very special tea with more crackers and sugar mice with long tails, jelly, bread-and-butter and cakes – even mince pies!

This was the human side of Wolverley that appeared once a year: that's all!

Then, about a week before Christmas it was time to go home, and there the festivities were in anticipation.

This particular year brought much discussion about Father Christmas himself. My brother Harry, who had just left school at fourteen, humoured the rest of us. He knew! My eldest sister, Lily, at twelve, also knew, but would rather not know! Marjorie was eleven, and had her suspicions, but clung on to the hope; whilst Betty, my youngest sister and I were totally convinced that Father Christmas was real, and that they all diced with danger to suggest that he wasn't!

It was all so exciting – all over again! Mum managed to get some new 'trimmings', i.e., paper chains, which we put together with much hilarity. The old box of well-worn decorations was brought from the cubby-hole in mum and dad's bedroom; the contents sorted, straightened out and put up. Wonder of wonders too – we always managed to have a Christmas tree! In the fun and anticipation of the season, we almost forgot that there was a war on.

On Christmas Eve, we went to bed in a ferment of excitement, our hearts beating fast, and with little hope of getting to sleep. Dad went for his usual walk 'round the corner', which we all knew to be a visit to the 'Dog and Partridge', whilst mum got some last minute jobs done.

It was late when dad returned, and we had drifted into a shallow sleep. Mum was ready for bed, but waited up because there was still one important task to perform. There were the Christmas stockings to fill. An apple, an orange, nuts and a new penny, plus a toy for me and a doll for Betty. (I forget what my older sisters had, but I remember being quite disgusted when my brother only got a jar of salted peanuts!)

Dad was to do the distribution honours, but unfortunately, his sojourn earlier that evening at 'The Dog and Partridge' had rendered him weak and somewhat unstable as he picked his way unsteadily up the stairs. Halfway up, his legs gave way and he fell with a heavy thud, accompanied by some surprisingly well-articulated language! He tried to hold on to the presents, but lost control of the oranges, apples and nuts, which bumped spectacularly, back down each stair to the bottom with a variety of fascinating bumps, bangs and clattering!

Fortunately, dad wasn't seriously hurt. He had had a bad knock, but then, so had our belief in Father Christmas!

Next day, when Marjorie was recounting the episode to one of her friends, she said, "Father Christmas doesn't 'alf swear!"

Mum got up early on Christmas morning in order to introduce the turkey to the oven. We were up even earlier, investigating our Christmas stockings, and playing with our toys. In those days, there was still a post on Christmas morning: cards would arrive, and sometimes little packages from relatives which augmented the gifts of the night before.

Christmas dinner was served when dad got home from having a drink with his mates. I was content to listen to the B.B.C.'s special greetings programme to the Commonwealth and Empire: and at 3 o'clock, whilst we were having our dinner, we had to listen to the Christmas message broadcast by King George. Royalty was held in high esteem then. There seemed to be much more respect for authority generally. I seem to remember that, just before the King spoke, we had heard, from the princesses Elizabeth and Margaret Rose. Dad insisted on complete silence when listening to the King.

Christmas night would be party time! Because we had a fairly big living room and a piano, often the parties would be at our house. There could be as many as forty people present, dancing, laughing, feeding, drinking, and totally unconscious of the noise that the neighbours must have heard. Yet I don't remember any complaints being made. Beer had been bought in for the occasion, and a limited amount of spirits. Uncle Fred would be there with his accordion, and Uncle Harold and Uncle Hiram, my mum's older brothers, would have a go on the piano.

But my dad's brother, Uncle George was a star on the piano. I would stand by him, marvelling at the way he played, never having had a lesson in his life!

All the furniture had been pushed to the sides of the room, the rugs rolled back, or taken up completely to expose the floor lino. The party would go on till the small hours of the morning, and Boxing Day would be spent in recovering! But there would be another party that night.

Chapter Six

Kinlet Hall

I WAS AT WOLVERLEY for just over two unhappy years. I'm sure it's fair to say that relations between supervisors and their charges were at best strained, at worse hostile. Perhaps we were too young and immature to appreciate the pressures they were under. The anxieties throughout the country at this difficult time were doubtless reflected among them, and yet I have sunny memories of the maids that served us. When we spent those nights in the dank cellar, I recall being awakened by their singing some of the old music-hall songs. It wasn't the recognised supervisors that presided over our sleeping – it was the maids, those that served in the kitchen, waited on us at tables, and attended our ablutions. They were our consolation at Wolverley.

As far as I remember, I was given no clue as to my transfer on 29th October 1941 from Wolverley to Kinlet Hall. I have since wondered why I didn't go there at the beginning of the autumn term in September. But out of the blue, it seemed, I was packed off on that Wednesday morning in Mr. Myers's car – another strange thing! I arrived after the boys had finished their dinner. Mine was cold and unappetizing as usual. The pudding was cold sago, and just as I was about to give up the battle, trying to get it down me, who should appear in the dining-room but my good friend Joe. What a joy that was to me: some one so familiar in so strange a place.

There were to be many differences here at Kinlet Hall. Although there were two female teachers in the shape of Miss Thomas and Mrs. Cotterell, we also had male teachers: something we never had at Harborne or Wolverley apart, that is, from Mr. Clarke and Mr. Whitton, the music masters.

I was going to get to know Miss Thomas very well; she was to be my teacher for my first year at my new school. She was actually a staff member at the Royal Normal College in Norwood, near London until the disruption caused by the war. The pupils from that college had been disseminated to Great Matham in Kent, Bockleton Court, Worcester College and Kinlet Hall. (In 1942 premises were found for the college at Rowton Castle near Shrewsbury.)

I am quite sure that Miss Thomas was very kind, having the welfare of us boys very much at her heart. However, I, and others, found her somewhat imposing! She spoke with a masculine kind of drawl, and even smoked a pipe! To hear her recite Shakespeare was hilarious. I can hear her now – "Blow, blow, thou winter wind, thou art not so unkind as man's ingratitude."

She was a disciplinarian of the 'old school', being constantly irked by what she considered to be our untidiness of appearance. In her drawl she would cry at us: "your hair, boy! why don't you comb your hair? Where's your parting? if only you would train your hair..."!

We had had virtually no training with regard to personal appearance. We had never seen ourselves in a mirror, and weren't actually shown how to part our hair. We could never judge each other's appearance, because we didn't know what we looked like!

When I meet a person, there are only two physical criteria on which to make any kind of judgment: the person's voice, and their handshake. I never think particularly of a person having a certain type of nose, hair, ears, face, etc. The most ravishingly beautiful girl can stand in front of me, and I would be totally unmoved! Our judgments start from a different point: because it's the person's voice, their accent, innuendo, that give us first clues.

In our class was a boy called Bob. He would sit quietly rocking backwards and forward, lost in his own world. Psychologists today recognise this as a symptom of chronic insecurity. It was an attempt to simulate pre-natal security, when the baby is safe, being rocked in the womb. Quite a number of my contemporaries suffered in this way, but there seemed to be no understanding – and therefore – no treatment of this problem.

Miss Thomas made every effort to rid Bob of this habit. Whenever he started to rock, She would drawl threateningly: "It's coming, Bob!" Then she would hurl a book at him. If her aim were good, she would hit the defenceless Bob as he tried to protect his head with his arms. Sometimes, however, her aim went awry, in which case some other unsuspecting boy would be struck by the dangerous missile.

Compared with Sion Hill House, Kinlet Hall seemed to be immense to me at ten years old. The hall used as the 'Assembly Hall' was positively baronial, with marble pillars, which always felt cold to the touch.

This was where all the main activities happened: morning assemblies, indoor physical training, literary and debating society, socials, concerts, etc. Off this hall was our dormitory, which was known as the Kindergarten dormitory, because we ten-year-olds were regarded as such – sub-junior. Juniors were aged eleven and twelve; intermediates were thirteen-year-olds, and seniors were from fourteen to sixteen.

Mr. Williams invariably took the morning Assemblies. As we were taking our places, copies of the hymn to be sung were passed around. Before a new hymn could be introduced, Braille copies had to be made. Volunteer groups did this work, and it was a wonderful way of learning the words of a hymn.

As well as the well known, mainstream hymns, I recall some less well known ones such as 'Glad that I live am I'; 'Lord, while for all mankind we pray', and

When a knight won his spurs in the stories of old,
He was gentle and brave,
He was gallant and bold.
With a shield by his side,
and a lance in his hand:

For God and for valour

He rode through the land.

For us lads, that seemed totally irrelevant to our situation: and we made a subtle change to the end of that verse:

For God and for Valerie

Rode through the land!

As well as necessary announcements, Mr. Williams would read from the Bible, and sometimes from a Commentary.

On my first Saturday at Kinlet, we were treated to a Punch and Judy show from a Mr. Worth. (I've often wondered since about putting on this kind of visual entertainment for us blind children.)

It was not long before the full rigour of the school's routine became my experience. Part of that routine was the Saturday afternoon walk. Usually the minimum length of the walk was about four miles, taking into consideration the length of the drive of almost two miles there and back. The drive was virtually unmade up; with stones of varied shapes and sizes, and it was an understood fact that new boys, in their endeavour to come to terms with its uncertainties, would come to grief by falling over. Especially on the return journey, tired legs were easy prey to the drive's mischievous trickery.

Typically, we would return from a harrowing walk at half–past four, weary and desperately hungry. But we knew we had to hang around, waiting for the intermediates and seniors to get back from Bewdley. Part of the privileges of these older boys was that they could go out on Saturday afternoons, but must be back by six o'clock. Tea, therefore, wasn't to be until six-thirty – two long hours to wait with gnawing hunger pains that we could hardly control.

Sometimes tea would comprise a baked potato, which was our favourite meal. Other times it was – unbelievably – carrot sandwiches! Any kind of cake was reserved for Sunday teas.

Saturday was also the day when we were given our sweet ration. Each of us was the recipient of exactly three ounces of sweets – slab toffee, caramels, or boiled sweets. We each had our own tin, for which we were personally responsible, and although some of the lads seemed to get through their sweets in practically no time, I was ever the economist, taking some pride in the fact that I could make my supply last for almost the week. Church attendance on Sundays served to help this economy. Sweets were definitely not allowed; and if anyone was heard chomping on boiled sweets during the services, punitive measures were taken, such as the permanent confiscation of the rest of your sweet ration, or the copying out by hand of a prescribed Psalm!

My first term at Kinlet Hall was a short one – just over seven weeks in length. Nevertheless, with all the rest of the boys, I looked forward to the Christmas holidays, as well as the concerts, socials, parties and Christmas dinner that brightened up the end of term. Spirits were running high as the great time approached, and on Saturday, 13th December, just five days before going home day, I was involved in a friendly charging game with Ron Gorton, a boy of my own age who previously had been at the college in Norwood. There was a long wall with a cupboard at either end. I stood at one end, Ron at the other end. At a given word "Charge!" we would charge at each other, to see who was the stronger. Ron was more well built than I, and I crumpled beneath a vicious charge, falling onto my left wrist, which subsequently bent, into a greenstick fracture. Amid all the pain and discomfort of it all, there was the consolation that I would miss the dreaded Saturday walk!

I was taken to the nearby town of Cleobury Mortimer where the lady doctor Fellowes gave me an injection and reset my wrist with a splint. Back at school, I was placed somewhat illogically in isolation in the sick bay! But Christmas was nearly here, and I would soon be home.

All through Sunday, Monday, Tuesday and Wednesday, I sat in that sick bay, huddled against the big fireguard that all but excluded the heat from a feeble fire. I remember being unutterably bored: I was unable to read a book, listen to the wireless, or occupy myself in any constructive way – it was sheer boredom. My friends were not allowed to visit me, and in any case, they were occupied with end of term activities, including packing their kit bags: Thursday, 18th December was to be going home day – but not for me!

To my horror, I was informed that I would have to stay at school through the Christmas holidays. I was devastated. I had been looking forward so much to the holiday – it seemed too cruel to keep me at school just because I had fractured my wrist. Surely I could manage at home just as well – perhaps even better – than I could here.

It was not until February that I was to discover the real reason for my detention at school. My mother had been taken into hospital for major surgery. My wrist injury had nothing to do with the reason for staying at school. But why didn't they tell me? Nobody saw fit to explain things to me. I was simply allowed to believe that it was my foolish horseplay that had brought this problem upon myself.

However, there were others who had to stay at school over the holidays, and as soon as the main body of children had left on that foggy Thursday, I was released from isolation in the celebrations. And amazingly, we did have celebrations!

From the usual austerity of term-time, we were pleasantly surprised to discover that a good time was to be had over Christmas. To begin with, there was more food. It was wonderful to feel reasonably full after a meal, and we livened up considerably at this welcome surprise.

By the pervading smell of cigarette smoke we realised that Mr. Whitton was to remain with us for the holidays. There were about a dozen of us boys, with a skeleton staff including some of the maids and cook. I seem to remember that Mr. Whitton was mainly in charge of us. Of course, Mr. Williams, with his wife and two daughters lived on the premises, kept themselves to their wider family. We felt positively liberated, and I actually began to enjoy the experience in spite of my limitations imposed by the splint and sling.

We had good food, lots of games, prizes and presents, and music! In spite of the fire earlier that year, Mr. Whitton still had a goodly supply of records, including the opera Hansel and Gretel by Humperdinck. I loved it all, and that Christmas of 1941 stands out in my memory.

On Monday, January 5th, those who wanted to go were invited

to a Sunday-school party in Chorley, near Bridgnorth. I believe the invitation came through Mrs. Joan Stubbs, the daughter of Mr. and Mrs. Tolley; a delightful couple who I would soon learn were very keen Christians. I was immediately attracted to them, and the attraction seemed to have been mutual. Before very long, Wilfred and Rose Tolley were going to be a major influence in my life. (Their daughter Joan eventually became one of our supervisors.)

Later that week, the other boys and staff came back to school, and things soon reverted to the norms of the previous term. What an incredible contrast it was! But for me, there was to be some consolation on the horizon.

Our principal, Mr. Williams, was a very kind man. He had a Devonshire accent, having been brought up in Brixham. He gave me the impression of sometimes being a little absent-minded – almost preoccupied with other things. A typical example of this was when he came across some of us boys having a rare old time in the washroom. We would make towels into weapons of attack by twisting them into thick, hard ropes and belt each other round the body and thighs. If you got a really good strike, you could temporarily disable your opponent who would limp away to take time out before renewing his attack. It was tremendous fun. However, as I say, Mr. Williams came into the washroom whilst the fray was in deadly earnest.

At the sound of his voice, everything suddenly became subdued as he announced our punishment. We were all juniors, nevertheless, our legs were slapped, and in those days, we all wore short trousers. And then we were told to "Go to bed at six!"

But by six o'clock, we knew that he was off duty and with his own family, with the result that that part of the punishment was never carried out. Why he didn't inform the next supervisor, we'll never know. This was his statutory punishment, and Mr. Williams would often be called 'Mr. Go-to-bed-at-six'.

Having referred to Mr. Williams' absent-mindedness and preoccupation reminds me of an incident which happened at a conference of teachers of the blind in Germany after the war.

Apparently he had a room on the top floor of the hotel, and as he took the lift to go down for breakfast on the first morning, the lift would stop at each floor to admit another delegate. 'Morgen', politely greeted each new addition to the lift.

"No, no, the name's Williams!" he responded, quite baffled.

In spite of his seemingly ineffectual discipline, and his sometimes rather vacant manner, he was undoubtedly an intelligent man who tried to give the school a family atmosphere. I think he tried desperately to compensate for the fact that we were away from our homes and families. One of the ways in which he did this was to read to us each Sunday evening. When I arrived at Kinlet Hall, he had embarked on the Biggles books, and everyone enjoyed these Sunday evenings. We had 'Moby Dick', W. H. Davies's 'Supertramp', and Jules Verne's 'Journey to the Centre of the Earth'.

Half way through the reading, he would stop in order to have an interval, during which he would hand out 'Mint Imperials' to his delighted audience.

To my great surprise, (and again, due to the sympathetic kindness of Mrs. Williams), I was allowed to go home for ten days at the beginning of February. My mother was still in the early stages of recovery, and I was overjoyed to see her, and so grateful to Mr. Williams for allowing the mid–term visit: and, of course, I had my mum pretty well to myself, dad and my brother being at work, and my sisters at school – it was lovely!

I'm afraid to say that Mr. Williams was not altogether successful in his endeavours to provide a happy school. Other members of staff counteracted what they probably saw as too much indulgence, and were at times very unkind.

I was still only ten years old when I received a hefty boot up the backside from one of the staff for not managing to walk quickly enough. Fortunately, this member of staff left at the end of the Easter term, and I, for one, was glad! I was not alone.

One of my closest friends was Brian from Wednesbury in the Black Country. For some inexplicable reason we always referred to him as 'Tim'. We were all lined up in the hall – I can't remember why – and Mr. Strachan said to us: "I don't want to hear a sound from anyone!" There was an embarrassed laugh from Tim, and that was enough! The next sound was that of Mr. S. hurtling towards us. I was standing next to Tim, and I felt the wind of his hand as it crashed across my friend's face, knocking him off his feet.

I remember the feeling of utter helplessness – what could anyone do? We were miles from anywhere; the country was preoccupied with the war, and most of us just didn't want to talk about school when we got home for holidays.

Generally speaking, the food was substandard and totally insufficient for growing boys. We were aware, of course, that a war was on; that food was rationed: but it was the quality, as well as the quantity that was so deplorable.

Breakfasts consisted of porridge and bread and margarine. Dinners comprised the usual potatoes, vegetables and meat: but it was all so bland and uninteresting. Much of it was processed, and when pudding was served, things were little better. On Saturdays in particular, it was either boiled rice or barley, which was preceded by what we called 'Jacob's pottage' – the most revolting stew, to my taste.

For tea, we were treated to processed American cheese: a rubber-ised slab of the stuff, with bread and Marge again. To be fair, we did have jam sometimes, and on Fridays, a bun with a piece of candy peel in the top.

Grace was always sung before we sat down for our meals. There was a piano in the dining room, and a rota of pianists provided suitable accompaniment. We had a variety of table Graces including:

Be present at our table, Lord,
Be here and everywhere adored.
These mercies bless, and grant that we
May feast in paradise with thee. Amen.

Occasionally, another Grace was used, and it was much later on in my life that I realised how inappropriate it was. The words were designed for Holy Communion:

Author of life divine,
Who hast our table spread,
Furnished with mystic wine
And everlasting bread,
Preserve the life thyself hast given,
And feed and train us up for heaven.

We didn't know what we were singing, and often – in view of what was before us – why we were singing. One senior boy, however, was heard to be making a complaint to his mother about the food. It was on Whit Monday, which was a 'visiting day' when parents and relatives were allowed to come for the day. Mrs. Stanton came to visit her son Fred. He was overheard by Matron, and there followed a scene! Fred was dragged away from his mother; she remonstrated with the Matron, threatening that if she touched Fred, Matron would be the worse for it. It caused quite a stir amongst us all: reports of the confrontation circulated like wildfire. We wondered whether such a protest would make any difference: but we wondered in vain.

Each morning, before breakfast, we would have to cross the yard to the washroom where there was a large cylinder of hot water. However, its capacity was rather limited considering how many boys had to wash. If we were early, there was no problem; but if we were delayed, there would be only cold water left. So the first thing we did was to feel the tank to see if we were going to get a warm wash or a cold one.

After washing and dressing, we had to line up in the courtyard – rain or shine – for inspection, and we were required to wash according to the standard of the supervisor. If Mr. Houghton had decided that we had not washed sufficiently well, then 'measures' were taken.

I well remember the morning when Eric's cleanliness was brought into question. Mr. Houghton said that he could see a 'tidemark' around his neck. Eric, in his protest, took the unfortunate step of raising his fists in frustration. Mr. Houghton lowered his voice menacingly. "So! after breakfast we will settle the matter: we'll see who's right!" Even the fourteen-year-old Eric could hardly have been prepared for what was about to happen.

At the end of breakfast, Mr. Houghton called Eric to come out into a clear space away from the tables. We were to stay where we were to witness the humiliation of our friend Eric Cranmer. "Put 'em up then," commanded Mr. Houghton. "Come on, come on!

We weren't, of course, able to see what was happening, but suddenly this hard man began to taunt Eric: "I can use 'em, I can use 'em! Are you satisfied? Are you satisfied? Well I'm not!" Every time he said "I'm not!" he hit Eric, shouting at him the whole time. "You think you can dictate to me? Who do you think you are?" Under the vicious, merciless beating, Eric crumpled to the floor.

It had been a show of vicious vindictiveness, and we could do nothing about it. What amazes me now as I look back is the fact that surely some of the domestic staff must have witnessed all of this, or at least, overheard something of it. As far as we know, the incident never got to the more kindly Mr. Williams: Mr. Houghton had been guilty of assault and battery, and would never have got away with it today.

Meanwhile, the war dragged on, and we tried to keep up with all that was happening, rejoicing at every sign that was to the advantage of our forces and those of our allies. At the news of the Eighth Army's success at Alamein, one of the boys, in his exuberance, slipped out of school and ran down the drive to the church where he took the unprecedented step of ringing the church bell. This was only supposed to be done in the event of an invasion, and even then, certainly not by one of the boys. But by now, bells were being rung all over the country, and Bernard just wanted to be part of the excitement.

The vicar, however, who may have been disturbed from one of his frequent visits to the 'Eagle and Serpent', was not amused. He really never understood boys. They were only useful for one thing – pumping the organ at Kinlet church – and you had to make sure they did that properly! Rev. Hard never made any attempt to gear his services to us, and we provided the majority of his congregation. The ringing of the bell that day in celebration was in all probability the most exciting thing that had ever happened in that church!

During 1942 there seems to have been quite a migration from Kinlet Hall, both staff and boys. In view of the fact that the Royal Normal College was now established at Rowton Castle, near Shrewsbury, Miss Thomas left to resume her duties at the college. Mr. Whitton went, too, in order to head up the piano-tuning department, having succeeded Mr. Kelly who had been responsible for the training of piano-tuners at Norwood. quite a number of the boys who had been at the college before it moved from Norwood went too, in order to continue their education.

The senior boys that had reached the age of sixteen went for workshop training to Harborne. The Kindergarten school was now little more than a hostel for trainees.

My former music-teacher Mr. Clark replaced Mr. Whitton, and Mr. John Lorimer replaced Miss Thomas, and therefore became our teacher.

Chapter Seven

Back from the Brink

I WENT HOME FEELING DRAINED AND WEAK, looking forward to my Mum's cooking, and the excitement of more seasonal celebrations.

Christmas and New Year came and went, and I felt more and more listless, and began to develop an irritating cough. I had been looking forward to the Sunday-school party on Saturday, 9th January – two days before I was due back at school. But on that Saturday morning, I awoke with a searing pain in my right side. My parents' bed was more comfortable than the one I was in which I still shared with Harry, my brother. I was duly transferred – at least for that day – and the doctor was called. Immediately he diagnosed pneumonia and prescribed tablets, which made me sick. With the effort of being sick, the pain became so bad that I found myself crying. I writhed in the creaking bed, but could find no relief.

Everything is so clear in my memory of that seemingly endless, remorseless weekend. I scarcely thought, in my preoccupation, of the party that evening, and all through the next day, Sunday, my temperature began to rise.

On Monday, when I should have been going back to school, mum sent for the doctor again. He called that afternoon, and – seeing the condition I was in – immediately called for an ambulance. I was rushed to Selly Oak hospital for an emergency operation at eleven o'clock that night. It was peritonitis.

The feel of the mask tight over my nose and mouth, and the suffocating smell of the chloroform filled me with fear, until I dropped into oblivion.

The operation, (performed appropriately enough by a surgeon called Mr. Gore!) was to be only the start of it all. Whether my doctor's diagnosis of pneumonia had been correct or not, it certainly developed after the operation, with the added complication of an abscess on one of my lungs – I was desperately ill.

For some time I hung between life and death. Because there was still so much poison in my stomach that couldn't seem to drain, I underwent a second operation.

This time, when they placed the mask over my face, I smelled oranges! This was obviously to assuage my fears: but soon the dreaded ether smell overcame me, and once again I surrendered to the anaesthetic.

Back at school an announcement was made that I was "at death's door". The boys were encouraged to write to me, but I don't know to this day whether any of them did: everything was vague; I seemed to fade, and then wake again.

I have memories of other men in Ward B3 of Selly Oak hospital: some having their daily pint of Guinness for medical purposes. There was a young boy called Teddy who screamed whenever his dressings were changed. A young man called Tony who was what we called an up patient, who brought the tea round at half-past five in the morning, and was generally very useful to the nurses.

I remember hearing news of the war in Russia; of the siege of

Stalingrad, and of German soldiers freezing in the dreadful Russian winter. There was even a Sweep Stake organized by Tony as to when Stalingrad would be secured.

The kind Mr. Williams even travelled the thirty miles from school to visit me, bringing me all sorts of goodies, but I was too ill to eat.

One Wednesday my parents were summoned to my bedside and warned, "He may not make the night." My mum's brother-in-law, Uncle Jim to us, came to support her. Uncle Jim was a cycle tester at the B.S.A. – a very practical, down-to-earth man. He placed a caring arm around mum's shoulder and said: "Never mind, love, perhaps it's a blessing in disguise; he may never have made much had he grown up!"

News of my illness reached Slade Lane chapel, where I had been to Sunday-school and the evening gospel services. Predictably enough, I was known as 'Blind Peter'. Wednesday evening was when the chapel met specifically for prayer. They were concerned for me, and most of the hour between eight and nine o'clock was spent in praying for me.

At the conclusion of the prayer meeting, they all felt that they had reached a place where they could trust and thank God for my healing. It was at nine o'clock that I came to, and attempted to reach for the headphones that hung on the wall just above my bed. But I couldn't manage it. The perspiration soaked me, and I was totally unaware of my mum standing by me.

I didn't know why she had come, and she was really hardly in a position to explain!

Of course, we didn't know then about the prayer that had been made for me. God's hand was upon me!

Shortly after this, as I began to gather strength, another operation was envisaged. I was actually being prepared for theatre when I was violently sick. Medically speaking, it was a defining moment. From then on, having cleared my own system in nature's way, I began to recover.

I can never forget the way the nurses and doctors cared for me. I remember particularly two staff nurses, Stockwell and Meddley: they were compassion personified. When staff nurse Stockwell changed my dressing, she knew that the plaster had to come off as quickly as possible – it would be less painful that way. The screens would be placed round my bed, and Nurse Stockwell would say, "Two shakes of a bee's wing!" and off would come the plaster with the minimum of discomfort.

It was now getting towards the end of February, and I was encouraged to try to take some steps in the ward. I shuffled rather than walked: the pain in the top of my feet was excruciating! But I remember chatting to the men, visiting this bed, and then shuffling to the next bed. Some of the men would tell me of their experiences of some twenty-five years earlier in the First World War.

During my last ten days in hospital, the nurses and sisters tried to tempt me to eat food. I was suffering from loss of appetite, and they would ask me: "What would you like to eat? Is there anything you fancy? You can have anything you like." It was the kind of offer I would have liked to have heard many times in the past, but I could hardly do justice to food of any kind at that time.

Some of my parents' friends came to visit in the latter stages of my recovery. Evelyn and Margaret from the local grocery store; even some friends from 'The Dog and Partridge' came – people were so very kind.

Eventually, I came out of hospital on Wednesday, March the third. It was a typically blustery March day, and I was carried into the waiting ambulance, made comfortable, and we sped for home! As the ambulance drew up outside our house, and the doors were opened, our dog, Ruff, jumped into the ambulance. He had to be restrained, and I was carried into the house, and propped up in my favourite armchair. Ruff came to sit by me, and stayed there for the rest of the day.

He was a rough-haired Irish terrier, and had been rescued from a bombsite by my brother. Normally, if ever anyone came to the door, Ruff would rush to the door, barking his little head off. People did come – plenty of them – but never did he move, and he never barked. It was as if he sensed my weakness, and sympathised.

I spent the next ten days at home, managing to walk as long as I was in the house. But a special wheelchair was provided for me so that members of my family could take me out for fresh air and sunshine. I was out with my mum one day; one of the neighbours came up to me and said: "Hello, grave-cheater!"

On Saturday, March 13th, I made the trip back to school, my mum coming with me. I didn't know just how I was going to cope with the rigorous routine and rough-and-tumble life at school. But

I needn't have worried; there was a surprise waiting for me.

Mum and I parted with a kiss and a hug: something that had happened all too often in the past. Then Mrs. Joan Stubbs came to where I was sitting by the fire. "Do you remember my parents, Mr. and Mrs. Tolley? You met them last just over a year ago at their chapel's Sunday-school party." "Oh, yes, I do!" "Well, you're going to stay with them at their home so that you can get strong again." How could I forget this kind, jolly couple? I was greatly relieved. I didn't feel that I could face school. The car came, and I soon was welcomed into the home of Mr. and Mrs. Tolley.

Chapter Eight

New Interests

As the car sped off to Chorley, Mrs. Stubbs driving, she chatted pleasantly about some of my fellow-pupils. But as I sat beside her, my thoughts were a veritable maze. I seem to remember something about an outbreak of chicken pox in the school, and that it was thought advisable that I should be taken out of any danger of the infection.

"You remember the chapel at Chorley, the Sunday-school party you came to, and of course, my parents? They're so much looking forward to making you well and strong again. You've been through a tough time, you know..." on she went, until at last we pulled in to the side of the road in front of my temporary home, Ebenezer Cottage.

For quite some time I didn't understand why it was called Ebenezer Cottage. We knew about Charles Dickens's classic 'A Christmas Carol' with its eventually reformed character Ebenezer Scrooge, but Ebenezer Cottage seemed very strange to me.

It was later that I realised that 'Ebenezer' "Hitherto has the Lord helped us". It was homely and comfortable – even though there was no inside toilet. This was to be found down the garden – past the pigsty!

I can't say I remember much about that first Saturday evening, except one thing that was a regular occurrence. After supper, whoever was staying with Wilf and Rose Tolley in Ebenezer Cottage was expected to join them in prayer. There was to be no sitting, slouched in an armchair, or even sitting forward with bowed head. We all knelt to pray, and that made a lasting impression on me.

Anglicans make provision in their churches by providing hassocks for kneeling, but it seems to me that nonconformists – for the most part – miss out on a special blessing in not kneeling any more. I say for the most part: there are exceptions, of course, notably the Wednesday prayer meeting at my chapel at home already referred to. When you entered the chapel at Slade Lane, as well as a fervent handshake, you were given a hymnbook, a chorus book, and a cushion, which was to serve as a hassock. When the serious business of praying began, everyone was on their knees – it was a wonderfully humbling, unifying experience. The Bible, after all, encourages us to kneel, both by exhortation and example.

In Psalm 95 we are exhorted to "Come, let us kneel before the Lord our maker, for he is our God, and we are his people". People like Abraham and Daniel knew the experience of kneeling when interceding for the people. Paul, the great apostle knew what it was to kneel in prayer, and best of all, the Son of God Himself knelt often. It was in the garden of Gethsemane that the Bible records that "He went a little further, knelt down, and prayed 'Not my will, but thine.'"

It has been said: "It's much more difficult to argue with each other when we're on our knees." "God has placed all his blessings on the bottom shelf."

Even when I was a young Christian I heard: "A Christian is like a camel: each morning the camel kneels in order to take the burdens of the day. Each evening, he kneels to release those burdens."

I was to spend three weeks with these lovely, caring people. They did all they could to make my convalescence as enjoyable as possible. It was wonderful to have good, wholesome food, to feel full after a meal, although it didn't take much to fill me – I was still trying to get used to eating proper meals. Mrs. Tolley worked hard on me in supplementing my diet with daily doses of cherry flavoured cod-liver oil and malt. (It sounds revolting – but I loved it!) I had to have egg beaten up in milk, and a strange medicament, which was known as my tonic.

There were all sorts of interesting things to do. Each day I would take a little walk in the village with Mrs. Tolley. In order to give me some respite, we would call at one of their many friends just for a little chat and rest. It wasn't long before the entire village knew that the Tolleys had taken in a sick, blind boy. I was unashamedly fussed over and spoilt.

I joined in with the weekly ritual of going on the Whittle's bus to Kidderminster every Thursday. The bus would be full of villagers going to market day. There were no such things as supermarkets in those days. We would have to get back to the bus for a certain time; clamber on, package-laden, and the bus seemed fuller than ever with parcels and boxes of all sizes. It was a merry day, with animated conversation: in fact, it was a weekly outing not to be missed.

I was never bored during the weekends. Mr. Tolley would be

home from the colliery where he worked, and he was such fun to be with. I remember thinking once: he ought to be called Mr. Jolly! If I wanted to, I could listen to the wireless: the Tolleys weren't in any way prudes. I would listen to Raymond Glendenning commentating on a football match – something I really enjoyed.

Sunday was a day for worship. There were services morning and evening, and in the afternoon the Sunday-school. I didn't find it at all difficult to relate to the other village children there. I already knew most of the choruses because I'd learnt them way back at Harborne from Miss Richardson.

As I experienced the unselfish love of the Tolleys, and listened to the simple preaching of the gospel in chapel, I began to understand more and more about their uncomplicated faith. I learned about a God of love who, as Jesus, came to earth to take the punishment for the sins of every person in the world – including me. The Tolleys' love of God began to make sense, and I realised that God loved me too. I enjoyed the services even more when I came to understand what the Lord Jesus had done for me.

My recovery began to accelerate: I was putting on weight, and I could walk further and further each day. The village doctor came to check up on me nearly every day. He was delighted at my progress, and expressed amazement when he saw me walking in the village.

The next day I was playing the Tolleys' harmonium. It was a fairly old instrument, which had to be pumped with the feet. I found it very difficult at first: the muscles of my legs having been out of action in hospital for so long. It was painful at first, but I persevered, and it gradually became easier until all the pain was gone. As the doctor came in, he saw me playing the harmonium with hands and feet going at it! He turned to Mrs. Tolley: "That explains it all," he enthused: "Finest exercise possible! No wonder his feet have improved so much."

As well as their daughter Joan, Wilf and Rose had a son Victor. He, too, was married, but all his childhood toys were summoned from remote cupboards and loft for my amusement. There was a prodigious collection of military badges; a thing called a gyroscope, which I never really got the hang of: cars, buses, tractors, and spinning tops – it was just like Toyland!

The older I have become, the more indebted I feel to those dear people. As a child, I could only partly appreciate their love. But now, I have much more understanding of their hearts towards me in opening their home and caring for me. They have long since gone to their reward, and I shall see them in that eternal day.

Will we have any kind of recollection of time then? I'm not sure. But I seem to sense, deep inside, that all they did for me has not been lost in time, but will resurface in eternity. The wood, hay and stubble will be burned up, to leave in glorious relief the gold, silver, and precious stones.

The end of my convalescence at Ebenezer Cottage co-incided with the end of the school term. This meant that I could continue my recovery at home for the Easter holidays.

Easter 1943 was as late as it could be. Early in the holiday 'our Joanie' came to our home, This was Joan Sidebottom, who was described as being our second cousin twice removed on my dad's side! (Who was responsible for working all that out, I never knew!)

Joan was keen that my sister Betty and I went to Sunday-school. We eagerly agreed, and Joan called for us on that Palm Sunday, 18th April. At the end of Sunday-school, I heard her talking with some of the other teachers about a radio presentation of Dorothy L. Sayers' 'Man born to be king'. She enthused about it, and I decided there and then to listen that night after the nine o'clock news.

It was an altogether splendid production. The one who took the part of Jesus had a beautifully modulated voice. Heron Carvic took the part of Caiaphas the high priest. Mr. Carvic had a menacing kind of voice – perfectly suited to the role. The music that was used in the play was Ravel's introduction and allegro for flute, harp and strings. It's eerie kind of music, with lots of atmosphere. I was immediately captivated, and every evening of Holy Week I was glued to the wireless.

On Good Friday, April 23rd, the crucifixion scene was acted out. I had never experienced emotions quite like it before. I was completely taken over by it all, so much so that – although there was an air raid that night, I didn't even bother to move! Normally, I would have been the first to get out of bed, slip on a dressing-gown and slippers, go down through the living-room, out of the kitchen into the garden, and climb into the Anderson shelter. But not this time!

Next day, with my mind still dwelling on last night's episode of 'Man Born to be King', I found two flat pieces of wood and nailed them together in the shape of a cross. I scrambled on top of the air raid shelter, and erected the cross there. I've only recently learned that that particular Good Friday raid was the night Birmingham received its last bomb. 'Our Joannie' had really started something that holiday!

I returned to school with the rest of the boys on Monday, 3rd of May. I hadn't been to school, of course, since the previous December, and had a good deal of catching up to do.

Mercifully it was a short summer term, in which my full recovery seemed very slow.

I think my teacher, Mr. Lorimer, understood. He had come to Kinlet – as I remember – when he was twenty-eight years old. (We prized that information out of him!)

He hailed from the Yorkshire town of Bradford, was very fond of classical music, and could play the piano. Although he hadn't come to teach music, nevertheless he introduced us to the Beethoven symphonies and piano concertos; Smetana's Vltava, The Vaughan Williams folksong suite, and much else.

John Lorimer was himself blind, and had learnt Braille as a teenager. He used to read to us on Friday afternoons from books such as R. l. Stevenson's 'Kidnapped'; John Buchan's 'Thirty-nine steps' and Prester John. Another of his favourites was the Arthur Ransome books like 'Swallows and Amazons'.

However, although we greatly enjoyed these classic yarns, because Mr Lorimer had come to learn Braille comparatively recently, and we had learned it from infancy, anyone of us was more fluent in our reading than he was. He would read slowly, and with some hesitation, but we bore it patiently!

I seem to think we were at the beginning of his experience as a teacher. He found us difficult sometimes. He introduced 'Question time', when we could ask him anything we really wanted to know.

One boy piped up: "Please, sir, where do babies come from?"

This caused great hilarity among the rest of us, so much so, that Mr. Lorimer refused to take the question seriously.

There was very little 'official' sex education at school. Such as there was came to us from the B.B.C.'s. schools broadcasts. 'General Science' did a series: but there was nothing from the staff in this respect. Like growing boys do, we tended to 'educate' one another!

Even when, later on, we became co-educational, there was no particular emphasis given to sex education, and yet I can't remember any serious incident, which might have led to the expulsion of a boy or girl.

The day before we went home for the summer holidays, Mr. Williams announced to us all that – within the next year or so, we would be moving from Kinlet Hall to Lickey Grange, a large house near Birmingham. One million pounds would have to be spent in altering and adapting the premises to make it into a school. That sum of money seemed positively astronomical to us. A year's work would be needed, and it was all very exciting.

At home, there was talk of the 'New front'. Nobody quite knew what it was all about, but there was a mounting confidence about the way the war was going. On the Russian front the Germans had sustained some crippling reverses. The campaign in North Africa was going well, and at home, there was very little enemy air activity. I remember hearing about a dear old lady in Scotland who was listening to the Scottish news. The news-reader said: "There was very limited enemy activity over Scotland last night. A few bombs fell at random." The old lady questioned: "Where's random?"

I gradually felt much better during the summer holidays, and would quite often go out on my own to explore the neighbourhood. I remember being delighted when I discovered where the shops were. My mother asked my older sisters one day: "Would one of you go to the Chemist for me for some head tablets?" They demurred long enough for me to jump up and say, "I'll go for you, mum." I held out my hand for the money, and to their great surprise, I was gone.

Round to the right from Sandmere Road into Moorside Road. Another right turn; passed three big trees whose roots were beginning to break through the pavement. Round a slight bend into Centre Way: cross the road, proceed along towards another large tree, before crossing the road again, which brought me to the shops.

I knew which shop to go in by the distinctive smell of each shop. When I got home, my sisters were suitably humiliated!

From then on, every Sunday morning that I was home, I was the one who went for my dad's newspaper and ten woodbines. Sometimes, when going further afield, I might get lost, and have to ask my way back. That was all part of the adventure! But most times, my sister Betty and I would be seen together, for I was closest to her. She was caring then, and has been caring since, for as well as bringing up her own five children, she then fostered two boys with learning difficulties right into their adult life.

When writing an autobiography, it's not easy to be wholly objective. Yet perhaps from this distance, it is possible. What kind of a boy was I as I approached my twelfth birthday? I can only try to look at myself as others must have seen me. I was short-tempered, especially at home where I felt that I was still a stranger to my family.

There were things I heartily disliked about my home: the fact that I still had to share a bed with my brother who was now nearly seventeen – and he must have hated it too. I found it difficult to come to terms with my dad's habits of smoking and drinking. As I have mentioned before, we had no bathroom upstairs. If I ever needed to go to the toilet in the night, I would rather make the journey downstairs to the back yard than use a potty. My dad used a bucket that was by his bedside, which meant that my parents' bedroom had a constantly pervasive smell of urine. I hated that! I never knew what my mother, or the rest of the family thought about that: it was just never discussed.

How my three sisters managed I just don't know. They slept three in the double-bed, and I never heard any complaints at all. They were mild-mannered girls; Lily was now fifteen and worked for a telephone cleaning company. Marjorie was to leave school at the end of the year, and Betty was almost ten years old. She was the one I was closest to, and even at that age, probably understood me better than the others did. With seven of us, in one living-room, we were cramped. It was not an ideal set-up.

Yet in spite of all that, home was still home: somewhere totally different from school, away from constant supervision and hunger. At school I was regarded as being pedantic, correcting people if I thought they were wrong. I could be moody and morose; and I recall one occasion when I told a bare–faced lie, which even now has left some kind of scar.

One of the buildings in the grounds of Kinlet Hall had obviously been servants' quarters. It consisted of a large scullery, and twisting stairs that led to several rooms – possibly bedrooms. The place smelt of antiquity, with plaster hanging off the walls. I remember sitting on the stairs, methodically stripping the inviting plaster! Eventually I stopped, and realised with horror the extensive damage I had created. I crept down the rest of the stairs, out through the scullery, only to be greeted by Mrs. Musgrove, one of the cleaners from the village.

Later that day, I stood in the staff lounge, and was cross-examined about my misdemeanour. But I protested my innocence vehemently, knowing that Mrs. Musgrove had not actually seen me stripping the walls. I bluffed it out, never admitting my guilt for fear of severe punishment.

I was not without friends at school. perhaps it was my music that made me bearable, and I did have a cheerful side. Even at that age, I loved cracking jokes, making people laugh, which all served to give expression to my gregarious nature. Yet my most consistent friend was the piano. Music was never just a 'subject' to me: it was too close to me for that. I had a gift of being able to express my deep feelings in improvising music – just playing whatever came into my head. Occasionally these improvisations crystallized into compositions, which I can still play today.

At the age of twelve, there were question-marks twisting themselves inside me. The previous year, Gordon had come to our school from Cardiff where, as a result of a direct hit on his home, he had become a blinded orphan overnight. He had a beautiful treble voice, and whenever he sang such pieces as 'Come unto him' from Handel's Messiah; I would fill up with sadness for him. I remember his being fostered out to folks living in Banbury. Ironically, – so I understand – Gordon has since spent most of his working life in the Ministry of Defence.

At this age, too, we were now considered to be approaching our intermediate status – we were, after all, in our thirteenth year. We graduated from short trousers to 'longs'. It makes me smile to think of that now. How fashions have changed! Until the age of twelve, we didn't think it unusual to show our bare knees. It never occurred to us to be embarrassed about not wearing underpants! We weren't very dress conscious anyway. War was a time of ration-books and shortages generally, and we experienced them too. There were occasions when Mr. Myers came from Bockleton Court, his car and trailer laden with vegetables and fruit from the Herefordshire orchards. In 1942 we'd had a shortage of water, and the sighted senior boys were 'drafted in' to help dig latrines in the nearby woods.

As the winter of 1943 approached, there was a shortage of heating fuel, and all of us were formed into logging parties, the younger boys restricted to collecting kindling wood. A boy with useful sight partnered each blind person, and inevitably, Joe was my partner. It was gruelling work in the cold, but in such an emergency, no one could escape! But that very winter was to be brightened up by something that we could never have dreamt possible. On Saturday, 27th November, some three thousand

American servicemen descended upon our quiet seclusion. They built an encampment on one side of the drive, and for the next six months, conducted manoeuvres in preparation for 'D-day' – although we didn't know that at the time. All we were told was that the Americans had come to help the war effort, and they opened up a whole new life to us.

The long drive was ideal for their purposes. There were plenty of trees and undergrowth – perfect for manoeuvres, and they soon established their bivouacs, tents, cookhouse, lorries, jeeps and other equipment in the grounds. Before long they were settled in, even to the extent of tarmacking most of the drive so that their army lorries and jeeps could be spared the rigours that we had endured. It was a treat for us to walk on such a smooth surface.

That Christmas term began a time of unprecedented fun and friendship for us, as the Americans responded so easily to the presence of lively, inquisitive blind lads. They spoilt us on every occasion possible. They came to give us a concert, and we were thrilled to hear them sing 'The Stars and Stripes' – their national anthem. I remember Colonel O'Shea coming to talk to us in class about life in the States. We were open-mouthed with interest and astonishment! They would give us rides in their jeeps, and on going-home day, they took our luggage and us to the bottom of the drive in a big lorry. We'd never before met such pleasant, jovial people with an unusually attractive accent. They were so friendly and helpful – we loved them! They augmented our meagre sweet ration with candy, and on one occasion, I was invited into the cookhouse and given a mug of steaming, sweet hot chocolate!

But they encouraged some of the senior boys to smoke Camel cigarettes, and this resulted in the whole school being subjected to a lecture from Mr. Williams. "On no account will this be tolerated," he said. "Any boy seen with cigarettes will be severely punished." A few special friendships were made – two of the soldiers, Ray Miller and Rusty Hendron built up a particular rapport with some of the lads, and would be remembered ever afterwards. It was a great time, but it ended all too soon for us in May 1944. As quickly as they had come, they mysteriously disappeared, and we were left with a disappointed void.

Because of the secrecy shrouding military operations, there could be no 'goodbyes' – no notice of intention given. It was a sad time for us when our American friends had gone. June 1944 began uninterestingly enough. The weather was cool and unsettled, and as far as we were concerned, we were already into the countdown for the summer holidays. But on Tuesday the 6th, news came through that the Allied Forces had landed in France – this was D–day! Even in our comparative isolation, the excitement was palpable. We listened to the radio that evening, savouring the drama of it all, thinking that it would only be a matter of weeks before the war was over. But we were to be proved wrong on that score. Nevertheless, preparations for leaving Kinlet Hall were well under way. A number of us were involved in packing boxes, many of which had been left by the Americans. So as we approached the end of our final term there, we were full of anticipation: and I was nearly thirteen!

Chapter Nine

Lickey Grange

I shall never forget my thirteenth birthday; that was the day when we returned to school – not to Kinlet Hall – but to Lickey Grange. I really don't think anyone regretted leaving Kinlet. We'd had so many shortages, so many leaking roofs – it was as if the old place couldn't stand the ravages of school-boys any longer. So we had, in fact, to move to Lickey Grange before the place was quite ready for us.

It was a large house situated on the Birmingham to Bromsgrove road that had been owned by Lord Austin of the Austin Motor Company. A plaque mounted on a plinth was affixed to a marble table in the hall, which read: 'The gift of Lord Austin to the Birmingham Royal Institute for the Blind'. The move meant a return to civilisation in the minds of most of us, but for me, personally, it was a welcome move nearer home.

Being thirteen meant that I automatically acquired the privilege of an 'Intermediate', which meant that I was able to go out on Saturday afternoons. We 'Kinlet boys' were to be there one year before going to the old school at Carpenter Road, Edgbaston, actually within the suburbs of Birmingham itself. The girls from Bockleton Court would join us there, whilst the children from Wolverley would replace us at Lickey. When we were there, Mr.

Lorimer's classroom was an outbuilding – little more than a hut. There was an asphalt playing area at the bottom of a fairly sharp gradient. In the playground was a hut that served as a place for polishing shoes, etc. This was known as the 'boot hut'.

In that autumn pine cones were thick upon the ground. We divided up into two armies, one to attack the playground, the other to defend it. Our ammunition was pine cones! We each had a formidable store of them, and battle commenced! I was a defender of the playground, and as the opposing army came down the hill into the playground, the air was thick with whirling cones, cries of "ouch!" and calls for more ammunition. It was tremendous fun, and we took great delight in taking prisoners and guarding them in the boot hut. We felt much more liberated at Lickey: it was to be a wonderful year, with new experiences of our surroundings, and new expectation as Europe was experiencing liberation too.

Whereas the dormitories, for the most part, were numbered at Kinlet, the dormitories at Lickey Grange were given names of famous hills that were not too distant from us. There was Malvern, Clent, Cotswold, Bredon, and Ankerdine. We were not far from Worcestershire, the county where Sir Edward Elgar was born. The whole place had a totally different atmosphere, and we were growing up and beginning to think for ourselves; to take more of an interest in the outside world.

Most Saturday afternoons, Joe and I would be seen together going to Bromsgrove, which was in easy walking distance. We would enjoy the bustle of the shops; we would go into Woolworths, and the 'Messenger' newsagents. But I particularly enjoyed going to Spain's radio shop. This was a popular shop for many of us, because making crystal sets was becoming quite a craze at school. It was at Spain's that we could buy crystals, headphones, and coils, etc. Ray Browning seemed to us to be a genius in the constructing of radios. I really think he started it all, and before leaving Lickey, he was into making valve sets. But I loved making up my own crystal set. Putting one together was really quite simple: a coil of wire, a crystal diode, (or Germanium valve) a condenser and a pair of headphones was all that was required. The set was earthed either to a radiator or a rod pushed into the ground. The aerial would be rigged up on to a beam, or better still, to a roof outside. External aerials always made for better reception. The circuit of the set was very basic, and virtually any reasonably adept youngster could put one together.

Where we were situated at Lickey was ideal for receiving the B.B.C. European news broadcasts. Even an aerial to your bed-spring would be sufficient to pick up a really good signal. We made all kinds of crystal sets, and we would compete with one another as to who could make the smallest one. I made one from a cotton-reel, using the actual reel for a specially constructed coil wound to receive the B.B.C. Home Service. Many happy hours were spent with these sets, and they were useful for listening to in bed!

Mr. Bentley, a local businessman and Methodist local preacher took a great interest in us boys. Mr. Williams welcomed him to the school to take services, and quite a number of us were invited out to tea in his home. He was undoubtedly a very kind man, having our welfare very much to heart; but I cannot remember any impact of his preaching. Maybe I wasn't really listening, except that I did have an appreciation of the gospel message, but didn't recognise it coming from this man. But it was probably due to his auspices that a number of us went along to the nearby village of Catshill, where we integrated with the young people from the Methodist church.

I remember the Wilks family, and a certain young man who rejoiced in the name of Grenville Wagstaff. He, too, had a crystal set: however, to my amazement and joy, he didn't listen to it through headphones, but fed it through an amplifier! This was a dream! The quality of sound was vastly different, and superbly clear. I'm afraid it was some years before I could acquire an amplifier; meanwhile, I continued to be satisfied with the intimacy of listening on headphones. Another visitor to the school was Mr. Cherry from Rednal. He became our scout leader, for we had continued our 'Scouting' right through the Kinlet years. Mr. Cherry was quite refreshing, coming as he did from the outside. I remember learning a concise summary of the scouting law, which, incidentally, adequately summarises the Decalogue of the Old Testament: a scout should be "Trusty, loyal, helpful; brotherly, courteous, kind; obedient, smiling and thrifty, clean in body and mind." It's a wonderful summary.

One day, I said to Joe: "If we get away straight after dinner, I reckon we could make the trip to my home, getting back by six o'clock." It was risky, depending on trams and buses connecting smoothly, but Joe was prepared to give it a go. We walked to Rednal, got the number 70 tram through Longbridge, past the Austin Motor Company factory, and so to Northfield, where we got the 18A bus from 'The Bell' to 'The Valley', both pubs! At 'The Valley' we got the 24 bus to School Road, Yardleywood, and then walked the mile or so to my home in Sandmere Road. It must have been at least 3 o'clock by the time we got home, and we had to be sure to leave by 4.30, and yet we deemed it all worthwhile. Gradually we stretched it a bit, having to make a hectic dash for it from Rednal back to Lickey Grange. The climb up Rose Hill was exhausting, and we had to be so careful not to be seen arriving some half an hour late. But there was never any trouble, and my family got to know and love Joe, even as I did.

I think Joe would testify even today that we became his second family. In November, Mr. Myers and Gwen Brown came to give us a piano recital, which included the Brahms' St. Anthony variations on a theme of Haydn. This was the same Gwen that had supervised us at Bockleton Court. In December, my brother Harry came to our carol concert. He was just eighteen, and he came to tell me that he was soon to get married to Roma Parr. This marriage had been hastened because Roma was pregnant, and because Harry had received calling up papers to join what was known as the 'Z Reservists'. My brother had all of a sudden grown up, and from then on, grew away from the family. He went on to serve in Northern Ireland, Egypt, Suez, and Port Said. The following April, on the Queen's birthday, the 21st, I became an uncle!

My nephew was also called Harry after his father as was the custom, but to avoid confusion, my dad was called 'Big Harry'; my brother, 'Young Harry', and my nephew was called 'Little Harry'! Later on he was to be known as 'Al', and showed some musical prowess in becoming the lead vocal in a pop group of the '60's known as 'The Applejacks'. 'Tell me when' was their best hit, and I have heard that still played on the radio over thirty years later.

Even though our relatives didn't know Braille, we were encouraged to write letters, one of the sighted staff writing in print on the same paper that we had written the letter in Braille. I wrote to Harry who was then serving in Egypt, but it was a long time before he got the letter. When it eventually arrived, he found it covered with 'British Intelligence' stamps. They thought that this was some coded message, which had to be deciphered. This innocuous letter must have gone through many departments; defying 'British Intelligence' to decode it, until it finally arrived at its intended destination.

Perhaps because of the general feeling that we were not so isolated now as we had been when at Kinlet, something happened in February that year which caused a real stir. Two boys, Jack Reed and Derek Shipp absconded. They were found sleeping in some one's garden, brought back, and were caned by Mr. Williams. Derek had tried to run away before from Kinlet, and was picked up by Mr. Williams when Derek put his hand out for a lift! In the early months of 1945 we knew that the end of the war was imminent, with Germany being threatened from the East by Russia, and from the West by American, British and Commonwealth forces. Although there were setbacks such as the battle of Arnhem, which went badly for our paratroopers, we knew that victory was in sight. On May 8th, the Prime Minister, Winston Churchill made the momentous announcement that Germany had surrendered unconditionally. Rumours were rife that Adolf Hitler had committed suicide in his own bunker; that Nazi leaders were being arrested, and were to be put on trial at Nuremberg.

We celebrated what came to be known as V.E. day at Lickey Grange. We were given one day's holiday with picnics and games in the ten-acre field. Even a threatening thunder-storm could not dampen our spirits as we rejoiced in the heady atmosphere of the day. But the war was not entirely over. The 14th army was still engaged in bitter conflict with the Japanese. Stories of terrible atrocities filtered through to us of the treatment of prisoners-of-war, and these combined with what we were hearing of the Concentration Camps in Germany. The emaciated corpses of Belsen, of Auschwitz and many others. By means of the radio, we kept up our interest in current affairs, following the Nuremberg trials and the Labour landslide of the general election.

We had been joined at Lickey Grange by Mr. Bill Arkinstall, a brilliant musician who was himself blind, and politically very much to the left. He once described himself to me as a free-thinker. As constituency after constituency went Labour, he rejoiced, as did so many others in the country. However, it wasn't going to be many years before Winston Churchill would become Prime Minister again. That term was to be my last at Lickey Grange, and I went home in the knowledge that I would be graduating to Carpenter Road after the summer holidays.

During early August, atomic bombs were released on Hiroshima and Nagasaki. I remember hearing about it on the news read by Frank Phillips. There was a sense of shock and shame that such measures had to be used to bring the war in the Far East to an end.

Around that time, I had spent some time suffering from 'flu. But in spite of that, when the announcement was made that Japan had surrendered, V.J. celebrations began in earnest on 14th August. There was a large grassy traffic island quite near to where we lived known to us all as 'the circle'. We allowed our piano to be taken out to be situated in the middle of this area. The neighbourhood came out in force; I played for hours, and it was a street party with a vengeance. We all felt exhilarated and full of optimism, sensing the promise of a whole new era. However, euphoria is, by nature, ephemeral, and so it was to prove. There is no doubt that the past twelve months had been a truly eventful year. The wars had ended; I had become an Uncle, and I had sensed a kind of liberty that I hadn't known before.

I had enjoyed being at Lickey Grange so much that there was no particular thrill in looking forward to the next chapter in my life. But at the end of that summer holiday, I made my entrance to the school at Edgbaston, and thus into new experiences.

Chapter Ten

Carpenter Road

I was now nearer to home than I'd ever been during my schooldays: just two bus rides! We were within easy reach of the centre of Birmingham, and sorties into the city would be really exciting. However, our arrival at Carpenter Road was to be more momentous than we could possibly have foreseen. This school was co-educational. We were to live and work alongside girls! To boys who had not had close contact with girls since Kindergarten days, this was to be a completely new phenomenon. We were really in uncharted waters. It's true to say that most of us had a blinkered view of girls – they were like angels to us – creatures who could do no wrong! We had little or no idea how to speak to them, and how to behave in their company. Many of us became quite inhibited by their presence. But in spite of all this, inhibitions were eventually overcome, and quite soon, boy-girl friendships evolved.

Our conversation changed: "Guess who so-and-so is going out with"; "She's keen on you, you know". "Is she really? How do you know?" It was to be quite some time before I had the courage to ask a girl to "come out with me". Although I had three sisters, this particular girl was different: but much was to happen to me before I was able to 'pop the question'!

As summer all unwillingly gave way to autumn that first term, Joe and I were just as inseparable. We went into Birmingham to explore: but our chief pleasure was to be able to spend much more time at my house. It was now so different from when we used to travel all that way from Lickey Grange. Instead of the seemingly interminable walk to Rednal, the tram, and the two buses and another mile walk, now it was just two bus rides of about quarter of an hour. When we came back from our visit to my home, the bus stopped right outside the playground, and it was a simple matter to shin over the low wall, and mingle with the folks in the playground – we were never late...Carpenter Road was nicely placed for an immensely exciting event.

Two miles away from the school were the Midland region studios of the B.B.C. in Broad Street. Some of the pupils and staff were asked to take part in a programme called 'The Future's Here'. This was a real mix of items, mainly of local interest that I was chosen to take part in. I had never before been in the actual presence of a dance band; I positively tingled with excitement at the all-round impact of its sound. I had actually heard the Alan Airs band on the radio a number of times, but to be in a broadcasting studio with them was ecstatic! And then, too, the pianist, Harry Engleman was to play some light piano pieces. I had heard him in his weekly series with 'The Harry Engleman Players'. I seem to remember that we were guests of the B.B.C. most of that day, during which, Mr. Engleman actually suggested that I played a currently popular song with him as a duet! So we played 'Chewing a Piece of Straw'! We were four hands on one piano: he played the middle and bass, and I did my best to provide a decorative performance on the mid and top treble. It was wonderful! Here I was, at last, playing – as it were – on the other side of the wireless! Listening on my crystal set would never be the same again!

Another man I met during that absorbing day was somebody called Mr. Bill Bowes. At first I only registered how big his hands were as we shook hands. During his interview in the programme, I suddenly realised that he was the famous Yorkshire and England cricketer! This was also the first time I met Mr. Cambray Jones, who was taking part in the programme. He was to feature later on in my adolescence. After the Alan Airs band had played 'Crazy rhythm', and Harry Engleman had played his first medley, it was our turn. As we stood around the microphone, Alan Howland whom I had heard as a news-reader announced us. I gave an account as to how blind people managed to play chess on a board with white sunken squares that had holes for the pieces to fit into. (the black squares were, of course, the raised ones.) I explained how we could differentiate between the white and black pieces: the whites having a sharp point on top, the blacks being plain. But that was not the end of my contribution.

I could perform the 'bones', or 'clappers'. These were two pieces of polished and slightly concave bone, which were held in one hand and separated towards the top by the fingers. Then, as the hand was shaken, the bones would click and tap out a lively rhythm. If you were really good at it, the rhythm could be very lively indeed. My friend, Ken Howarth played the mouth organ, and I would think that that was the only time the song 'South of the Border' was ever played as a duet by mouth organ and bones at the illustrious B.B.C.! I shall never forget the impressions made on me that day in early October 1945. We all had a wonderful time, and received the very handsome fee of – half a guinea! When the recording went out on 22nd October, all the school assembled to hear it: it was marvellous!

At just about that time, I was taken ill again. I developed severe rheumatic pains in my right knee, which practically immobilised me. My mother came to visit me in sick bay, and – realising the predicament I was in – was furious! My pain was so acute that I could not even bear the movement of the bedclothes. She wanted to know why I hadn't yet seen a doctor. She harangued the mild-mannered Mr. Williams who wilted under the onslaught. I was sent home, and an appointment with our family doctor soon saw me in Selly Oak hospital, where I had been so ill two-and-a-half years ago. As I lay on the couch, the hospital doctor examined me, and pronounced: "This young man is suffering from malnutrition." I was inordinately thin, for years of hunger had restricted my physical development. Then he diagnosed a peculiar heart condition that required complete bed-rest.

With another prolonged stay in hospital, my first thought was to get myself organised with my crystal set. Headphones to the main radio that broadcast throughout the hospital were provided, but I very much wanted my own creation. It was brought in to me, and I earthed it to the radiator, which made an excellent 'earth' because it was, of course, linked to all the hospital's plumbing system! However, the signal was not really good enough, probably because the hospital was in a built up area. What I needed was a good outdoor aerial. Amazingly the hospital staff moved into action. A maintenance engineer appeared who rigged up a superb aerial which went right along the ward and out through the window! I can hardly believe how kind they were to me. The result was marvellous! I had made the set in such a way that I could get the Home Service and the Light Programme with reception that was really clear.

The doctor (whom I suspect had organised it all) came to see me inquired about my crystal set: "Have you got it going yet?" I replied, "It's wonderful...listen to this," handing him the headphones. "Marvellous!" he exclaimed, "And it doesn't shout at you, does it?" And so I willingly rested, with my ears to the outside world, taking my medicine – which was the most revolting I have ever tasted. I couldn't take it without an accompanying fruit sweet – it was so awful! But I was glad to be able to go home for Christmas, with the stern warning, "Be very careful; don't get too excited, rest as much as you can. If you misbehave, you'll be back here with us."

These instructions were going to prove all too difficult for me, especially being at home with my family, at Christmas, the time I loved most of all. I managed well, though, until after the celebrations were virtually over. There had been a heavy snowfall in early January – snow was lying a good six inches deep, and deeper still in some places. I was quite content to stay indoors until my sister Betty came in, full of excitement, and urging me to come out and join in the fun. (Betty was twelve years old at the time.) "We're making a really big snowball!" she cried: "We've rolled it all along the road, and we're just going to get it up onto 'the circle': come and see it and help push it." This was just too much. I simply had to go and find out what was going on, and join in. It was amazing fun. The snowball had got so big that everyone had to get behind it to push. I couldn't resist it, and went to help. We pushed with all our might, the snowball getting bigger and bigger, and more and more difficult to roll. Suddenly I collapsed. Boys and girls converged on me, trying to lift me, but it was no good. Stronger hands were called for, and I was carried back to our house.

The doctor came and confirmed that I had done altogether too much, and that I would now have to rest in bed for a few days. However, resting did not solve the problem. When I was finally allowed up, I discovered that I was sometimes prone to fall over for no apparent reason. Then, too, when I held a cup of tea, my right hand would suddenly jerk violently, spilling the tea dangerously. Back to hospital I went. Then something quite inexplicable – and in its way – illogical happened. Mum and I were waiting for me to be admitted. We were told to go upstairs to the second floor, which was the cardiac ward. My sense of humour didn't fail me.

When we had climbed many stairs and had reached the appropriate department, a nurse asked, somewhat peremptorily, I thought: "Are you cardiac?" Before my mum could say anything, I replied: "Well, even if I wasn't before, I am now after climbing all those stairs." When the doctor came to examine me, he said: "Just what have you been up to? Too much excitement, I guess." I hadn't the nerve to tell him about the big snowball incident. I was now diagnosed as having a mild form of St. Vitus's Dance, the remedy for which was more rest and medication.

I eventually went back to Carpenter Road in March after pretty well five months' absence – just before the Easter holidays were due to begin! I believe, as a result of this long illness I missed the opportunity of furthering my education, and eventual training, at the Royal Normal College, near Shrewsbury. In your fifteenth year, if you were judged to have made good enough progress educationally, you either went to Worcester College for the Blind, or the Royal Normal, which specialized in music, shorthand typing, and piano-tuning. (Worcester majored more in academic work. People who had been there could graduate to Oxford or Cambridge, study law, etc.) But I missed the boat, and was bitterly disappointed. Now I would simply have to go to the workshops at Harborne to train for manual work such as Upholstery, mattress-making, brush-making, or mechanical engineering, which meant putting nuts and washers on bolts and screws: not a pleasing prospect!

After the recuperation of the Easter holidays I was ready for school. Mr. Myers had come from Bockleton Court with the girls, and he was now our teacher. He was the senior teacher with pretty progressive ideas. He made brave attempts to bring democracy into the school. His idea was to set up what was called 'The School Council Organization', which included staff and children. It was a good try, but not altogether successful – perhaps because we had been too 'institutionalised', and perhaps because we were enjoying a greater freedom now – whatever the reasons, it just didn't work out.

In a biography of Mr. Myers, 'And you a gentleman', the author, Cambray Jones explains that Mr. Myers was completely 'out of step' with the ethos of our school. He did not agree with the harshness of our treatment, or with corporal punishment. It tells how he hated the dreaded outdoor inspections, which he consid-ered degrading and unnecessary. Apparently on one occasion, he was told to cane a boy, but instead, he beat a cushion and told the boy to scream! He then warned him not to offend again; otherwise he would be forced to cane him properly! Mr. Myers wasn't really at Carpenter Road all that long. Eventually he went on to pioneer a school at Condover Hall, near Shrewsbury. This was a special school for blind children who had additional handicaps. Later he became an executive with UNESCO (United Nations Educational, Scientific and Cultural Organisation).

During the Easter term of 1946, my family started talking about a possible house move. For Joe and me, it would mean a minute's walk from the bus to our new home. The move took place sometime during the summer term. We were now living no longer in Yardley Wood, but in Warstock, still in Birmingham B14. The road had a pretty name, Daisy Farm, which must have had some historic significance of which we were totally unaware. Among other things, it meant that dad had to change his 'local' from 'The Dog and Partridge' to 'The Warstock', or even 'The Prince of Wales'. Generally speaking, I was glad of the move, principally because it was virtually on the bus route, and saved that mile walk which, in places, could be dangerous by virtue of a bridge with desperately narrow pavements.

By the time I was fifteen, I had developed a terrific 'crush' on a girl I had known in Wolverley days. Rene was quite small, and when we used to play 'hide and seek' all those years ago, she used to be able to hide in a school desk! For me, this was it! She was a wonderful girl, and I was quite distracted by my feelings for her. A boy's first love for a girl can be a painful experience. I wanted so much to be with her, and yet – when I was – I was tongue–tied and gauche. It was strange how much a physical contact simply by holding hands meant to me. And when we kissed...! I'm not sure at that time how much she reciprocated my feelings. She was indulgent of me, but years later, we almost became engaged.

By now, the senior boys were billeted at my old Kindergarten school at Harborne. We commuted every day, and began to feel rather grown up. From Carpenter Road we would walk along Calthorpe Road to Five Ways where we would get the 3A bus to Court Oak road. We learned to interpret where the bus was going by the turns, hills and islands. For instance, on that journey from Edgbaston to Harborne, we knew so well the way the bus would change gear for the quite noticeable incline, at the top of which was the bus-stop outside 'The Green man' pub and Nursery road. After another two stops, the bus would slow down, and a right bend before it stopped told us that we were at the Royalty cinema. Next stop was 'The Duke of York' pub with a big island. This was where one could change to take the number 11 bus, which went right around the edge of Birmingham. Two stops later was our stop. More often than not, a group of us blind young people were together on the bus.

I remember one particular occasion when we were having a really good laugh – behaving as typical teenagers, thoroughly enjoying ourselves. Suddenly, we heard two women talking. One said to the other: "In't it a shime for 'em: they ought t'ave been shot out of their misery!" Well, you can imagine our reaction to that! In January 1947, we commuted to Harborne as usual. As we walked, the snow began to fall. It had been very cold for some time, and people were bracing themselves for this very moment. A typical remark was: "It's too cold for snow, and it won't get any warmer 'til we 'ave some". We reached Harborne safely enough that January day, and didn't realise that we wouldn't get back to Carpenter road until mid-March!

The BRIB staff must have been very stretched, for we had to have members of staff who could continue our lessons, even in a limited way. We really enjoyed ourselves, and at that time, certain 'mature' students were given supervisory duties over us. There was a Mr. Davis who had been in the Royal navy. When he got us up in the morning, he would come rushing into the dormitory saying: "Feet on the decks, boys!" There was a Mr. Beynham who once took some of us to the Aston Villa ground to see the Villa playing Stoke City. At the beginning of the second half, with the match at 2-2, it had to be abandoned because of a blizzard. Then there was Mr. Marshall, who had been in the army, and had witnessed something of the battle of Arnhem when so many of our paratroopers were killed. Mr. Marshall would bring a radio into the dormitory so that we could hear 'The man in black' in Saturday Night Theatre. He was a really good sport – in fact – we got on well with all of these men, and they got on well with us.

The snow seemed to go on and on. I was fascinated with the weather situation. There was a persistent anticyclone over Scandinavia, which was linked to a high pressure area over Siberia. This forced depressions, which would start moving from the Atlantic in an Easterly direction to go South-East, and then move along the English Channel. Over and over again the forecasters were duped into believing that the warmer air at the centre of a depression would gradually bring about a thaw. But it only needs a slight deviation to change potential rain into snow. The Easterly type that was generated by the positions of the two pressure systems meant snow...and more snow. Buses eventually stopped; people couldn't get to work, but somehow or another, milk was delivered, at least, to cities. There was one cartoon that represented a table set for tea. People were sitting round, and somebody comes in with a milk jug. "How many lumps do you take?" Even the sea froze!

The building hadn't changed since I had been a little boy there some eight years before. Nowadays it's known as Queen Alexandra College, and it's almost unrecognisable from what it used to be. I usually visit there every year when attending a technological exhibition. I remember being at this exhibition one year, standing in the room that used to be Miss Richardson's classroom. A young lady asked me: "Are you a Braille user?" I replied, "It was over fifty years ago when I started learning Braille in this very room!" "Oh, that's really interesting," she said.

The thaw came in late March, and things began to revert to normality. 1947 was the centenary year of the BRIB. We had been told that special plans had been made for a very special celebration that would include all the senior boys and girls, and all the trainees together with some of the training staff. We were to go to a holiday camp in Prestatyn, North Wales for a week! This was tremendously exciting for us, and on a drizzly Saturday in early May, the coaches were packed with animated teenagers. It was a totally new experience for many of us, and we thoroughly enjoyed ourselves.

For me, one of the outstanding memories was to go to the ballroom and listen to the 'Norman Collins broadcasting band'. Sadly for me, Joe wasn't part of this celebration. He had left just before this took place in order to make his way in the world of industry – he was judged to have too much sight to go into sheltered workshops. It was to be two years before he got his first job in Wolverhampton, sweeping up! That lasted a week, and thus began the unequal struggle for a partially sighted man in open industry. Of course, I wasn't aware of Joe's struggles at that time, but I missed his friendship, and his companionship during this particular week. I completed my schooling at Edgbaston. Through the summer holidays, I anticipated the next chapter in my life: being trained as an upholsterer at the Harborne workshops.

Chapter Eleven

A Wonderful Opportunity

I RETURNED TO HARBORNE in September 1947, and resumed residency at the old school where we seniors had been for the last twelve months. But, instead of taking the bus back to Five Ways, and walking to Carpenter Road, the workshops where we were to train were just a five-minute walk away. I remember that first morning of 'going to work'. I recall vividly the smell of pitch, which emanated from the brush shop; heard hammering from the boot and shoe repairers, and was conscious of the whirr of machinery from the engineering shop. I was shown to the upholstery workshop and introduced to my trainer, Mr. Thatcher. He had, in fact, been a supervisor at our school, and he seemed genuinely pleased that I was about to join his work force.

It was a bad start! I knew, then, that this wasn't where I wanted to be, nor what I wanted to do with my life. Nobody else in my group of school leavers was with me: I was a boy among much older men, feeling alone and rebellious. To the accompaniment of

'Housewives Choice' on the Light Programme, I remember using a ripping chisel to prize out tacks that had held webbing at tension for years. I had to cut springs free, disembowel old armchairs and sofas, the dust of decades rejoicing in its release! There was no possibility of my acquiring upholstery skills, so I was transferred to the bedding shop: still under Mr. Thatcher as my trainer. For me, this was equally soul-destroying, and I was becoming more and more depressed, and more and more rebellious.

I was then transferred to the care of Mr. Cambray Jones who looked after the basket-making. My fingers just weren't made for soaking, bending and weaving of willow and cane. Frustration began to set in – there seemed to be no way out. I was virtually unteachable, because I was a round peg in a square hole! I was, of course, having no more piano tuition, and because of my circumstances, I wanted to play as much as was possible. So I spent from Mondays to Fridays longing for the weekend when I could do what I really wanted to do. I would spend hours lost in the world of jazz and popular dance music. I would do my best to emulate the pianists of the day. One that I particularly admired was the legendary 'Fats' Waller. Like me, he was a rebel! I knew the story of how he had horrified his father, who was a minister, by playing jazz on the church organ. His father threw him out, telling him never to come back. He never did! 'Fats' combined his rebel spirit with a weird sense of humour. Who else would write songs like: 'Your feet's too big!' or, 'Your socks don't match'? His playing was much better than his singing, and yet without his singing, it just wouldn't have been 'Fats' as we knew and loved him. I suspect, like him, I was sick of being 'pushed around'. I had been told what to do by other people all my life. I wanted to break out and do "my own thing", as the vernacular has it.

One Friday evening I was having one of my 'Fats Waller' sessions on our piano. 'My very good friend the milkman' was going well, when there was a knock at the door. I took no notice as the man from the Prudential came in. My mother gave him the weekly payment, but he didn't rush away. He waited until I had finished what I was playing and said: "That was terrific! I've got a twelve-piece band, and we have a regular Saturday night at Cateswell House dance hall. I'd like you to come and, when the band has its intervals, you could play to the folks. How would you like that?" I was overjoyed; this was more like it. At last I would be able to entertain the public. My playing would have a real purpose. Betty came with me: she could sing, and possibly fancied herself as Birmingham's answer to Vera Lynn! Betty and I went on stage for the interval. She sang a few songs that went over well, and then I launched into jazz and ragtime. The people loved it! My first exposure to public playing (apart from the street party of V.J. day) was an unqualified success.

Soon I was accepting bookings for parties. In the days before fitted carpets became so fashionable, parties would be held in people's houses. Our family parties were held either in our house or at my maternal grandparents'. We would push the three-piece suite to the sides of the room, roll the rugs up against the furniture, which exposed the lino, and folk would be able to dance. Next morning the lino would be cleaned, rugs put back, furniture resume its normal place, and nobody would have known there'd been any kind of celebration the night before. My mum and dad were members of a working men's club in King's Heath, and when there wasn't a party to play for, I would go on stage at the club, playing background music, or accompanying soloists and community singing. It was a kind of a double life I was leading. Bored to bits during the week, but able to let off all my pent-up frustrations at weekends.

On October 22nd we experienced our first family loss. Our grandmother – mum's mother – died. Ironically enough the funeral took place on 27th October, mum's forty-third birthday. From then on, things were never quite the same in the family. Parties were never as many, and the only times we got together were for weddings or funerals. The one who had seemed to preside over us, and unify us had gone. She died at the relatively young age of sixty-five. My Auntie Edna, mum's youngest sister looked after granddad for the next five years or so until he died.

Early in 1949 I walked along Woodville road to the workshops as usual, not realising what this particular day would bring forth. But, as I was enduring the drudgery of basket-making, the patient Cambray Jones said to me: "Your presence is required in the general office." I made my way to where I knew the office to be, knocked on the door, and at the curt invitation to 'come in', walked rather timidly into the office. I don't remember being asked to sit down by Mr. Edkins the superintendent, but was conscious of a number of people sitting at a long table. Mr. Edkins began: "We've been trying to train you, giving you opportunity after opportunity to learn a craft so that you can be usefully employed. However, you don't appear to want to co-operate with your instructors: in fact, you show no interest in their efforts with you." I felt very small, standing there in front of what almost seemed to be a jury that had already passed sentence on me. What was going to happen now? What would become of me? These questions flashed before me, and I could only lamely apologise and admit that they were right. Suddenly, I heard my previous instructor, Mr. Thatcher speaking to me. "I seem to remember you playing the piano at school." "That's right," I said: "I've set my heart on playing the piano to entertain people, and that's what I'm already doing at weekends and in the holidays."(It's strange that, although one is blind, one can still be conscious of people turning to each other, and making some kind of exchange of looks.) Mr. Edkins again: "We understand your interest in music, and considered that that's where your talents lie. So, we are making a proposition to you which we hope you will consider carefully." I waited anxiously, wondering what my fate would be. I was totally unready for what was to come.

"The Birmingham Authority," continued Mr. Edkins, "is willing to sponsor your attending the Royal Normal College at Shrewsbury, where you will be able to take up your studies in music, and also learn to be a piano-tuner. How does that appeal to you?" My face went hot with excitement, and a lump in my throat all but prevented speech. I was overwhelmed with a sense of profound gratitude as the facts of the situation dawned on me. I thought I had lost my chance for ever to go to college, robbed as I had been by illness. But the opportunity was actually being presented to me now

– at this very moment. I stammered out my reply: "I-I would l-love that, sir: I really would. Thank you, thank you very much." "Furthermore," continued Mr. Edkins, "assuming you complete the course and gain your tuning diploma, we can offer you a job here." I was ecstatic! I realised that it would curtail my embryonic career, but I had enough sense to grasp that it would only be a temporary lull whilst I trained for a profession. I could return to the circuit later. My tenure at the workshops finished straight away. I went home that next weekend to spill the good news to my parents. "I'm going to college," I blurted out, "And I start at the end of the Easter holidays."

The Birmingham Authority could do no more for me than that. I have an enduring debt of gratitude for their help – they were wonderful!

Chapter Twelve

A New Beginning

I was well into my eighteenth year when I went to college on April 28, 1949. My mother came with me to Shrewsbury on the Midland Red X96 bus from Birmingham. When we arrived at Claremont Street bus station, there was quite a crowd of students getting on the coach, which would take us the seven or so miles to Rowton Castle. I remember that ride well. I didn't feel that I could be part of any conversation: after all, nobody knew me except one lad who had been with me at school, years before. He was asking one of the masters about the coming term's work – Keith Bradley wasn't even aware of my presence.

You can't get eye contact with fellow-blind people, and I felt really alone! Sighted people, even though they may be strangers can engage one another with a smile. Such is denied to us. Even now, in my own church, I have to wait for people to speak to me before I know where they are! It's therefore not normal for a blind person to make the first approach where sighted people are concerned. We have to wait for people to make contact with us, however outgoing our nature might be.

So here I was, with no one to talk to about what awaited me: I just sat there, wondering...anonymous. We arrived in good time for tea; I followed the rest into the dining-room, and after Grace was sung, we sat down to discover a shelled, rubbery hard-boiled egg on our plate. This, I felt, was a singularly unappetising welcome! But at least meal-times provided opportunities for getting to know one another, and as a result, friendships were soon formed.

After tea that first evening, I was shown 'the huts', which were built during the war to accommodate the senior boys. They were little more than nissen huts, but were destined to be the centre of most of our activities at college. There was the tuning block and practice-rooms, which included two organs and twenty-six pianos. The sleeping quarters were housed here too, including three dormitories, with some twenty boys in the one where I was to sleep. Right down the centre of the room were metal lockers for our possessions. It was very Spartan, and maybe partly because of this, we all associated with one another easily and readily.

As I look back now, I really can't recall much in the way of pettiness or squabbling: we were all in the same boat, and determined to make the best of our situation. My first morning was taken up with the daily Assembly, and the sorting out of time-tables. Tuning lesson, tuning practice, music lessons and practice times; English, economics, physical education, choir, etc. etc. I felt I was in at the deep end, and was conscious of a strange exhilaration. Assemblies were presided over by the college Principal, Dr. J. N. Langdon. He was authoritarian, having difficulty in maintaining the respect of the students. His manner of speaking and the frequent clearing of his throat made it easy for some of the lads to imitate him.

We had to negotiate a narrow slab path from the huts to the Assembly Hall, collect our Braille hymn-book, selected hymns from Ancient and Modern, and take our places quietly: college choir at the front. A hymn was sung, followed by a reading, usually from the Bible or a Bible commentary. After two or three brief prayers, announcements were made, and sometimes a lecture given by 'The Doctor'. As well as the morning assemblies, there were also evening prayers, with a similar procedure, but this time taken by a member of staff. Most of us had a very flippant attitude to these religious practices. Some of the hymns were archaic, unrelated to us or to our situation. We drew what consolation we could, sometimes at the expense of the hymns. For instance, there was what we called the anti–smoking hymn. (Notice especially the third line):

Sun of my soul, thou Saviour dear,
It is not night if thou be near.
O may no earth-born cloud arise
To hide thee from thy servant's eyes.

More boyish hilarity was realised in yet another evening hymn:

At even, ere the sun was set,
The sick, O Lord, around thee lay...

A rather more delightful story to tell concerned another hymn, 'Ye servants of the Lord'. Our bursar was a Methodist lay-preacher. He had a very gentle way of speaking, and I was hard put to it to think of him as a very dynamic preacher. He was precise, and extremely efficient at his job. He had his own office, which brings me back to the hymn. Whenever we sang it, our thoughts invariably turned to Mr. Lidster, the bursar: the first two lines especially: Ye servants of the Lord, Each in his office wait...

One more quirky bit of memory concerned yet another hymn. Bathing arrangements were pretty primitive for us boys at any rate. (How the girls got on, we never knew!) We had communal showers, which I did not like one bit. Imagine coming out of a shower with many naked bodies around the shower–room. Just because most of us couldn't see, we had to be very careful in other ways: the trajectory and position of one's hands when looking for a clear space for the operation of drying oneself.

My shower was always on a Monday evening after prayers. On quite a number of occasions, we would have the hymn 'Pleasant are thy courts above, In the land of light and love.' Bearing in mind what was to follow prayers, here is the last verse of that hymn:

Lord, be mine this prize to win:
Guide me through a world of sin;
Keep me by thy saving grace;
Give me at thy side a place.
Sun and shield alike thou art;
Guide and guard my erring heart:
Grace and glory flow from thee;
Shower, O shower them, Lord, on me!

Although I was very glad to be at college, I had to get used to being under authority again. Having had a time of relative freedom, I was now back in what amounted to residential school, and that meant regimentation, rules and regulations. I could no longer get home for weekends because the college, being situated between Shrewsbury and Welshpool, was fifty miles from Birmingham.

Another factor was the constant lack of money. My parents just couldn't afford to subsidize me. I was the typical impecunious student. Now I was away from the clubs and party scene of Birmingham. But at least there was the Saturday night dance, when fellows and girls had the closest contact of the week! This was inevitably a supervised affair for which pianists were provided, sometimes by staff, sometimes by students.

As soon as it was discovered that I was a strict tempo pianist, I was asked to go on the rota. It was no problem to me to play waltzes, foxtrots, quicksteps, tangos, and all the other forms of ballroom dancing that made up the evening's entertainment, so I willingly agreed to go on the rota.

When I duly turned up for my stint, I was stopped in my tracks by the sound of the pianist who preceded me. His technique, his chord formations and harmonic progressions astounded me! "Who's that?" I asked in total admiration. "Oh, that's James – John James: he's just a junior and we seniors don't fraternize with juniors." "This senior does!" I retorted quickly, and went straight over to the piano. "You're just great," I said to him, "absolutely marvellous!" Shyly he answered: "Oh, thanks. You're playing next, aren't you?" The word "Yes" came out, but in my mind I was thinking, "Too right I am!" That was the start of our friendship.

One of the things I hated most about institutional living was the obligatory church attendance. All through my school days church had been incredibly boring and unrelated to us as blind people. I had determined that at the first opportunity, I would stop going. Of course, the one exception to this general opinion of church was

Slade Lane chapel at home. But even that was now in the past, and didn't seem to relate to me. I was ambitious and self-opinionated: I knew where I was going, and nothing was going to hinder me. But, for the time being, I had to knuckle under, I could not avoid going. I was angry. I was not a child any longer, and they had no right to insist on my complying with this stupid rule. I was perfectly willing to comply when it came to my training – that was necessary. But I couldn't see that church attendance was essential to my training as a piano-tuner and musician. But here we were on a bright morning in May, my first Sunday at college, forming the usual 'crocodile' – just like a crowd of little children – leading off to the weekly dose of boredom.

I fumed as I walked along in the line – I didn't need this. Religion was a 'crutch' for the young and the elderly who had nothing else in life to keep them going. I was still of a mind to make my way in show business, and church would not form part of that. I had no intention of submitting to religion simply because it was 'the thing to do'. As we entered Cardistan church, I anticipated the usual musty smell of old pews, worn hassocks and damp hymn-books. But to my surprise, a smell of fresh paint met my critical nose. This church had a strange 'clean' smell to it, and did not have the kind of atmosphere I expected at all. I knew the service would be the same old form, though, and I continued to rebel as we stood, sat and knelt in the appropriate places. As the sermon droned on, I fidgeted and scowled for twenty minutes. Then came the familiar "Now to God the Father, God the Son, and God the Holy Ghost...". It was an unusually warm May morning, and as we all made an effort to stand for the last hymn, there was a rending, ripping sound that met our ears. The pews had been newly varnished very recently, and twenty minutes of close encounter with the still tacky pew backs provided a physical, if not a spiritual, adherence. The students could hardly contain their mirth, but I didn't find it funny. To me it was a kind of symbol as to the 'holding' power of institutionalised religion upon the masses. I was not only forced to attend – it seemed as though they were even trying to keep me here!

During the afternoon of that first Sunday, I took part in a hand-ball game, where at least I could vent my spleen! By the end of that first weekend, I was already well integrated into the Royal Normal College. I had begun to meet people whom I had known years before, including a young man, Alec Thomas who had been at East Grinstead. There were boys who had come to the junior department when they were fourteen. And then there were some staff members, including Mr. Arkinstall, who had been at Lickey Grange, and especially my tuning instructor, the much-loved Mr. Whitton! These reunions were of great help to me, and my gratitude to Mr. Whitton for his excellent training was going to know no bounds.

I loved piano-tuning right from the word 'go', and was determined to get on. So as well as tuning, music studies, and other ancillaries such as English, etc., another ingredient was typing. Although we weren't to be involved in the courses for shorthand and typing, nevertheless it was felt that even we tuners should have a working knowledge and skill in being able to manage our own letters and invoices. The head of the typing block was Miss Penny, but my instructor was a very pleasant man from New Zealand – Ian

Doull. Looking back now from the computer age, how glad I am that the college insisted that we learned to type. It has proved to be of inestimable value to me.

There was one disappointing aspect to my growing friendship with John. It wasn't a serious one – not until, one day, he asked me if I would care to come to 'The Christian Fellowship': a small group of fellows and girls that met every Sunday afternoon. Sundays for me were 'recovery' days after Saturday nights! I scarcely was up much before mid-day. Having been up for some six hours or so, it was then time to make my way to Cateswell House to play for the officers' dinner. This was quite a different style of playing from Saturday night parties, dances or club work. This was a gentle playing such as you would hear in fashionable restaurants: a background to people's conversations, unobtrusive music.

I had felt that they were pleasant evenings – a class above, and with a fee at the end! And now, here was John, asking me to go to yet another 'religious' meeting, on top of compulsory attendance at church, and college prayers every morning and evening through the week: that was more than enough for me! "The great thing about it is that there are no staff there!" urged John. (He knew where to hit me hardest!) "Well," I said hesitantly, "That perhaps makes a difference." Here, at least, would be a place to get away from the endless supervision. "What do you do there?" I asked. Now it was John's turn to be hesitant. "Well, ... well, we sing some good hymns, have a chorus-time..." "Do you ever play the piano there," I interrupted. "Yes," he confirmed, "We have a rota, I take my turn." "Okay, then," I told him, "Next time you're due to play,

I'll definitely come." "Good!" he replied, "Because, actually, I'm playing next Sunday!"

It seemed like a continuing conspiracy to get me involved in religion! I didn't seem to be able to get a break from it at all. But I must be as good as my word, and so I duly went to the next meeting. There was only a small group of students that met in the big Assembly Hall, but what they sang and said was all too familiar to me. For the most part, the choruses were those I had learned as a child at Sunday – school and in the evening gospel services of seven years before. The prayers were extempore, like Miss Richardson's had been, and like those in the chapel. They were talking to someone who was vitally real to them – a personal friend and loving father. It was not a bit like the pompous religiosity I had experienced in church. It was like a step back into the past.

Nostalgia swept over me, and I remembered the time those years ago when I had asked Jesus to come into my life. Then someone read from Psalm 139. The Psalmist was saying, "Lord, you know when I go to bed, when I get up, when I sit down and when I'm about to stand up. You know what I'm about to think before the thought is in my head! You know what I'm going to say before I say it. You're in front of me, behind me, and your hand is laid on top of me. I can't cope with that knowledge – it's altogether too wonderful for me. I've tried to get away from you, but I can't. I've tried distance, but everywhere is near to you. I've tried darkness, but everywhere is light to you. So, Lord, I just give up. I want you to search me, try me, and then lead me in the way everlasting."

This Psalm really summed up my situation perfectly. It spoke to me loud and clear, although I didn't intend it to – for one thing, I just didn't like Psalms. They were usually badly chanted in church by understaffed choirs, and this offended my musical ear. In school, the Psalms had been synonymous with punishment. If one misbehaved in church, one had to write out a Psalm. But this Psalm spoke to me in spite of myself. It told me that I could not avoid God. I couldn't hide from someone who is everywhere. So I was inevitably drawn to the Christian Fellowship for most of the Sunday afternoons that first term at college.

By the end of that term, I was invited onto the piano-playing rota. But other than that, I was not at that time prepared to make any firm commitment, but simply keep my options open. I hadn't been at college very long before I was taken into Shrewsbury to get my eyes seen to. That may sound strange, but the fact was that my artificial eyes had never been updated from when I was a child at school. My natural eye sockets had grown, but – of course – my artificial eyes had remained small. My eyelids had no support, and if things continued for much longer, my muscles would begin to waste away. So I was fitted with new eyes, plastic this time as opposed to glass – much safer!

When I got home for the summer holidays, I was able to tell the family that my tuning had gone well. It seemed as though I was born to it. I had already passed two tests, and was therefore well ahead of the usual time-scale for the course. My keenness, however, did not impress the lads who came round for a band session. I was no longer very interested in this kind of thing, and they turned away scornfully. "One term at college," they said, "And he's a snob already!" It wasn't that, though. My appetites and ambitions were changing subtly. My life was already beginning to go in a different direction.

Chapter Thirteen

Surrender!

As I remember it, the summer of 1949 was a fairly settled one. We'd already had two quite spectacular thunder-storms on the 11th and 13th July, but the weather settled fair after that. Even though my sister Betty was now almost sixteen, she remained very loyal to me. We still went places together: going into the big city, taking picnics in the local parks, etc.

On Friday, 2nd September, she suggested that we went that evening to the town-hall where there was a visiting team of evangelists from America. The main attraction was David Walker, a boy preacher of fourteen who had an unmistakable charisma. The Americans, perhaps somewhat unwisely, made much of child evangelists in those days, and 'Little David' toured with the team, telling about an amazing experience. Betty and I went on that Friday evening. We had never been in such a huge meeting before – there were over two thousand people there, all singing rousing hymns such as 'What a wonderful change in my life has been wrought', and 'What a friend we have in Jesus', complete with descant! The atmosphere was electric! This was nothing like any religious meeting I had attended before. It was not in the least dull or boring. It was vibrant and meaningful, making God real to us, rather than being a remote entity somewhere above the clouds.

We went again on the following evening, and by this time I was coming to a crisis point. All I had heard and seen over recent months was going round and round in my mind. I felt compelled to go on until I reached some kind of conclusion. I could not quite grasp it: yet the exciting meeting fired me, and the next morning, Sunday, I made a decision to go back to Slade Lane chapel where I had attended Sunday-school. I had not been forgotten. As I walked in, I was welcomed with open arms and a great deal of adulation! Straight away I felt that I belonged.

By now, my cousin Joan was married and attending another church near where she and Ray Mills lived. But other old friends were there: my Sunday-school teacher Mr. Bynham; Mr. Parkkes, George and Albert Berks, Miss Smith, and John Baker and Hilda Felton: it was just great to be with them all again.

There was to be an afternoon meeting at the town-hall, beginning at three o'clock. Betty and I were determined to go, although it meant missing dinner. Dad never got home from the 'Dog and Partridge' before half-past two, so dinner was always late. We couldn't wait, but went straight to the town-hall, not feeling hungry for physical food.

I listened enrapt as 'Little David' told his story. It was an extraordinary story. He had always been something of a 'mystical' child, going often into the woods to pray. One afternoon when he was only seven years old, he was in his bedroom praying. He felt himself being lifted. Suddenly he found himself walking through fields by a river. He could see fruit trees – beautiful trees – he had never seen anything so beautiful. He had never seen a river so clear – it was clear as crystal. There was a city in the distance, clothed with light. He took in the glorious scene, noticing that there didn't seem to be any weather. There didn't even seem to be any sunshine, yet a soft, beautiful and wonderful light pervaded everything. Then he became aware of someone coming towards him in a kind of cloud. He didn't want to go back, and he began to cry. Whoever it was in the cloud spoke to him, telling him that he must go back to earth to tell people about the peace, the joy and the happiness of the place where Jesus wanted them to be. David knew, then, that he was in conversation with Jesus himself. There was something beautiful and calming about his voice, and yet Little David cried because he didn't want to go back. Jesus told him, "You must go, but you will come back again." When he found himself back in his room, it was seven o'clock in the evening. His body had been in a praying position for five hours!

There were no doubts in my mind that what 'Little David' had described was true. The importance of his experience seemed to reach right into my soul and fitted together with all the other experiences I had had recently. I knew that Jesus Christ was challenging me to place my life and my whole future in his hands. I had nothing but an orange to eat that day, and when we got home, I made it clear that I didn't need any tea, and I wanted to be alone in my bedroom. As I knelt by my bed, I thought over all that I'd heard. I did not expect to be 'lifted', like Little David – that was a one-off experience for people who came from America to tell people like me that heaven was real – but I was conscious of a deep sadness. I became aware that even as a child growing into a young man, I had let Jesus down. Seven years before, I had received him as my Saviour. I had taken him at his word, but I had not continued to love and trust him. And, supposing I was to start all over again, could I sustain such a commitment? I had no doubts about the faithfulness of Jesus to me – it was my faithfulness to him that gave me problems. Would I be able to withstand the pressures of college life – pressures such as academic, intellectual, scientific and perhaps even philosophical arguments? And what about myself? Did I have what it takes? Did I have the moral fibre, even the faith to make a real Christian? Would I fail Jesus again? I didn't want to put my hand to the plough unless I knew I wouldn't look back.

For some time I was obsessed with difficult problems. I struggled – O how I struggled! Then suddenly it came to me. Jesus didn't die for people who would be successful – he died for failures! His death on the cross was the price he paid, whether I failed or succeeded – there could be no change in that. There was no altering the fact that Jesus died for me whether I failed or succeeded. So to refuse what he had done for me would be the biggest failure of all! That was the end of the line. I had no further arguments. It was at that point, whilst still kneeling, that I became overwhelmed by what can only be described as an intense feeling of being loved.

The death that Jesus died, the forgiveness implied and imparted by that death, became personal to me. A sweet joy had overcome the sadness, and I melted! I 'caved in', and surrendered to the Lord Jesus. Then I prayed: "Lord, whether I fail or succeed, I want to belong to you – that's all that matters." Verses I had learned as a child came back to me. "Him that comes to me I will in no wise cast out"; "Behold, I stand at the door and knock; if anyone hears my voice and opens the door, I will come in and sup with him and he with me". "I am the door, by me if any man enters in, he shall be saved...". I know now that these were promises from God's Word of accessibility – Jesus giving me access and I giving him access.

The gospel is mutual – I possess him, but he possesses me. We possess each other. This was a relationship that was being born in me by the Holy Spirit. I was being called into relationship. I understood that Jesus had won the victory on Calvary, so I was reconciled, restored! In surrendering, Jesus gave me the victory he had won on Calvary. In being conquered by his love, he would make me more than a conqueror through his love. What a transaction! What a transformation!

Years later I would recount this experience when speaking to young people who, like me, had made a commitment in childhood, but who had fallen away, counting it for nothing. It is never 'nothing', – it is a foundation that God will work on in time and through circumstances. From God's side, the relationship had not been broken. It was only broken from my side. He had held his end of the bond, and all the time had been waiting for me to take up my end.

Later that evening I went to the Youth Club where I was to play for a service. Afterwards we had 'canteen' – tea, coffee, squash and biscuits. During this time I would usually play requests of the popular music of the day. Soon someone asked me to play, and the young folk gathered round the piano as I began to play 'Twelfth

Street Rag'. Suddenly it all felt out of place. I had to stop and explain. "I've had a wonderful experience with Jesus," I began. "I just can't play that kind of music any more. I am in love with Jesus, and everything else seems unimportant."

Being 'in love' was the only way I could describe my feelings. I had been 'in love' in a youthful fashion with Rene, and the experience I was now going through was quite as emotional as that. It welled up from inside me together with a feeling of gratitude and assurance. It was tremendous! No one understood, of course, but it marked the first time I had witnessed for my Saviour. I believed, then, that Betty had received Christ as her Saviour, but our experiences were evidently not comparable.

No one can explain the ways of God in his sovereignty. All this was to mean little or nothing in Betty's life, but for me it was complete revolution. The family put it all down to a typical teenage infatuation – it wouldn't last. It's true to say that if my experience rested on that initial surrender, perhaps it wouldn't have lasted. In the Old Testament, all the sacrifices that were demanded were to be placed on the altar as dead sacrifices. But in the New Testament, we are exhorted to "Present your bodies as a living sacrifice..." Dead Sacrifices stay on the altar: living ones have a habit of jumping off! In other words, our whole lives must be a series of 'surrenders'. I know only too well the products of an unsurrendered life: wanting my own way, insisting on my rights; a critical spirit; short temper, and general lack of self-control.

The Bible puts it very graphically when it talks about our being "Crucified with Christ". It's a daily business, even a moment-by-moment experience – it becomes a whole new attitude.

Term was to start soon after my eighteenth birthday. That first Sunday back saw me in the Christian Fellowship, really fired up. I asked if I could be allowed to give my testimony of all that had happened. Most of the folk were delighted that I had had such a convincing experience, out of which nobody could talk me out of – although plenty of the students tried! I told as many as possible about Jesus, expecting that, as soon as they knew, they, too, would believe and be saved. I couldn't understand why they didn't! I didn't know why the same experience shouldn't happen to everyone else!

But there were those who, during the course of my stay at college, did come to know the Lord. We used to hold counselling sessions for them to help them on their way. From that time on, the meetings of the Christian Fellowship had a different emphasis as I poured everything into evangelism. Perhaps I was not too wise, but God beautifully overruled in my enthusiasm.

One fellow-student who sought to advise me was Albert Pemberton. He was one of the gentlest people I have ever met. I had got to know him during my first term, and towards the end of that term, Albert became ill. I was to know him only a matter of weeks after my salvation; Albert died that term, leaving an impression of sadness throughout the college. He had run his race, and I took the baton from him. The one thing that began to puzzle me was, how was I to serve God? How could I give him what I had to offer? I longed to give him my gift of playing the piano, but Christian music was very staid and plain in those days. Most of the hymns were to be played in four-part harmony, with no scope for the kind of playing I enjoyed. I prayerfully thought and wondered what God had in store for me.

Meanwhile, my college work seemed to be going well, in tuning, music and typing. They were wonderful, formative years, and probably the most productive of my life in terms of learning. I could relax in the knowledge that the crisis for me was over. I was now related to God by receiving Jesus Christ as my Saviour, and I could therefore confidently face the future, whatever it held.

Chapter Fourteen

Winning for God

My GOOD FRIEND FAITHFUL JOE, had been to visit me during the summer holidays. He said he would come to Shrewsbury, and we could spend a Saturday afternoon together. Sometimes he actually came to the college, which meant that I could play the piano for him. Another interesting thing about Joe at this time was his love of T.V. wrestling. It seemed out of character with his gentle disposition. He would assure me that most of the antics were contrived – a lot of acting up to the audience and the camera. On one of his visits, he brought me a little battery-driven radio. I thanked him profusely, but had no idea what it was going to mean to me.

It was late one Thursday night when I was exploring the medium wave that I heard the sound of amazing piano–playing. But it was not just the playing – it was what was being played that attracted my attention. It was a gospel chorus: 'Heavenly sunshine, Heavenly sunshine, Flooding my soul with glory divine...' There was no four-part harmony here – it was brilliant, lively music, with copious chromatic octaves in both hands! Here was a pianist who was obviously not inhibited in his playing at all! Then the cheerful voice of Dr. Charles E. Fuller urged the audience to sing along, then turn round and shake hands with a neighbour and enjoy the 'Heavenly sunshine of the Lord!' I no longer wanted to go to sleep, but listened on in rapt attention as Rudi Attwood drew wonderful sounds from the piano. There was the singing of the quartet and the choir, accompanied by Rudi on piano, and George Broadbent on the organ.

There I was in bed, but catapulted in my memory to the Birmingham town-hall where I had heard gospel playing for the first time, and where my experience of God coming into my life had begun.

At that time I don't remember possessing a headset, which meant that I couldn't stay in the dormitory with the others to hear the programme. They had no interest in the gospel, so I would get out of bed every Thursday night and go along the corridor to the wash-room and close the door behind me. On the right side of the wash-room was a line of hand basins situated under a wide window sill. I would count to the third basin, climb onto the sill, and sit with my feet in warm water. This was a good way of keeping relatively warm while listening to 'The Old-Fashioned Revival Hour' on Radio Luxemburg 208 metres. Every Thursday night I would be blessed in the third hand basin, being entertained by gospel music at its best, and edified by the simple, direct preaching of the Word of God. (That third basin on the right became more sacred to me than any font!)

On Friday mornings, I reckon I had the cleanest pair of feet in college! I regret to this day never having written to the programme. Dr. Charles Fuller's wife, (whom he always referred to as "Honey"), used to read letters from listeners. I had only just been introduced to typing lessons, and just didn't have the confidence to write. If I had, I could just imagine Mrs. Fuller reading: "Now we have a letter from a young man who listens to our programme over there in England. Apparently it's late at night when he hears us, and the only way he can keep warm is to keep his feet in hot water!" I reckon there would have been great amusement in the auditorium at Long Beach, California.

I distinctly recall, as I listened to the masterful playing of Rudi Attwood, that I prayed a significant prayer. "Lord, if I can play even half as well as Rudi Attwood, I'll be a gospel pianist for you one day." God answered that prayer – I'm just about half as good as Rudi Attwood! I guess I should have prayed: "...if I could be as good as him..." – I might have been twice the pianist I am today!

During the Easter holidays of 1950, I experienced another spiritual high. On Easter Monday, April 10th, I, along with a number of other young people, was baptised by immersion. I remember having to borrow a pair of flannels from my friend John Baker, as he was then (later to become the Rev. John Reeve-Baker, Elim Pentecostal minister). The sprinkling that I had had as a baby meant nothing to me, or to my parents, and I simply wanted to follow in the steps of the Lord Jesus who was himself baptised. It was an altogether wonderful experience! There was the meeting of the Easter Convention in the morning when the baptisms took place; a ramble in the afternoon with the young people; tea at the chapel, followed by the evening Convention service. The place was packed, the atmosphere charged with praise, the preaching powerful and relevant.

I returned home after such a wonderful day in a state of euphoria, and tried desperately to convey to my family all that had happened, and the way I was feeling. But they didn't understand: they just couldn't seem to be part of it all, and I longed for them to come into the experience of knowing Jesus. They didn't realise what they were missing.

Peter with Grace and Reg Tomlinson.

As I reflect back on all that happened that day, I now realise that it was a precious seal on my friendship with John and Hilda who were then going out with each other. They came to see me twice at college, and I always looked forward to the holidays when we would be together, sometimes at John's home in Sparkhill. We would have tremendous fun playing indoor cricket using a table tennis ball. John would take me to the central library and read the letters of Leopold Mozart to his son, and Wolfgang's letters to his father – all very fascinating! And, of course, John, Hilda and I revelled in the activities at chapel: the worship service on Sunday mornings; the gospel service in the evenings, and the prayer–meetings and Bible studies – I was being strengthened in my faith, more and more convinced of the truth of God's Word.

I remember the time when John and I were travelling together on a Birmingham bus. We were discussing music and its place in our lives. The question came up: if we had to choose between making music or preaching God's Word, what choice would we make? Both of us came to the same conclusion – we would prefer to preach the Word of God. It's by the 'foolishness of preaching' that men and women are saved, not the playing of music. Music can be a bridge-builder, but it must never replace the clear, authoritative statement of the Good News about Jesus.

At this time, we were both beginners in the preaching ministry, and I remember another bus journey when I was feeling quite discouraged about my preaching. I wondered whether I would ever really make a preacher, and was quite prepared, after all, to give it up. I got up, made my way to the platform, and was in the act of getting off the bus. A man got on the bus, and as we passed, he said: "Hello, Pete, how's the preaching going?" I was both amazed and encouraged. To think that anyone would ask that vital question at that precise moment settled it for me. I would do all I could to cultivate any preaching gift I might have, and I've been ministering the Word ever since.

Throughout my remaining time at college, my willingness to speak about the Lord to anyone who would listen – and some who wouldn't – earned me the nickname of 'Father Jackson'. (Apparently there was an 'old boy' from the college who went out to do missionary work for the Catholic Church with the same name as mine.) But at least everyone knew that I was a Christian, and what I stood for. Of course, Joe and I had known each other for a good many years by now. He had proved himself to be a really good friend. His visits to me were no small sacrifice, travelling for long distances so that we would keep in touch. He, therefore, was one of my chief concerns, now that I had discovered the truth of the gospel. Joe had been brought up as a Roman Catholic, and although he still kept a tenuous contact with his priest, there was not much more to it than that.

I wanted him to have the same vibrant faith as I had found, and so I prayed for him often. I was particularly burdened one Friday evening. Joe was due to visit me the next day. I determined to spend some time in prayer on his behalf that evening. I took myself into one of the practice-rooms, which was not in use, it being after eight o'clock. I set myself to pray for Joe.

As a new, enthusiastic Christian, I became very emotional when anything touched me deeply. I felt a desperation for Joe that drove me into fervent prayer. In the cold light of the following morning, I told myself that perhaps I shouldn't have got so 'het up' over it all, and that, maybe, I had gone a bit 'over the top' in my efforts.

I met Joe in Shrewsbury that Saturday afternoon, and we went to the Prince Rupert restaurant for a bite to eat. I hadn't realised the extent to which Joe had become quite fussy about what foods he could eat, and what he mustn't. I remember being quite appalled when, after ordering our meal, he whipped out his own wholemeal loaf that he'd brought with him. I remonstrated with him: "You can't do that, Joe. Whatever will the management think, bringing your own food?" But Joe was totally unperturbed: nothing would move him to put that loaf back in his bag.

We finished our egg and chips and went to the area of parkland known locally as 'the quarry' and sat down for a while. I handed Joe a small tract which read: "For God so loved the world that he gave his only begotten son, that whosoever believeth in him should not perish, but have everlasting life." But where the word "Whosoever" should have been was a blank space where one could place one's own name. I said to Joe: "Do read this, Joe, and see if you can put your name in the blank space."

We eventually strolled off in the direction of the bus station. As we got to Claremont Street, we came across an open-air Salvation Army meeting. We had some time to wait for the bus, so we mingled with the folk. Suddenly, to my amazement, one of the officers came to me and said: "Brother, come and give a word." It was a total surprise to me, but as it happened, that week I had noticed a lovely verse in the first book of Samuel, chapter nine. it said: "Stay here awhile, so that I may give you a message from God." What more appropriate text could you have for an open-air meeting? It actually asks the people going by to stay and listen! I jumped up onto the rostrum and preached.

When I had finished, we hurried off to the bus. Joe and I shook hands, and we parted. By the middle of the next week, I had a letter from Joe, which read: "I listened to what you said; I read the tract, and I filled in my name. Then I went to the priest and said: 'With great respect, I've no longer any need for your services, because I have found Jesus as my Saviour.'"' I cannot explain just how much that meant to me. It encouraged me as nothing else could have done. Throughout my college years, however, I was to come under influences, which were to challenge my young, developing faith.

There were times when I had to reassess what I had learned. But instead of shaking my faith, it served to strengthen, clarify, and consolidate it. One of these influences came from a Mr. Sanderson to whom I was introduced by the girl who lived next door to us at home. Sheila was a Christadelphian, and wanted very much for me to become one too.

Mr. Sanderson was one of the leaders of the meeting, and his job as a travelling salesman in ladies' fashion hats often brought him into the Shrewsbury area. Whenever he could, he would visit me and talk to me about the Christadelphian way. He was a very kind, considerate man: generous to a fault. Yet he told me various things, which were in direct conflict with what I thought I knew about Christianity. He said that Christadelphians do not believe in Satan as a person; that evil is simply thoughts and inclinations.

He explained that the Bible's description of Jesus facing the devil in the wilderness was mere imagery: there was no being involved; Jesus was on his own, with negative and positive thoughts battling in his own mind. I wasn't prepared to dismiss all that I was told, yet I had to make some kind of assessment of what these very kind people were saying, and try to find out where the truth really lay.

In spite of the limited resources at my disposal, I studied as much as I could about the origins of evil, using the scriptures – the

Word of God – as my basis. (We had unfettered access to a Braille Bible at college.) Gradually, I came to the conclusion that evil could not be reduced to mere thought patterns; it had to be a definite power, generated by a created being known as Satan, or the devil. In my quest for the truth, I 'discovered' C. S. Lewis's masterpiece 'Mere Christianity'. This illuminating book, so well reasoned, provided me with a fuller understanding of 'dualism' – the battle between good and evil.

This was a tremendous help to me. I also had to find out the truth about the Holy Spirit of God. Again, the Christadelphians maintained that this was just the breath or influence of God. I really had to get to the bottom of this one! When I came across the verse in Ephesians, chapter 4, where it says, "Grieve not the Holy Spirit of God", I wondered how one could 'grieve' a breath or influence. 'grieve' is a word which expresses emotion, and could therefore only allude to a person. Furthermore, Jesus constantly referred to the Spirit in personal terms: he, him. On these grounds, I had to reject the Christadelphian position.

But there was one more thing that gave me concern about them. The Word of God talks about "The full assurance of faith". The Christadelphians seem to lack any real assurance of eternal life. It was as if they were on probation of some kind. I remember discussing this at great length with Mr. Sanderson, who maintained that one could not presume on the promises of God. Promises were yet to be fulfilled, so by their very nature were to do with the future, and not with the present. If only I had been aware then of the scripture in the second letter of Peter, chapter 1 verse 4! "By the exceeding great and precious promises given to us we become partakers of the divine nature, whereby we escape from the pollutions of this world". In other words, these are not promises which are merely futuristic, they are for us in 'this world', for the here and now.

So my researches were serving to strengthen my faith. At about this time, another influence came into my life, this time from the Seventh-day Adventists. I found their arguments more convincing. I began receiving a magazine from America whose material was generally very good. However, there were articles about the Sabbath being the seventh day of the week, not the first: these arguments were powerful. I went to some of their meetings, and I found them more of a challenge in a way, because this argument seemed to have more credence – especially when I read the Old Testament, which said over and over again, "This shall be a Sabbath unto you for ever and ever". I found I had more in common with the Seventh-day Adventists who did believe in the Deity of Christ, and in his sacrifice for sin, but I had difficulty with their legalism in other areas.

I had just one adventure with another group in Shrewsbury that was to leave its mark on my experience. Donald was a Christian who didn't associate with us in the Sunday afternoon Christian Fellowship. In any case, he wasn't much around on Sundays because, every morning somebody came from Shrewsbury to take him to a morning meeting there. But Donald respected us as Christians, and one day asked me if I would care to come with him to his meeting in Shrewsbury.

He explained that each 'Lord's day' they broke bread and took of the cup. I understood perfectly, because this is what we did in our chapel at home. I was delighted with the invitation: this would be better than the formal service in Cardistan church. We were duly picked up one Sunday morning, and I found myself in a chapel, which was nicely filled. Visitors were welcomed by name, (including me), and then there was what I considered to be an uneasy silence. Maybe the unease was in me, but I found it strange. A hymn number was announced, and some of its verses read out before we all stood and sang unaccompanied. Again, this was very strange to me. We sat down, and another silence ensued, which I found more difficult. Eventually, I rose to my feet nervously to do what I normally did in my home chapel: I began to pray, praising God for sending His son to die for me at Calvary. It was such a usual thing for me to do, that I can't exactly remember the form and content of the prayer, except that it was praise and thanksgiving, and given in all innocence. Did I detect more uneasiness, this time among the assembled throng? And when the bread and the cup came, I was passed by! I didn't understand, and felt injured.

We went to the County Surveyor's house for lunch. Mr. Pook was an elder at the Assembly, and Don normally went to lunch with him and his wife. After a good roast lunch, I was escorted into another room where I was asked to sit down in an easy chair. I was then interrogated. Which chapel or church did I go to at home? When I declared that it was a Pentecostal church, I got the shock of my life. My host told me unequivocally that the Pentecostal church was of the devil. I was reprimanded in no uncertain manner, and was never invited again. At that point in my life, I didn't know that there was such a movement as the Exclusive Brethren. But I knew what it was to be excluded!

But the greatest influence and challenge came from another direction. As the evangelicalism of the Christian Fellowship became more and more overt in the college, a counter-culture began to develop, which proved to be far more sinister. One of the students at college was possessed of mediumistic powers, and he was responsible for what was called 'The Circle'. These folk were not members of our fellowship, of course, but very much wanted me to be part of their Circle. So they invited me to one of their meetings. I had read nothing about Spiritualism, and had absolutely no idea as to what to expect. But I remembered that I had read in the Apostle John's first letter chapter 4 which said, "Test the spirits to see whether they are from God".

These young people used that reference to point out that the spirits "Come through and talk to us". I was fascinated and went along to the meeting of 'The Circle'. Bernard, the Medium, could fall into a trance almost at will. His normal, rhythmic breathing gave way to long drawn-out breaths. It was eerie – he didn't seem to draw normal breaths at all, it was just a long, long breath. I sat there, enthralled. Sure enough, before very long, a voice began to speak – but it was not Bernard's voice, although the words came from his mouth. Members of 'The Circle' asked the voice questions, and at one point, I was welcomed into 'The Circle'. I sat amazed as I was then told that if I continued in my zeal by attending the meetings, I would get wonderful revelations from the spirit world and the astral planes. I could hardly believe it! It was obviously very real, and the voice was addressing me! This was really something! Of course I would attend the meetings – I was a young Christian, very keen to learn as much as I could.

However, my keenness made me very vulnerable. There was only one problem which niggled in my mind. I knew that the Bible said that there was only one Mediator between God and man, and that was Jesus Christ. Yet all the voices, which we were hearing, seemed to be trying to mediate too. Therefore, to me it seemed that Christ was being de-valued. I would need to find out what it all meant.

When the holidays arrived, I went hotfoot to my Pastor. I was overflowing with the wonderful revelation and the 'outworking of faith' as I saw it. This man of God did not rebuke me, or condemn anything I told him, but quietly responded: "Right. Let's see what the Bible says about it – as we usually do." That was fine by me. I had nothing to fear by looking into the Scriptures. So I went round to his house, and we sat down to see what we could discover from the Bible. At this point, having prayed together, the Pastor stressed the supreme authority of the infallible Word of God. As we went through the Scriptures, it became more and more apparent that God was against all mediumistic practices such as communicating with the dead. Any manifestations of this kind were forbidden, including crystal ball gazing, fortune-telling, witchcraft and so on. From time to time God gave prophecies, but these were not meant to be peeps into the future. They were given for specific reasons as signposts along the way. The Pastor showed me Scriptures that talked about wizards that 'peeped and muttered'. I came away firmly convinced that spiritualism is not only wrong, but positively dangerous, and I thank God that in my keenness and profound respect for my pastor, I saw the truth of what he was teaching me.

When I went back to college, I told the people in 'The Circle' that I wanted nothing more to do with their practices, because they were contrary to the Word of God. The voices they were hearing were challenging the person and work of Christ, de-valuing him, even to the point of trying to de-throne him! I could not go along with anything like that, and I determined in my heart that the power of spiritualism should be smashed.

The matter came to a spectacular head – significantly enough – on 31st October, at Halloween. 'The Circle', which included well-meaning, sincere people who claimed that they were on the side of the forces of light, met on 31st October – Halloween ostensibly to combat the forces of evil. On this night of all nights of the year, evil forces – according to tradition – predominate.

The meeting this night took place in the organ practice–room which was larger and therefore more accommodating for the purpose. I set myself to pray in the practice-room next door. As I knelt on the hard floor, I began to feel that same desperation in my spirit that I had felt when praying for Joe's salvation. I prayed for a mighty deliverance from the powers of evil, and I claimed the whole armour of God to protect me.

It wasn't very long before there was a knock at the door. It opened, and someone said: "Who's in here?" "Me," I answered, and added, "I'm praying against all that's going on next door. I'm asking God to destroy your Circle." "Ah, we thought so", responded the voice, "we were told by one of the spirits that there was someone evil in the next room." "Be careful," I warned, "you're on dangerous ground."

About a quarter of an hour later, the door burst open. There was no knock this time, just a person in a desperate panic. "Please come and help us," the voice pleaded, "The spirits are threatening that they will either send our medium back to us mad, or else they will kill him...!"

Quickly I followed him into the airless room. Their medium, whose name I forget now, was not the 'experienced' Bernard. But what I do remember clearly is what happened as I was given access to the middle of the circle, and approached the lad who was acting as medium. I said the first thing that came into my head: "If God be for us, who can be against us..." And then another powerful verse came into my mind: "Thanks be to God who giveth us the victory through our Lord Jesus Christ." I then took his stiff, unresponsive hand in mine, and commanded: "In the name of Jesus Christ who was manifested to destroy the works of the devil, I command that you come back!"

Strange noises came from his mouth as he came out of the deep, deep trance. As he returned to consciousness, he asked for a drink of water. We gave it to him, and then I called the group to prayer. Firstly, I prayed a prayer of thanksgiving that this lad had been delivered. Then I prayed that God would cleanse the place of this evil, and grant his mercy on all of us.

When he had fully recovered, the boy told us what he had experienced. He had been in a temple-like area; he was encircled by beings who were dancing, and as they danced, they got closer and closer to him. He knew they were evil, and he felt threatened and very frightened. Suddenly he saw a soldier coming towards him. He recognised him as a soldier because he carried a sword which had fire all around it.

The soldier simply 'mowed through' the evil, dancing hordes with his burning sword, and they seem to melt away. Then he found himself back in the practice room.

I needed no more convincing as to the dangers of the occult, and of the importance of the teaching of the Bible, especially when it tells us that we must "put on the whole armour of God". This was not figurative language in the spirit world – it was literal!

But that was not entirely the end of the matter. In view of the scare that the episode had caused, I decided to take some very practical action. I went to the Principal, Dr. Langdon, and reported that a group of students were holding regular séances. He was horrified, and made an announcement in morning assembly to the effect that if anyone were found dabbling with the occult, they would be immediately expelled. The evil one had overplayed his hand, and God had won a decisive victory in the lives of gullible young people.

But of course, my own Christian faith was simple enough. My involvement in the Christian Fellowship was a great stimulus. There were plenty of times when it was impossible to get a speaker for the Sunday afternoon meetings, in which case, we had to look to ourselves as budding young preachers. This meant that we had to read the Bible intelligently, and present what we read intelligibly. It was excellent discipline. Neither were we permitted to preach at great length. We all possessed Braille watches that had a glass cover that one opened in order to tell the time by lightly feeling the position of the hands. When the lid was closed, it made a very definite 'click'. It was a novel and effective way of dropping hints to the speaker when twenty to thirty watches started to click! It was all done in a spirit of good humour with no-one taking offence.

Another feature was the prayer-meetings. We had one before breakfast on every week-day, with a midweek one which was held in the typing building. This meant that the fellows and girls could meet together, and we had some lovely times of fellowship, praying for specific situations, and praying for fellow-students who were seeking for a living faith.

During my last term at college, that midweek prayer-meeting was held in the assembly hall: it had grown so much.

I enjoyed college life to the full; the work, the societies, going to concerts in Shrewsbury, and the friendships that were formed, some to last many years after leaving. I enjoyed the ritual of the last morning of each Christmas term.

On the day we were to go home for the Christmas holidays, a group of us lads would get up at about five o'clock. We would let ourselves out of our department to go round the college, singing carols underneath the windows of staff and students. Our efforts would often be rewarded by gifts thrown to us by the staff. Sometimes we would get the carefully parcelled up remains of the girls' midnight feasts – it was all tremendous fun, and sadly enough, Christmases have never been quite the same since.

More often than not, I would come home to find my Father in the throes of pneumonia and pleurisy. He was unable to work now, and the doctor would call, and after examining him would say, "You must take it easy, Mr. Jackson." My Dad would reply with stolid cheerfulness: "If I take it any easier, Doc, I'll stop!"

By now my sisters were married, and mum was keeping the home together by her earnings. This was a great concern to me as I returned to college at the beginning of 1952, my last year.

Chapter Fifteen

A New Direction

TWO GREAT NATIONAL EVENTS took place in the years 1951, 1952. The 'Festival of Britain' was particularly marked with the opening of the Festival Hall on the Thames embankment. Had we been at the college when it was on its original site at Norwood, we may well have been delighted by the prospects of attending London concerts. But we had to be content with taking part in concerts in Shrewsbury where there was plenty of infectious excitement.

In 1952, on Wednesday, February 6th, King George the 6th died, and the second Queen Elizabeth acceded to the throne. The morning lessons were cancelled, and as Wednesdays were half days, we listened to the radio for most of that day. We all felt part of the subdued mood of the nation: such a contrast to last year's celebrations.

In the summer of this, my final year at college, there was to be another big event for me: the obtaining of my piano-tuning diploma.

As I remember it, there were three of us that took our journey to London, staying at a person's house in the Regents Park area. I remember being really keyed up, and sleeping fitfully that night before I was to take the exam.

We arrived at the Northern Polytechnic, and I was shown the piano I had to tune. I expected that I would have to raise its pitch, something I had done frequently in training. To my surprise, however, I was told that I had to lower the pitch to a specified level. This was a tricky one, but I set to work with a will. The result was that I was able to obtain an Honours diploma, and I was thrilled! The three years and one term it took to train me was worthwhile, for it meant that I would be able to earn money in my own right, helping my parents at home.

Prizes and diplomas were presented to us on Speech day, an annual college ritual. A well known person would be the college guest, and this year it was to be the celebrated conductor Sir Adrian Boult. I hardly know which gave me the greater joy, actually to receive my diploma, or to have shaken the hand of such a notable musician. I felt doubly privileged, and deeply grateful.

At this point, I must mention another activity that I got involved with this last summer of my college life. John Wells had got together an accordion band, and although I could play an accordion, I hadn't got one of my own, so I was to be the pianist. We were asked to do some outside 'gigs', and at one such, we discovered that this was an outdoor engagement, and there was no piano! At first we were non-plussed, then I decided to brazen it out. "Never mind, chaps," I said cheerfully, "You just play normally, and I'll conduct you, no-one will know any different!"

So the performance proceeded. They played all their usual numbers, and I stood in front waving my arms like I imagined a conductor would. And no-one realised a thing! We had a good laugh afterwards, and joked that it had brought new emphasis to the saying "The blind leading the blind!"

That Summer holidays I went home, a very proud young man, with a tuning certificate and a slim, shiny case filled with the tools of the trade. Dr. Langdon, the Principal, had given each of us a lecture, and all I remember of it was the last phrase: "May you earn many an honest penny". And although I actually tuned some pianos that summer, I wasn't quite ready to leave college. For one thing, I had to report to the Birmingham workshops, with my diploma: and I wanted to pass one of the advanced grades in music, and needed another term to do it.

Always keen to savour the dramatic, I waited until September to present myself to the Superintendent, Mr. Edkins at Harborne. I was shown in to the Superintendent's office, and Mr. Edkins greeted me with a warm handshake. I explained to him that I had now passed my final tuning exam, and presented him with the evidence. He had a glossary on his desk that contained something of my history. As he looked from the diploma back to the glossary, he said: "I see that this is your twenty-first birthday. Let me congratulate you, and my birthday present to you is to tell you that, from next January, you can take up a post with the Birmingham Workshops as a piano-tuner."

Gratefully, I went back to college, secure in the knowledge that I had a job and an income guaranteed. This was no small gift in those days. The advent of television was causing a severe slump in the piano trade. A number of my contemporaries, having gone through all their training, just couldn't find enough work on their own account, and had to re-train as telephonists or typists. I was so very fortunate! So I commenced my last term at college with enthusiasm and anticipation. Twenty-one was considered to be the age of responsibility – a watershed in the life of a young man. As long as college work was attended to, and we were there in time for our studies, we were allowed to go anywhere and do more or less as we liked. Thus, in my new status as an official adult, I was now allowed to stay away from college for weekends if I so wished.

By now, I was in touch again with Rene, and it was quite a simple matter to visit her by means of the X96 Midland Red bus that went from Shrewsbury, via Birmingham to Northampton. This passed right through the village of Hillmorton, where Rene lived at a hostel. I would travel on Saturday afternoon, book myself in at 'The Red Lion', for the night, and spend the remaining precious time with her before making the trip back to Shrewsbury on the Sunday afternoon. As I remember it now, I must have made that trip about three times, not being able to afford the bus fare, but knowing that, before very long, I would be earning a wage, and in any case, the journey would be shorter from Birmingham, and I'd be able to see her much more often.

There was, too, another important claim on my weekends. During the previous summer term, I had been introduced to Mr. & Mrs. Ramsey & Muriel Maule, and their daughters, Joy & Jill. Ramsey was a Sergeant in the Shrewsbury constabulary, and all the family were keen Christians. They came to the college that summer on a beautifully sunny day. I showed them round, and as we sat in the grounds, Muriel became quite emotional. "All this beauty," she said, "And to think, you are denied seeing it!" She was really quite upset, and there was nothing I could do to console her. But from that moment, a lovely friendship blossomed, and they were to be such an encouragement to me in many ways.

They invited me into their home where they had a Danemann baby grand. As soon as I started to play it, I was unhappy with the tuning! Next time I came to their home, I laid hands on it, and from that time, became their regular piano-tuner.

Sergeant Maule, as he was popularly called, was secretary and leader of a little church known as Radbrook Evangelical Church. Although I was very young in the Christian faith, Radbrook welcomed me not only to play at their Saturday rallies, but also to preach. It was valuable experience for me, and they were really very indulgent.

I spent several weekends with the Maule family, and on Sunday evenings after church, we would join scores of mainly young people who had made their way from their own churches to the C.A.W.G. hall in Shrewsbury for an after-church fellowship. (C.A.W.G. – Christian Alliance of Women and Girls.) They were great times of fellowship, and I met so many lovely young people including some nurses from the Royal Salop Infirmary, and was invited to speak and play at their Nurses' Christian Fellowship. Sergeant Maule was a big man with a commanding disposition. But he loved a joke too.

I remember the story he told about the time he popped into his local barber for a hair cut. There were already quite a few waiting, so he asked the barber to give him a call at the police station when the queue had gone. "Certainly, Sergeant Maule," he said.

Some time later, a 999 call came into the station: "Tell Sergeant Maule I'm ready to cut his hair!"

During this busy term I made it my business to go to Chorley to seek out the Tolleys. It was all of nine years since I'd seen them, and I had never forgotten their kindness to me when I had convalesced with them. They were absolutely overjoyed to learn that I had found a living faith, particularly when I told them that it had largely been their influence and love that had much to do with it.

Mrs. Tolley was fully convinced of my conversion after she accompanied me to the bus that would take me to college. She watched to see if I would light up a cigarette when I thought I was out of her view! I didn't light up, since like her, I found difficulty in equating smoking with being a Christian. Our bodies are temples of the Holy Spirit, and mustn't be defiled. Anyway, Mrs. Tolley went away both convinced and happy.

I took my final piano exam for which I had officially stayed that term. Arnold Goldsborough was my examiner, and I had heard him broadcast both on piano and harpsichord a number of times, so I was genuinely pleased to meet him. We got on very well, and then he said: "Now we come to the sight-reading." (We had to read with one hand, and play with the other – we weren't spared! Mr. Goldsborough continued: "I don't know how you do this – it's very clever!" To which I replied: "Well, just give me an average mark, and we can skip it, if you like!" He didn't spare me either, but he did give me a pass mark.

My last college days were exciting and fulfilling. I shall never forget the last meeting I attended of the Christian Fellowship. It was a carol-service, and between fifty to sixty students attended – a record. I look back on those years with gratitude in my heart – so grateful that I had been delivered from the aimless life I had been living before coming to college, and finding Christ as my Saviour. Because I had extra luggage to bring home at the end of this, my last term, my sister Lily made the journey to college to help me. I had been at Rowton Castle, Royal Normal College for just over three-and-a-half years, and I had undergone in that time a transfor–mation in all sorts of ways. I was now ready to take my place in the outside world after most of nineteen years in an institution!

I reported for work at the workshops for the blind in Harborne, Birmingham, just walking distance from the Kindergarten school to where I had come just over sixteen years and four months before. I introduced myself to the foreman, Fred Thomson, and he in turn introduced me to the other men – Frank, Sid, George and Jack Turland who was just twelve years my senior. These were the 'Inside men' whose job it was to repair broken bits from customers' pianos. Sometimes, pianos came in for major work, which kept the workshop busy. Another 'Repairer' was needed, and it was hoped that I would fit the bill. But over the next nine months, it became more and more apparent that I was much more of a piano tuner than a repairer. I left college, knowing this fact. Mr. Adams, our repair trainer had been a Broadwood man, and was an expert repairer, but everyone knew that he failed to be able to see things from blind person's point of view. Not many of us, therefore, left college with much confidence in this respect. Tuning was a different matter, and that's what I wanted to do.

So in September 1953 I joined the 'Outside men' – the men on the road, and my first assignment was to go to Kingsland Road

School in Kingstanding to tune their pianos. I really knew now that I had started to do what I really wanted to do.

Each morning we would come in from our homes to the office where Mr. Thomson would give us our day's assignment. Imagine my surprise, then, when I was given my list that included, 'Miss M. Colquhoun of 18 Tustin Grove, Acocks Green'. I was to tune my one-time music-teacher's piano! She had a 1930's Challen piano, and from then on, I was her tuner. We became firm friends, and would go to the Thursday evening concerts at the town hall. I remember being taken aback by the sound of a live orchestra. All the instruments seemed to have a kind of edge on them – so much more defined. The sheer breadth and volume of sound thrilled me in a way that I could never have believed possible.

The first concert pianist I heard play was a Russian called Pushinov. He performed with the City of Birmingham Symphony Orchestra the Brahms second piano concerto. It became an instant favourite then, and has remained so. (The third movement of this particular work was to feature significantly at a later date.)

Recently I heard a story about Pushinov, which gave me great amusement. My friend, Rev. Paul Bassett told me of when he was a young man living in Weston-Super-Mare. Pushinov was billed to play at the Winter garden theatre there. However, as soon as his hands were on the keyboard, he got up and walked out in disgust. The piano was out of tune! Next day, the caption in the Weston-Super-Mare Mercury read: 'Pushinov pushes off!'

When John and I used to meet, we would whistle the opening phrase of Beethoven's eighth symphony. John would whistle part of the phrase, which indicated that he was about to meet me, and I would respond with the next part.

Often, when we were in a crowded room or hall, and I needed, say, to obey the call of nature; I would slip my comb out of my top pocket, and gently drag my finger down the teeth of the comb. John would notice and come over to me. I would casually take his arm, and off we would go. Nobody else quite knew how it all worked! At this time on Saturday mornings, I was a regular passenger on the X96 Midland Red bus, either going to Shrewsbury to take part in meetings on Saturday night and Sunday at Radbrook with the Maule family, or going the other way to Hillmorton to see Rene. Sometimes she would make the trip to my home, and the family began to like her very much. She would come with me to some of the meetings, but somehow couldn't grasp all that was implied in becoming a committed Christian. We were already planning to become engaged on her birthday in October, but I began to have misgivings.

I was absolutely certain that I was very much in love with her, and after a meeting one day I just had to bring things to a head.

We began to talk about future plans, but somehow I was unable to be as enthusiastic as I should have been. I sensed a reluctance on Rene's part when I talked about my further involvement in Christian work and what it would mean to me. Then came the moment when she tried to settle the matter by saying: "Well, when we are married, you could still have your friends and I could have mine." This, I instinctively knew, just wasn't going to add up.

For weeks I prayed and agonised over the problem. For me to

break off our relationship was unthinkable. I had loved this girl for years, and even apart from my own feelings, I hated even to think of causing her to hurt. "Oh, God, what am I to do? Help me to do the honourable thing as your child."

Finally, and with great reluctance, I had to admit that it wasn't going to work, and we would have to part. I believe that Rene was quite upset; she tried to contact me from time to time, but I was becoming increasingly busy in Christian work, and eventually she gave up. Perhaps I was conceited in thinking that I had in some way spoilt her chances. But I needn't have worried: a year or so later, she married Don, and they had four boys.

My church attendance at this time was at a Pentecostal Church in Camp Hill, a twenty-five minute bus ride from home. One evening on my way home, two couples boarded the bus, and I heard them talking excitedly about the prayer-meeting they had just attended. They spoke of the sheer beauty of the presence of God amongst them, the reality of the power of His Spirit upon the whole meeting. That was the kind of thing I was looking for. I made up my mind there and then to start going to that church. In any case, it was only a ten-minute bus ride from home – much nearer.

I showed up the following Sunday; the place was packed, the people enthusiastically friendly, and the preaching of Pastor Len Middleton was powerful and relevant. I had found a spiritual gold mine!

I hadn't been going to the Full Gospel Tabernacle, Yardleywood Road very long before Reg & Grace Tomlinson introduced themselves to me. At that time they were lodging with a Mrs. Waugh in

Moseley, and they invited me round one evening. Reg & Grace were soloists in their own right, and also sang duets. They began to teach me gospel songs, and I was only too ready to learn.

Before long, we were in demand in many churches in and around Birmingham, and not least at the Tabernacle.

I've always been possessed of an impish sense of humour. One Sunday evening, Reg was introducing their first duet at the Tab. I was waiting at the piano, and noticed that there was a music book perched on the music desk. Whilst Reg was speaking, I turned over the pages as if to look for the appropriate song. Just as Reg was getting to the end of what he was saying, I smoothed down one of the pages, and started to play the introduction.

I was totally unaware of the consternation I had created. A deputation from the elders accosted me after the service: "We don't understand, were you actually reading the music? How could you do that if you can't see?" They didn't know me very well at that time, but they were to learn...

Back in 1948 the evangelist Billy Graham and his team visited Britain. During that time they launched 'Youth for Christ' monthly gospel rallies, and these were extremely popular in many cities and towns in this country. Birmingham 'Youth for Christ' was no exception. Queues would form right around the outside of the town hall whatever the weather, and age was no barrier. There was always a resident choir, (in Birmingham's case it was the Ambassador choir), visiting singers and a national evangelist. Reg Barnes was the pianist in residence, and he was a great encouragement to me when I came to accompany Reg & Grace.

Until then I hadn't done much composing, but I was invited, with many others, to write for a chorus competition. I entered two such competitions, coming second in one, and first in the other. This succeeded in bringing me into the Christian public arena. Reg, Grace and I began to appear at other 'Youth for Christ' rallies in such places such as Derby, Walsall, Coventry, Dudley and Banbury.

The Banbury 'Youth for Christ' was held in an upstairs hall. Some way through the proceedings we heard, to our amazement, a dance band start up downstairs – right underneath us! Rev. Hugh Butt of Dudley Baptist Church was the evangelist, and he battled against the thud-thud of the drum beats, and the sounds of saxes and brass. As he was making a gospel appeal against this racket, I leaned over to the girl pianist and whispered, "May I play some background music?" I wanted to try to mask the noise coming up from below. Eventually she 'got the message', I moved into her seat, and started to play quietly. The understanding girl then let me play the last hymn, and that marked the beginning of my role as an accompanist for congregational singing.

These were wonderful days of evangelism with a great deal of input coming from our American friends. They showed us that the technology of the entertainment world could be used in the service of God. The Billy Graham organization did most to put it into action by professionally made evangelistic films, which were shown in many churches and halls throughout the British Isles.

The first we had at our church was 'Mr. Texas'. Here was a new phenomenon, the Christian message put across in the same manner as the media marketed their products. We were agog at the audacity of the production, and at the immensity of the costs involved. This was working for God in a really big way!

I was awed by the sheer professionalism of the musicians: Ted Smith on the piano; Paul Mickleson, organ: and when George Beverley Shea began to sing 'Just a closer walk with thee', I melted! I simply started to cry. Somehow I had become used to the brashness of the pop world, where people were promoted with their songs. Here it was so different. There was virtuosity, but with humility. The message was the all-important thing, not the performers, and yet the message was promoted in the best way possible.

Other films followed: 'Oil Town U.S.A.', 'The Heart is a Rebel', 'Souls in Conflict' and many more. The results were dynamic. Thousands of people were reached and lives changed. This was the age of top line evangelism.

Billy Graham's London crusade held in Haringey Arena was, I believe, supposed to last for two weeks, but was extended over almost two months to accommodate the thousands upon thousands of people wanting to attend. We filled several coaches from our own church, and as we travelled to London, more and more coaches from other parts of the country were to be seen. It was an operation requiring military precision to accommodate coaches and people on site. It was wonderful to be part of that atmosphere, with Cliff Burrows and the choir singing Fanny Crosby's 'Blessed Assurance' in the 'Crusade Manner'! George Beverley Shea sang, and then Billy Graham preached.

I must say that I expected the same kind of fiery preaching that we had heard in the Mr. Texas film. In fact it was nothing like that.

The preaching was chatty more than confrontational, intimate rather than intense. But at the conclusion of the message, people came forward in droves to be counselled for salvation: it was moving, and very wonderful.

I had brought an accordion with me on the coach, and we sang nearly all the way back to Birmingham, and this was some five years before the M1 was officially opened.

By now, Reg & Grace had bought a house in Hollywood, near Birmingham, about two miles from where I lived. I thought nothing of walking those two miles unattended, and without a white stick. I was possessed with the confidence of youth, and to be fair, there wasn't the traffic then that there is now. We would learn and practise songs together, increasing our repertoire because we were going further and further afield.

Reg bought a motorbike and sidecar, and I well remember my first pillion ride from Birmingham to Chepstow in Monmouthshire for a Mission. I slept in an adjoining bedroom to Reg & Grace, and as I was getting undressed, I suddenly heard Grace raising her voice to Reg: "Catch it, Reg! There it is – quick!" Then I heard a crash, and Reg's triumphant voice exclaiming, "Gotcha!" It was a flea!

I was, of course, still working as a piano-tuner, and I well remember one lady saying to me: "You're a bit young to be doing this, arencha?" At that time, the nearest in age to me of the other tuners was Sid Parry, some twenty-four years my senior. I invited him home, and we struck up a firm friendship. He came to our church, and was first of all impressed by the firm, warm handshake at the door that welcomed him. He listened to Pastor Middleton's preaching and was captivated. Sid came several times to church, and on one Monday morning, he drew me to one side, blurting out the news that he had come to a living faith in Christ. He said to me: "As I was going home on the bus last night after the service, I felt as though the bus was a chariot! I could hardly contain the joy that thrilled me through and through – it was wonderful!"

He was forty-five, and I shall never forget the time we went to a Christian bookshop in Birmingham. As we stood there listening to George Beverley Shea singing "I've wandered far away from God, now I'm coming home", became aware that Sid was very quiet. Then the singer got to the verse: "I've wasted many precious years, now I'm coming home..." Sid began to weep openly, and we had to leave the shop. He said to me later: "I've lived a miserable life of luxury, and I've come home!"

In the 1950's my holidays were spent at Hildenborough Hall in Kent, and Frinton, Essex. The well known evangelist Tom Rees ran these holiday weeks, and after my first experience of such a week of blessing, fellowship and ministry, I got some of my friends to come with me, including Joe, Sid, and a couple who had been at college with me, Ray & Norma.

There was a morning session of Bible ministry, and an evening session which was rather more informal, but where the Word of God was central. The songwriter Gordon Brattle was the regular pianist, but I well remember that there was a student at Bible college who also played: the now well known Bible teacher, minister and Keswick speaker Eric Alexander.

Tom Rees's secretary, Joyce Silcox was also his main soloist, singing at the great rallies in London's Royal Albert Hall, and throughout the country on Tom's whistle stop evangelistic tours.

Mr. Rees often referred to me by my college nickname, Jacko. One day he said to me: "Jacko, I want you to accompany my secretary in a song tomorrow evening."

I could hardly believe what I was hearing: me, accompanying Miss Silcox whose record I had just bought!

We practised together, and everything seemed to go well on the night. For me, it was a great encouragement, and that's exactly what Tom Rees wanted it to be.

I once said to him when we were at Frinton, "You know, there isn't a copy of the Braille Bible here. Do you think it would be a good idea to get one?" A month later – so I was told – there was a Bible installed!

Reg & Grace had hardly been in their house two years when, in 1956 they started talking very seriously about the possibility of going into gospel work full-time. They asked me what I thought, and of course, I was all for it. But now, as I look back, they had much more to sacrifice in terms of their home than I had. My only concern was my parents: mum was still working part-time, and dad's health was continuing to deteriorate.

The more we prayed and talked it over, the more aware we became that this was God's leading for our lives. We canvassed opinions from evangelists we were already working with, notably Don Summers: and they all seemed of the same mind. They would welcome us to look after the musical side of their work, and I was getting more and more excited.

But my good friend Sid was not quite so sure. He struck a note of caution in saying: "You do realise that you'll have to sacrifice a certain amount of confidence and independence, don't you? Things will never be the same again."

No doubt there was plenty of logic in what Sid said, but I hardly thought it was worth consideration: the nation was waiting for us; God was surely with us, added to which – in my case – there was still a certain arrogance which was waiting to be chipped away.

Chapter Sixteen

On the Open Road

BY NOW AT THE AGE OF TWENTY-FIVE, I was still having a job to shake off the trappings of institutionalism. I was still working for the Birmingham Royal Institute for the Blind, although that was soon to end.

I seem to remember that I had no real 'pride' in my personal appearance. I washed my hair infrequently, never having applied shampoo – I thought that was something only girls did! I realise now just how self-centred I was, and I had no idea then of the difficulties I would experience in my thought life, living with a married couple in the confines of a caravan. Early in 1957 the Tomlinson's sold their house, and bought an eighteen-foot caravan from a firm in Evesham. This would give us freedom of travel and serve as a hide-away to escape from the public eye. It also meant that we wouldn't have to impose ourselves on people.

The caravan was towed by a canvass-topped land rover, which we called Abraham, the caravan being named Isaac, who always followed Abraham!

My bedroom was a tiny, cramped affair to the front of the caravan over the tow-bar. I literally had to thread my way into bed, but I didn't mind: we were on the King's business, after all.

Having given my notice in to the workshops to the consternation of many, I was ready to set out with Reg & Grace in early May as 'The Gospel Witness Trio'. Our first crusade was in Doncaster with Rev. Roy Hession as the evangelist and team leader. This was the beginning of intensive travel. For us, spreading the gospel was more important than anything, and we appreciated the privilege of being able to throw ourselves into this vital work for God. During that time we met and worked with those who were at the hub of large-scale evangelism – Ray Castro, Frank Farley, Marshall Shallis, David Shepherd (Welsh evangelist), and Don Summers.

Sometimes we would undertake Missions on our own, including beach missions on the Lincolnshire coast. I now recall those two-and-a-half years as frenetic and frantic!

In March, 1958 I was admitted to the Queen Elizabeth hospital, Birmingham, suffering from acute sinus problems. This had been getting worse and worse for years, and sometimes – before preaching – I would have to inhale nose drops to free the congestion. I had already undergone some minor nasal operations under local anaesthetic, but now I had developed a chronic condition.

It was a horrible operation: the nose had to be straightened, and my sinuses stripped.

One of the nurses that 'specialled' me was a Christian from Rugby named Mary Martin. She told me that she rode everywhere on a scooter. But shortly after my discharge from hospital, I heard that Mary had been tragically killed whilst on her way to a Bible Study. She had been a splendid nurse, and it was so very sad to think that such a lovely girl had to go that way. These are some of the unanswered questions we have to live with. One day we shall know, even as we are known. But now we see through a glass dimly. As Christians, we know that the supreme question has been answered in Jesus Christ, but there are many secondary questions for which we shall have to wait for the answers.

As well as Mary Martin, there were a number of Christian nurses at the Q.E at that time. Many of them joined the Faith Mission, some going overseas. There was a meeting of the 'Nurses' Christian Fellowship' every Tuesday evening, and in my latter stages of recovery, I would be escorted from the ward to the chapel to play the organ. (You can just imagine some of the remarks the other men made as they saw me going out of the ward with a pretty nurse!)

A number of us with nasal problems had to endure 'packing' in the nose. This prevented normal breathing, and one night when sleep was difficult for many of us, one of the men addressed the night nurse:

"Durse! durse! I can't breathe. What can I do?"

"Die!" said the nurse.

I was glad to be able to rejoin Reg & Grace and be on the road again, and in the following September, we went to Guernsey in the Channel Islands, to be part of the National Young Life team for the 'Guernsey for God' Crusade. We didn't take the caravan this time, but flew there in a small Dakota aircraft. It was the first time any of us had flown, and all three of us were very excited. Unfortunately, however, Grace did not enjoy the experience very much because, for some reason, the pressure and altitude caused great pain in her ears.

As we came in to land, we were amazed at the prospect of landing on a grass runway. "This is a bit like an incident from a Biggles book" I commented to Reg. It seemed adequate for the job, however, and we landed perfectly safely.

We were met by our host, Mr. Ozanne, who was a grower, specialising in tomatoes and freesias. He was also a very active member of the 'States' parliament of Guernsey. He drove us to his beautiful farmhouse called 'Lilyvale', and we were introduced to his Scottish wife, Peggy. We had been briefed beforehand that the family had recently experienced a tragedy. Their son Harry had been fatally injured in a car crash. He had been a popular lad on the island, a bright Christian with a promising career. He had won a scholarship to study farming in Finland, and would have taken the family business on. Now they had lost him, and were still trying to come to terms with this disaster.

Margaret, who had trained as a nurse at University College hospital in London had been very close to her brother Harry. After the accident she returned to Guernsey, and was reluctant to go back to her nursing, having become rather quiet and withdrawn. Being a member of the local 'Young Life Campaign', she was encouraged to join the crusade choir by her friends. They felt this might help Margaret to "Come out of her shell". We were welcomed enthusiastically, however, as Mrs. Ozanne set our first meal before us. "Right, stick in 'til you stick oot!" she laughed, with her characteristic Scottish accent.

The crusade really 'took off', and we all had a great time except Reg. Just after our first weekend in Guernsey, Reg went down with an attack of shingles. This was a real blow; he was the song-leader for the meetings, and of course it meant that Grace was now the soloist for almost the whole of the crusade. But she was well able to handle that.

As well as daytime opportunities in schools and coffee mornings, meetings were held each evening in Ebenezer Methodist church, St. Peterport. It was a large church to fill, but crowds came in from all over the island, many people being reached who otherwise wouldn't have been.

Derek Cleave, David Pawson, John Blanchard, Peter and Eric Clarke at Millmead Baptist Church, Guildford. (1972)

The local 'Y.L.C.' committee included two young men who were later to become well known internationally in Christian circles. One was John Blanchard, acclaimed convention speaker and author of many books. John was at that time working in the legal department of the courts of Guernsey. The other young man was Peter Smith who had a beautiful baritone singing voice. Little did I realise then that I would in future often be working with them.

I also met a man who was already well known as a gospel pianist, songwriter and recording artist. Jack Ward was not actually on the team, but happened to be on holiday in Guernsey. He attended some of the evening meetings, and on a couple of occasions we played duets to the assembled company. I was thrilled to have these opportunities of playing the piano with him.

In those days when it was reckoned that there were more feet of glass in Guernsey than roads, the island had a kind of magic about it. There were times when we could go walks along the cliff paths, or even go into the comparatively warm sea. I was attracted, too, by its recent history of German occupation, and Mr. & Mrs. Ozanne would recount stories of those difficult times. So it was music to my ears when Ray & Peggy thanked us for our visit and assured us that we would be most welcome to return whenever we wanted.

MWE team on a Crusade at Toxteth Tabernacle, Liverpool. (1971)

"Do come back," they urged, "You will be welcome any time."

And so we returned to the mainland, a busy schedule ahead of us. Most of the campaigns and meetings in which we took part were events that had been planned as major projects for the churches or towns involved. This, however, did not always mean that we had good equipment to use. The absence of musically gifted folk in the churches usually showed in the condition of their pianos! Often, churches acquire their pianos through some kind of gift or bequest. These I call 'a gift with strings attached'! These are usually pianos that no-one wants, and which can't be got rid of for fear of offending the donor. I have experienced all too many of these 'gifts'!

One memorable example was at a church in Neath, Wales. The piano was so damp that I had to ask the minister's son to stand by it and continually flick back the hammers so that they could be played again!

On another occasion, I felt the black notes coming off as I played them. I could do no more than slip the loose notes into my top pocket so that they wouldn't impede my playing. Eventually there were so many that I had a job to get them all in my pocket!

I've played pianos in some unusual places, too. Once, in Herefordshire, a meeting had been arranged to take place on the lawn of a big house. The weather had been very wet, but everyone was pleased to see the sun come out. It had been a lovely day, and during the afternoon, in preparation for the open-air meeting, the piano had been man-handled out into the garden (which probably didn't do it a great deal of good). It was placed on its castors – on the lawn!

As the meeting progressed, I became conscious of a diminishing pedal movement – the piano was sinking further and further into the soft lawn. Then, sure enough, both pedals were flat against the grass, and were quite unusable! Maybe they stopped the piano disappearing altogether!

During our travels we met some wonderful people. We were often quite overwhelmed by the welcome we received, and the kind way in which our every need was anticipated. We gradually learned, however, to be careful what we said.

We were on a Mission at Pentyrch, near Cardiff, and were guests for tea. As we sat down, Grace made an innocent enough comment to our hostess. "Oh, what a pretty cloth!" "Do you like it," asked Mrs. Jones. "It's really beautiful," exclaimed Grace.

Nothing more was said. After tea, however, our hostess shook the cloth outside the back door, folded it, and presented it to Grace.

Grace protested in great embarrassment, but all to no avail.

Another time, Grace passed a comment about a particularly lovely vase standing on the side-board. When the lady had gone into the kitchen, I quietly said to Grace:

"I'm not sure you should have said that, you know. She'll be wrapping it up for you!"

"Surely not," said Grace ruefully, "I was only being polite – mind you, it is nice!"

All went well, and the incident was all but forgotten. At the end of the evening, just as Reg was on the point of driving away back to the caravan, the lady suddenly called out: "Just a minute!" and dashed back into the house. A moment or so later, she returned, carrying the wrapped-up vase! "Here," she said, thrusting the vase into Grace's hands: "You liked it so much: you shall have it!" Grace had learned her lesson. Never again did she pass comments about the fittings and fixtures after that.

Anyone in Full-time Christian service will know that they are never likely to be wealthy. We were never actually in want, though, because God's Word says that he will supply all our needs if we trust him. We did trust him for everything – even our clothes.

We visited a Methodist church in Hull, and towards the end of our stay, the church felt that they would like to buy me a suit! Very few people in that church would have given much thought to that wonderful gesture for long. I never forgot it!

There was the time when Grace was in great need of a warm coat. She did not acquire one by remarking on the excellent taste of one of our hostesses – no, we prayed about the need.

We were involved in a Mission with Don Summers in Tetbury, Gloucestershire, and were staying with the Rev. & Mrs. Pople. For no apparent reason, she suddenly brought out a superb coat, which she offered to Grace with some apprehension. With a gasp of astonishment, Grace cried: "What an answer to prayer – it's just what I needed, and it's a perfect fit!" We were all amazed, and it struck me that this reaction is typical of us Christians – we pray for our needs as God commands, and then we are surprised when our prayers are answered! I remarked: "Why should you be so surprised at it being a perfect fit? The Word says: "...Their sighs went up to heaven! ..."

We met some real characters during our travels. One dear old farmer in Somerset showed concern about the decidedly uncooperative weather. The evening campaign meeting began at 7.30 each evening. At 7 o'clock, without fail, down would come the rain! The farmer was anxious that people were deciding to stay at home, rather than come to the meetings.

The early morning prayer-meeting was set for 5.30, in order to fit in with the milking.

Suddenly, the farmer blurted out in prayer: "Lorrrd, I wants to pray about this 'ere weather. You know wass 'appning, Lorrrd – each nightat seven a'clark the 'eavens open: an' in fact, Lorrrd, some of us are beginning to wonder who's side you'm arn!"

When we arrived in Essex to work with Mr. Dennis Brooks of the 'Friends' Evangelistic Band', we had to make a slight adjustment to our eating habits. We had pitched our caravan in Hadstock, a village quite near the county borders of Essex, Cambridgeshire, Hertfordshire and Suffolk. It was a quiet rural spot, and once a week the fish-and-chips man would come round in his van. His time of arrival...eleven o'clock A.M!

It was during that spell of village evangelism that we went to have supper with an old lady who had been housekeeper to an evangelist over many years. She spoke with an East Anglian drawl, and she was so very caring. She said towards the end of supper:

"Would yer like annuver cuppa tea, Reg?" "Just half a cup, if you don't mind," answered Reg. "Are yer quite sure, dear?" queried the lady. "Quite sure," said Reg firmly. After some activity in the kitchen, she returned with a cup positively brimming! As she handed the cup and saucer to Reg, she said: "Yer could 'ave 'ad a full wan if you'd 'a' warnted it."

There were so many lovely people and wonderful experiences, and yet my health was causing problems. Again, in 1959 I had to undergo more hospital treatment for the nasal and sinus problems. A young pianist, John Gilmore, took my place. He was very able, and was a great asset to Reg. & Grace. I rejoined them in a crusade in Wrexham under Marshall Shallis.

It was at that time that we all decided to have a medical check-up. A doctor friend who was concerned about our general health and welfare had made the suggestion.

It was discovered that I had a hiatus hernia under the left rib cage, and it had probably been congenital. For some reason not known to me, it was regarded as potentially dangerous, and it was recommended that I should seek further advice in Birmingham.

Reg & Grace were clear at the time, so it was very surprising that, later in 1959 Grace was taken very ill with abdominal problems, and was admitted to a hospital in Watford. (Grace's sister Edna and her husband Fred were then living in Watford.) Suddenly, all our engagements were abruptly curtailed, and I returned home, my own health still under suspicion.

Grace eventually came out of hospital but was far from well, and it was some two years or so before she was admitted again, and when opened up, it was discovered that she had been suffering pain and discomfort from adhesions resulting from her previous operation.

So our time of serving together came to an abrupt end. We sadly faced the inevitability of it all – our ways would part, our destinies are quite different. In the late 1970s, Reg and Grace went to Canada. A lady from Guernsey had emigrated to Canada, and because she had got to know Reg & Grace, suggested that there was a church vacancy in Bosano, and that they would fill it in a pastoral capacity. What happened in Canada remains one of the unanswerable questions.

We received a newsletter saying that Reg had slipped and injured himself in the bathroom. The newsletter spoke of the fact that drink was rampant in this little town, and that Reg felt constrained to preach against it. "Please pray for us," pleaded the letter, and I confess to having strange vibes about the whole business of them going out there.

Then came the altogether shocking news of a terrible injustice. Reg & Grace were in the church basement, and the husband of one of the members of the church rushed in upon them in an uncontrollable rage. He had a gun in his hand, and before Reg & Grace could do anything, they were both shot and killed outright.

The man then went to his home, shot his wife and children, and then turned the gun on himself.

It was devastating news, and I often think about these two wonderful people, lovely in their lives, undivided in their death. I think of them on their birthdays just as I think of my parents on theirs. Was their work really finished? Should they have gone to Canada? Might they still be alive today if they had taken a church here, and now be quietly retired? Questions, questions: yet I know that one day the puzzle will be completed to be a puzzle no longer. But I do know that they are now experiencing that eternal life which they sang and preached about; that one day we will all meet up again in glory.

It was probably cowardly of me not even to face going to their Thanksgiving Service at the Full Gospel Tabernacle where we first met. It was all so very painful, and still is.

So in 1959 a phase of my life had come to an end, and I was very unsure as to my future. I consulted my good friend Sid, who had by this time married Eileen from Kidderminster. I poured out all my troubles over a meal with them, and Sid tactfully reminded me of the misgivings he had experienced those two-and-a-half years ago. Now he was somewhat doubtful as to whether I could return to the workshops. Not so many tuners were needed now.

It's hard to imagine just how dejected I felt in those days. By way of trying to cheer me up, Sid said, "The M1 has just opened, let's go for a spin – see what it's like." That was quite an experience, and it lifted me for a little while. Added to all of my problems was the fact that my father was now very ill. His prognosis was very depressing, and the strain on my mother was taking its own toll.

The words of a hymn came forcibly to me at this time:

...Oh, what peace we often forfeit,
Oh, what needless pain we bear:
All because we do not carry
Everything to God in prayer.

So I prayed, pouring out my heart to God. "Lord," I begged, "What am I to do? I wanted so much to serve you, and now it's all gone!" No revelation came whilst I was on my knees: instead, it came when I was bringing some coal in to make up the fire. A Bible verse suddenly flashed into my mind: "This is the will of God, even your sanctification." It hit me like a bomb! God was saying through his Word that although I wanted to be in the big time, the first thing he wanted from me was not my service for him, but my separation to him. He wanted my commitment, so that however I served him, our relationship would be secure.

I realised that in all the work I had been doing for him, it had done surprisingly little for my relationship with him. This was to be a time of consolidation with God.

Chapter Seventeen

A Funeral and Two Weddings

In January 1960 I took courage in both hands, went to the workshops and had a chat with Mr. Fred Tompson, the foreman of the tuning department. He was very understanding, and promised to do his best to present my request to the appropriate authority. He must have done a good job, for before long, I was reinstated and actually welcomed back. The other tuners were keen to know how I'd got on in the two-and-a-half years I'd been away. Sid was especially glad to see me back.

It wasn't long, however, before I was summoned to the Queen Elizabeth hospital to see a Professor De Brue. I was examined thoroughly, and he agreed that an operation was necessary, and that I would be called some time during the summer.

It was in that summer that a big crusade took place in the Bingley Hall, Birmingham. The Eric Hutchings team were to lead it: Eric being the preacher with Geoff Percival, piano, Russell Mills, organ, and soloist Betty Loo Mills – Russell's wife. The weather was fine and hot, and I remember touring the Birmingham streets in a van, playing the on board piano! It was hot work, and my good friend Dennis Guest bought me several ice-creams in an effort to keep me cool.

The meetings were well attended, and my mother came and actually made a decision for Christ, but alas, she didn't really get involved with a helpful church, and so never grew spiritually.

During the early part of the crusade, dad grew much worse, and was taken into Selly Oak hospital again, and we knew that the lung cancer was now in its final stages.

My father's brother, Uncle Bert, who had been our milkman when I was a child, was now in the blood transfusion service. In order to visit at any time, he only had to don his white coat, and no questions were asked.

During one of these visits, dad poignantly asked Bert to take care of Lily – my mother. "I haven't got long, Bert, and I want to be sure she'll be all right." The undertaking that was given that day proved to be prophetic.

We had always assumed that, as he was invariably ill with bronchitis, pleurisy, pneumonia, etc in the winter time that he would be bound to succumb to the cold eventually. However, true to my father's innate sense of humour, he actually died on Saturday, 25th June – just after midsummer's day! Uncle Bert reminded us later that his wife, Aunt Mary had died two years before – on 25th June!

It always seemed to me to be a strange custom that, the day before the funeral, the coffin was brought home together with its occupant. It was as if dad was lying in domestic state in the open coffin, and because I couldn't see him, I remember placing my hand on his crossed hands – O, how cold they were!

It's hard to express how I felt, remembering things that dad had said. He was a materialist to the very end. "When you're dead," he would say, "You're just a box of cold meat!" The book of Ecclesiastes tells us that "God has put eternity into the heart", but it didn't seem to be in dad's heart. I had tried so hard to explain the way of salvation, and now the evidence of my failure was before me, and it was in those moments that I became less sure of eternal banishment to hell – my mind simply refused to entertain those kinds of thoughts.

The day of the funeral came; a harrowing day. The undertaker came into the house, placed the lid on the coffin, and there and then began to screw down the lid. My poor mum gave a cry, and we all surrounded her, and at that moment, to everyone's surprise, I began to pray for mum, that she would be strengthened and surrounded by God's love. I shall never forget that day of utter sadness, trying to come to terms in my own mind with truths about heaven and hell. Often my dreams would be haunted by vivid flashbacks of my standing by the coffin. Dad's voice would come to me, and I would awake with morbid fears in a sweat. Much later, a Christian couple prayed with me about these awful recurring dreams. They asked that God would put his hand on those fearful days and heal them. Since then, I have never had morbid dreams of my father. I know that God can see our lives from their beginning to their end, and can (as it were) place his healing hands on any year, month, day or hour. He knows the end from the beginning, and – as the Psalmist says: "My times are in his hands".

In early August I received my call to the Q.E. hospital. The operation was a massive one, which included having to have several ribs sawn through in order to reach the hernia. When I came round, and was back on the main ward, a physiotherapist was in attendance trying to make me cough. It was the very last thing I wanted to do: the pain was excruciating.

I can't fault the care and attention I received during those difficult weeks. Some of the Christian nurses came to visit me, and during the latter part of my recovery, I went down to the chapel to play for the Nurses' Christian Fellowship again.

Around my bed, one day, came a group of medical students, led by the consultant. (I've always thought it strange how one becomes the subject of discussion across the bed.) "This young man's eyes were shot to hell when he was a baby," said the consultant. Quickly I retorted: "Yes, and I'm not going there to get them back!"

One morning I was having a shave in the washroom. One of the other patients came out of the ward inquiring as to whether I was managing all right. I said I was, but things were a bit difficult because there didn't seem to be any mirrors in this place. Before I could stop him, he was away to find a mirror for me! ...

On another occasion, a little boy came over to my bed to ask a question:

"I've been thinking," he said, "When you're blind, how do you know when to wake up?" For once, I was stuck for an answer!

My good friends, Sid & Eileen came to visit me; I noticed, too, that my mother seldom came alone – Uncle Bert was already looking after her! Joe was also a frequent visitor, and he was so concerned to see how ill I was. I know that he prayed for me often: in fact, I would probably be amazed to know just how often Joe interceded for me. I thank God for the gift of one who still remains the embodiment of a truly faithful friend.

I was to be in hospital for about a month, and during my recovery a medical social worker came to talk to me about convalescence. She had a list of places to which I could go, but somehow or other I just wasn't willing. I mentioned this to Sid & Eileen on one of their visits. "Well," said Sid, "What about Guernsey? You've always said you'd love to go back there. What about writing to Mr. & Mrs. Ozanne and asking if we could all three come?"

That was a brilliant idea, and I remember typing the letter in the day-room, and wondering whether the response would be as cordial as it was some two years previously. I needn't have wondered. Back came a letter saying that we would be very welcome, but that the Ozannes would be away in Canada at the time. The letter went on: "If you would like to fend for yourselves, our home is open for you to stay. Margaret is nursing at the Princess Elizabeth hospital, and will be in and out: just help yourselves."

I returned home feeling distinctly fragile. The wound in my side was very sore, and I wanted to do as little as possible. I reckon I was suffering from post-operative blues and, switching on the radio one afternoon, I heard Yehudi Menuhin playing the Brahms violin concerto. At that particular time I don't think any other piece of music could have so adequately expressed my feelings. And it was the way Yehudi Menuhin interpreted it that moved me so much.

What a genius he was! I shall always be indebted to him for that performance.

Sid & Eileen put all the arrangements in hand for our trip to Guernsey, and we flew from Elmdon airport, Birmingham on a Monday in late August.

The first thing I noticed on landing was the hard core runway: so different from two years before. Mr. Ozanne's brother, Uncle Les, had been deputed to keep an eye on us in case we needed anything. He it was who met us at the airport, and transported us to Lilyvale.

On Wednesday, we went to Sark where we hired a pony and carriage for a trip round the island. However, every time the carriage jolted, I was conscious of a searing pain that grew worse and worse. By the time we got back from Sark I was very much the worse for wear.

We shared the problem with Uncle Les who, incidentally, owned a hardware shop nearby. His first language was a kind of Patois known as Guernsey French, and quite often, Patois words would come into otherwise English sentences. "Mon vieux," he said, "You must go to hospital." it was discovered that I had developed a stitch abscess, which would have to be dressed each day for the rest of the holiday. Then I would have to report back to the hospital in Birmingham.

Margaret asked how we'd got on at hospital, and when we told her about having to go each day for a dressing, she asked the doctor whether she might attend to the dressing herself. This would save my having to keep on going to the hospital, and inhibiting Sid &

Eileen's holiday plans. The hospital readily agreed, and so for the remainder of the week, Margaret looked after me very efficiently.

Just before we left Guernsey, we bought Margaret a 'Thank you' box of chocolates, which she delightedly accepted by saying, "These are lovely! You've picked the ones I like – I'm not normally a sweet lover!" Of course, Sid made as much of that as possible, and Margaret's blushes were cloaked in gales of laughter!

As we returned, plans had already been discussed for a visit next year. Margaret had suggested that she would take a week's holiday so that she could show us round the island, and maybe we would go to France for the day. It was all so very exciting!

The Queen Elizabeth hospital confirmed the stitch abscess, and this set back my recovery for quite some time. It was well into the autumn before I was able to work again, and another surprise was in store for me.

At an appropriate moment my mother began to share with me what was obviously very much on her heart. "Your Uncle Bert has asked me to marry him," she began tentatively. I wasn't really all that surprised: I had noticed things – starting with his coming to hospital with her, and his frequent visits, and taking her out from time to time. "What did you say to him," I asked. "I told him I would have to ask you first," she replied. "Why ask me," I questioned. "Because," said mum, "This is your home, and it would mean our having to move house to Hadnsworth, the other side of the city." I was grateful for her concern about me, but I really couldn't see any problem. I assured her that I felt it would be the finest thing for both of them. I liked Uncle Bert. He was a jovial character and comfortable to be with. He compared favourably with my father whose illness had often made him morose. Uncle Bert was always in good health, and was a very kind man.

I still remembered him from when I was a child, and he had been our milkman working for Midland Counties. He would call with a cheery greeting: "Good morning, Mrs. J.!" Once, he gave me half-a-crown, which was a princely sum in those days. I certainly approved of Uncle Bert!

Their wedding was a lovely occasion, and I am one of the few people who can say that I played at my mum's wedding! But my mother was unique too, because she not only married two brothers and therefore didn't have to change her name, but eventually had two silver weddings! The Birmingham Evening Mail got to hear of this phenomenon, and photographed her and Uncle Bert on mum's eightieth birthday.

In the summer of 1961, Sid, Eileen and I fulfilled our plan of a year ago and went to Guernsey. This time I was able to introduce my friends to Mr. & Mrs. Ozanne, and, of course, we met Margaret again. She had taken a week's holiday, and showed us many sights on the island including the German underground hospital, the shell chapel, and lots of other places – many of which were connected with the German occupation, and which had now become tourist attractions.

We also made the short air trip across the channel to Dinard. It was a very hot day, and we sat on the beach eating luscious peaches. Nearby was a woman with her children, and I remember her calling to her son: "Andre, Andre, Ou est ton chapeau?"

Having made the mistake of eating too many peaches during the morning, we made another mistake in ordering a 'Menu Gastronomique' in the local restaurant. It seemed to me to be a gigantic meal, and since I was still recovering from last year's operation, I could not manage a quarter of the meal. But we laughed a lot that day, enjoying ourselves tremendously.

It was during this week that I began to realise that I was going to miss Margaret a great deal when the visit was over. She herself was due to visit some friends in Kent later in the year, and she asked me how far Birmingham was from Kent.

"Oh, just a couple of train rides," I answered truthfully – not mentioning how long the rides were!

At the end of October, she came to visit us in Handsworth. She was soon completely at home with mum and Uncle Bert, and – like everyone else – they loved her easy nature and quiet, loving ways. It would be difficult not to like Margaret.

On the day I asked her to marry me, I listed all the cons. "You know that I have serious limitations," I warned. "I can't paper the walls or paint the ceilings, and I won't be able to drive or even navigate for you." But Margaret brushed all my negatives aside with the comment: "Well, I know of a lot of men who wouldn't paper the walls or paint the ceilings even if they could, so we won't worry about that!"

So we decided to get engaged at Christmas, and although I hated to see her return to Guernsey, I was left feeling that maybe, at last, there was hope for the future.

It was only a week or so later, that my 'future' nearly came to an abrupt end.

On November 5th, I was coming back from a Sunday night meeting in Northfield. My driver, Winston Simon, was a baritone gospel singer who had taken part in the meeting. He was an excellent soloist who had been a Carol Levis 'discovery' in the radio days before Hughie Green's 'Opportunity Knocks'. Winston would say in a word of testimony: "Carol Levis discovered me, but Jesus Christ recovered me!"

On the way home we gave someone else a lift, dropping him off at Winson Green. Since I was in the back seat, Winston asked if I would like to change to the front passenger seat. As there was not far to go, I decided to stay where I was.

We were just crossing a junction on the outer ring road, when a car came hurtling from a side road from the right, smashing into our car. We swung violently around, hitting a tree. The car was a total write-off, with the near-side door and wing completely stoved in and shredded. Had I been sitting in that front seat I would undoubtedly have been killed or at least seriously injured. I was taken to hospital for observation, having lacerations to my arm and eye, and a severely bruised rib. Miraculously, the side on which I had had the operation was undamaged.

News got to Margaret in Guernsey, and remembering Harry's death in a car crash, I wanted to assure her that I was all right. As soon as I was well enough, I arranged to fly over on the 25th November. The engagement ring had already been bought, and there seemed little point in waiting until Christmas to announce our engagement.

Ever a romantic at heart, I chose my moment carefully, and as we were sitting, listening to that delightful cello passage in the third movement of Brahms second piano concerto, I brought the ring from my pocket and slipped it onto Margaret's finger.

I had already done the honourable thing of writing to Margaret's father, asking for his blessing on our intentions. Both our families were overjoyed at the news, and our future happiness was assured.

In the following March, Margaret came over for a short time to do some house-hunting. Our friends Geoff & Winnie Bowater had met Margaret, and were keen that we should look at a property in their road.

Now I've never been a betting man, especially with regard to horses. But the Grand National was being run that Saturday, and there was a horse by the name of Kilmore, a complete 'outsider'. The house was in Kilmorie Road, Acocks Green, and almost as soon as we entered, we somehow knew that this was going to be our house. I said to Margaret on our way back to Handsworth, "There's a horse running in the National called Kilmore, and they reckon he's fifty to one. Now if we were to place twenty quid on him, that would go a long way to paying off our mortgage."

By the time we got back to Handsworth, one of the main events of the racing year was over. "Who won?" I asked Uncle Bert. "A rank outsider," he replied, "Kilmore!"

We were married on June 6, 1962, in Holy Trinity church, St. Peterport, Guernsey. My old friend Geoff Bowater was my best man, and the evangelist with whom I loved to work best, Frank Farley was a guest. Frank recorded his impressions of the church and the scenery in his inimitable way.

The Rev. Arthur Geary Stevens officiated, and it was a great moment for me when Margaret stood next to me in my top hat and tails – I felt justifiably proud!

It couldn't be a long drawn-out reception as the manner of some is; we had to be at the airport to get a plane to Heathrow, for we were to spend our first night together in a London hotel before flying to Switzerland the following morning.

We had planned an 'away from it all' honeymoon, as my life had already become a constant round of meeting people and speaking at crowded gatherings. It seemed that wherever I went, I would come across someone who knew me.

We would ensure at least one week of quiet and privacy before I had to begin it all again. The ideal place would be Switzerland – Margaret had always wanted to go there, and it would be a place where I could enjoy anonymity. We had booked our honeymoon at Hotel Rosat in the village of Chateau D'oex, in the Bernese Oberland. As we walked into the hotel, I mentioned to Margaret: "Well, now we are completely away from everything and everybody who knows us!" (Meaning, of course, "Who knows me!")

We had hardly reached the end of the foyer before a man came up and said: "Hello, Margaret! how lovely to see you!" He was from Guernsey who had married the hotel proprietor's daughter. I was amazed, particularly because it was Margaret – quiet Margaret, who liked to stay away from the limelight, who was the one that was known!

The next morning, like true honeymooners, we took breakfast in our room. Suddenly there was a knock at the door. In my best French I called "Entrez", and in walked a girl who said: "Hello, Mr. Jackson, I'm Christina Winterburn. Do you remember – you came to our church to do a gospel campaign with Reg & Grace in 1958?" The world is, indeed, a small place!

It was a lovely week. Even in June there was still snow in the sunshine on the mountains, which we climbed – in a cable car, of course! But we managed to extend our week for one extra day when we completely failed to realise that we were supposed to change trains on the journey home. Instead of arriving at Geneva, we found ourselves at Frieburg, and so, by the time we got to our destination, our plane had gone! We had to spend a night in London with Mr. & Mrs. Francis who had befriended Margaret when she was in training.

Eventually we arrived home which was, to begin with, in Handsworth with mum and Uncle Bert. It was a frustrating time for us, having to wait for the occupants of 69 Kilmorie Road to vacate. They had to wait for the folk in Scotland to sell, and so on.

We were in Handsworth for some two months, but finally we moved in early August, and then we gave the signal for all the presents to be transported from Guernsey. There was some damage in transit, as well as the fact that Custom and Excise made a meal of examining and approving of everything. Electrical goods seemed to pose the biggest problem.

I soon began to realise that it was one thing to have enough money to look after myself, and quite another to keep two of us, a car and a home. I began to think of becoming self-employed. It might be that I could earn more this way: at any rate, I was prepared to give it a go.

An appointment was therefore made with the management of the workshops, and I explained my intentions to them. They were very helpful to me, suggesting that I joined their 'home-workers' scheme. It was an incredibly fair – and in those days – trusting arrangement, which meant that I would declare what I earned each week, and they would make up the money to a minimum wage until I got on my feet. Even then, all holiday pay would be based on my average earnings over the year.

At first it was a struggle to find enough work; Margaret got a job in an out–patients' department at Little Bromwich hospital, as it was then called.

The winter of 1963 was particularly severe, and that didn't help at all. At one point, we didn't know how we would get the money for a meal! Then, suddenly, I got the very thing I needed. A 'House of Fraser' store in the middle of Birmingham asked me to maintain their pianos. This gave me one full day's permanent work each week, providing some security. Then, too, I was given the after-sales service on pianos sold, as well as being a living advert in the store itself. So work began to come in, and the Birmingham Authority didn't have to make up my wages at all as my averages crept up more and more. I remember receiving a congratulatory letter from them.

There was never any difficulty in deciding where we would

spend holidays – it was always delightful Guernsey! We spent the first Christmas after we were married with Margaret's family, retu-rning on boxing day with her parents, for we were to spend a few days in Birmingham, and then to Scotland for the New Year celebrations.

As we came over the channel that Boxing Day of 1962, there was a force seven south-easterly blowing, causing the boat to do all kinds of gymnastics. That was the first time I experienced the horrors of seasickness. When we finally boarded the train at Weymouth, we discovered that there was no heating in the carriage. During the journey, ice formed on the inside of the windows. The only uncomplaining friend was Ginger, Margaret's cat who went virtually everywhere with us. He had missed his mistress so much after she'd left home that he would sit on the wall, waiting for her to come from the hospital. Then, when she failed to arrive, he would go upstairs and sit mewing outside her bedroom.

Margaret's parents had mercy on him and sent him to Birmingham by air! We had to meet him and bring him home – and wasn't he pleased to see Margaret again! All the time we'd crossed the channel and made that freezing journey home, we didn't hear a squeak out of him!

The snow came with a vengeance that night, covering the South of England, the Midlands, and the North, except Scotland. When we got to Motherwell, there was not a snowflake to be seen, and on New Year's Day we went to hear Geoffrey Bull – author of "When iron gates yield". We'd had a very late night, as was the custom! Perhaps Mr Bull had also followed the custom; at any rate, he seemed less than dynamic that morning, added to which the warm, bright winter sun was shining right where we were sitting. My dear mother-in-law went sound asleep, with plenty of 'sound'! I couldn't resist teasing her by posing the riddle: "When is a mother-in-law not a mother-in-law?" Answer: When she's a 'bull-dozer!'"

Chapter Eighteen

Mission Accomplished

In 1963, our friends, Geoff & Winnie Bowater were becoming concerned about developing an embryo church in Shirley, near Birmingham. A work amongst boys and girls had been started by Eddie & Betty Jackson who were members of the Tabernacle where I had been a member.

Geoff knew that Margaret and I were not really settled in any of the Acocks Green churches, and so he approached us to see if we would be interested to join the founding team. As we talked and prayed together, we felt of the same mind as Geoff & Winnie, and in October, Shirley Mission was born! That first Sunday evening saw eleven of us in the Warwick room of Shirley Institute because, of course, we had no building of our own. It was hard, pioneering work, but we prayed a lot, and the Mission gradually began to grow. It was a lovely experience to see new members come, and sad to see some go.

But they were great days of battling through disappointments, and as co-pastors of the work, Geoff and I constantly had to cajole, encourage, and remind people that we were veritable missionaries in a mission field.

I remember one time especially when we hadn't seen any signs of growth or progress for some months. We called a crisis meeting. The motion was: "Do we want to give up, or go on?" It was as simple as that. Because we rented the room, we reminded the folk, we had no obligation to stay – all we had to do was to give notice that we were quitting.

During that meeting, people were galvanised and motivated to continue, and we began to see growth again, but it had been a necessary and decisive meeting. Not long after this "Crisis" meeting came a breakthrough. The famous Arthur Blessit from America came to Birmingham as part of his extensive travels, carrying a cross. Arthur was a typical guy of the 1960's – a drop–out from society. He had thrown off society's constraints in order to 'do his own thing'. But the difference between him and other drop-outs was that he had found a living faith in Jesus Christ, and was fully committed to serving him. This outrageous personality who didn't seem to care what anyone thought about the way he looked or dressed, attracted many young people, but directed them persistently toward the Lord Jesus.

After his visit, many young people came into Shirley Mission, and the work really 'took off'. These young people who were confused by the contradictions of life, were looking for answers. They found them, as so many others have done, not in Eastern religions, which seemed to be a growing trend in the sixties – but in the person of the Lord Jesus.

From this point in the Mission's history we became a church. It was a case of 'Mission accomplished'. We now had a church structure, but still no building of our own. We applied to the Council for a building plot. After much consultation, we were disappointed to learn that there were no plots available, but we continued to pray.

Then, to our amazement, two ladies who had heard that we were looking out for somewhere to build a church, came to us, mentioning that they knew of a possible plot.

"It is right beside Shirley railway station," they said, "And we stood in the middle of it, claiming it for God some twenty years ago!"

They had simply seen it, noticed its potential as a site for a work of God, and had repeatedly 'claimed' it by prayer in God's name.

There was a Christian solicitor, known to Geoff who had undertaken our conveyancing – in fact we regarded Mr Peter Lovesey as our solicitor and friend. He was appointed by the Shirley Evangelical Church to negotiate with the Council. The subsequent story of God's faithfulness is well documented in the annals of Shirley Evangelical Church. But amazingly too was the fact that, shortly afterwards, Mr Lovesey died. Our project was one of the last transactions he made. Today, the church has two to three hundred members, and Geoff & Winnie's son Anthony has been the pastor for a number of years. Their other son Chris, is the well known Christian songwriter.

By now my piano-tuning business was really established; I was travelling around Birmingham, Sutton Coldfield, Lichfield, Solihull, and even as far as Stratford-On-Avon. I was quite accustomed to using public transport to get myself from place to place, finding most people willing to lend me a hand when I needed one.

Some blind people find it very difficult to accept help. Part of growing up is to achieve some measure of independence, and suddenly to become dependent on a stranger seems to be a denial of one's dignity – a reversion to childish dependence. This is not often understood by sighted people, but my view is that it's up to us to create an understanding of the problem. In my younger days I battled against this feeling of being 'patronised', but now I realise that being patronised is nothing less than injured pride. I have learned that, by accepting help, I value another person. Conversely, by not accepting help, we can injure a person who genuinely wanted to help, and we do ourselves no good turn.

A defining moment in this kind of thing came when I was making my way to a bus stop in Solihull. As I was walking along, a man approached me and surprisingly asked: "May I walk with you?" "But of course," I said, and for a while we chatted. He asked me questions about my blindness. How long had I been blind, and my attitude toward life. I was able to assure him that I had no regrets about being a blind person because I lived such a full life as a Christian. When we reached the bus stop, he gripped my hand fervently, and I thanked him for walking with me. "No," he remonstrated, "I want to thank you. You see, when I came up to you, I was actually thinking of taking my life, but meeting you has made me think again." As I got on the bus, I was dizzy with amazement. What might have happened if I had taken his overtures as an offer of unnecessary help, asserting my independence? I was so glad I had reacted sensitively, and mentally chalked it up for future reference.

Knowing my exact whereabouts has never been a problem to me at all – with the possible exception of that little incident on the return journey from our honeymoon – and that was entirely different! However, I have to admit that I did have the occasional collision with pavement furniture such as lampposts, which I think should all be made of rubber! And then there was the memorable time when I actually fell down an unguarded manhole in Edgbaston. Fortunately I was virtually unscathed, and my family fell about with laughter when I described the incident as graphically as possible!

But things literally came to a head one day when I was walking down a fairly narrow pavement in Shirley. A lorry came along, totally masking the sound of my own footsteps. I really should have stopped in my tracks until the lorry had passed, instead of which I came into collision with a concrete lamp standard, gashing my forehead badly. How I carried on working that day I'll never know. I managed to make my way to the house where I was to tune the piano, and they were horrified at the sight of my head. They cleaned me up, put a plaster over the wound, and I carried on.

When I got home, it was decided that I should go to hospital. Three stitches were inserted, and I actually took a day off from work.

It was then that I began seriously to think about applying for a guide-dog.

Chapter 19

One Man and His Dog

MARGARET AND I DISCUSSED this new idea, and eventually we agreed that it would be for the best. I knew that I would have to surrender my relative independence; Margaret – being essentially a cat-lover – had some misgivings too. I rang the 'Guide-dogs for the Blind' centre and asked tentatively: "Do you think I could be considered for a guide-dog?" The response was reassuring and friendly, and in a matter of a week or so, a trainer came to assess me. We talked; he took in our home situation; and then we went for a walk together. He noticed my pace, and my anticipating of kerbs etc. "It's going to be a struggle for you," said Brian Moody. "You're going to have to learn to trust the dog in the same way that you trust your wife when you go out walking with her."

Confidentially, Mr Moody assured me that I would be accepted, but that I would need to wait for official confirmation. It came, and I was delighted, even though it would mean that we would have very little income for at least a month while I trained.

So in 1964 I was to commence training with my guide-dog at Leamington Spa, one of only three Centres then, but in recent years many more have been added. Any potential guide-dog owner is required to spend up to four weeks learning how to control and care for their dog.

Training a dog to be a guide-dog is a highly organised process. The 'The Guide-dogs for the Blind Association' was started in 1931 in this country, and is a privately funded charity.

Dogs used are mainly Labradors, Retrievers, Collies and Alsatians. As far as possible, the trainers have to suit the dog to the person. For instance, I heard of a lady in Scotland who was so small that a Shetland sheep-dog was trained specially for her, with the appropriate diminutive harness! On the other hand, I met Mr McGregor, a large man in height and girth for whom a Malamute was trained. (Malamutes are used in Alaska to pull sleds.) I remember giving this huge dog a friendly pat, and it was like patting a bale of closely woven blankets.

Normally, the dogs are chosen from specially bred puppies for their character and suitability for training. They spend nine or ten months with a 'puppy walker', learning the rudiments of obedience, and becoming acclimatised to many different situations. At any one time, the Association would have nearly eight hundred puppies in preparation, of which about eighty percent will become guide-dogs. When they are ready, they go to a Centre for nine months for serious training. They begin to learn specific skills – how to respond to certain commands which use words like "Forward!" "Right!" "Left!" "Back!" And, of course, "Sit!" They must learn how to avoid obstacles, taking into account the height and width of their owner – and how to deal with near and far traffic. The dog learns to wear a harness – a handled frame which gives freedom of movement, and through which his owner can sense his every action.

Before long the dog realises that as soon as the harness is in place, he is 'on duty', and his behaviour must reflect that fact.

The dog doesn't instinctively know what is expected of him; he learns by discipline and encouragement. Should the dog forget what he is supposed to do, he is reminded by a sharp command. If the aberration still continues, a jerk on the harness usually puts an end to any preoccupations. But when the dog does well, he is rewarded by a loving pat, an exclamation of praise, and other displays of affection. I've even known times when I have put my arm around the dog, giving her a hug. Dogs respond to love, and will usually willingly obey if they know and feel that they are appreciated.

Andy

The last month of this intensive training is shared with the eventual owner. As has already been hinted, the staff at the Centre will have completed a surprisingly in-depth research into the blind person's character and habits – even style of walking – in order to match him or her with the right dog.

The owner, too, has to learn. He discovers that very strict rules must be obeyed if his dog is to remain healthy and happy, and therefore able to serve efficiently. One rule is regarding meals. With some exceptions, the dog needs only one good meal a day of a prescribed content. He is not to be fed between meals. This can often prove difficult for the blind owner when well-intentioned people try to offer the dog biscuits, cake or sweets while he is on duty. If only people would realise that indiscriminate feeding can lead to weight problems, can be a distraction from work, and that it militates against the dog's very dependence on his owner.

I had been at Leamington Spa Centre for a couple of days, during which time we would talk of little else other than dogs. I didn't know what dog I would have, and we were told that each dog differs in much the same way as humans. We were introduced to the mind of a dog, and by the time Sunday came – the day we were to be introduced to our respective dogs, we were all at a pitch of anti–cipation. In those days, we waited in our bedroom with some lean cold meat on a shelf. There was a bed for the dog because – once we came together as a unit, we would stay together – day and night.

I have always had a soft spot for dogs. As I waited in my room, my mind went back to our faithful pet who had sat by me for hour after hour when I had come home, having been so very ill. And yet I knew, after all the talks we'd had that this would be a relationship on a higher, deeper level. Somehow I harboured no doubt that whatever dog had been allocated to me, we would get on fine. And so I waited…

Soon I heard the approach of Estelle, one of the kennel girls, and the accompanying sound of a jingling bell, and the unmistakable sound of a dog's pattering paws. I was almost sick with excitement; the door opened, and Estelle proudly announced the arrival of Donna! She was a pale yellow Labrador, fourteen months old, and it was quite obvious that Estelle was really quite fond and proud of her.

Donna came straight to me as Estelle left us and closed the door. I introduced myself to Donna, chatted to her; patted and stroked her, and now and again, reached up to the shelf where the meat was, and gave her some from the palm of my hand. This was to indicate that, from now on, her food was to come from me, and nobody else. I was now to be her pack-leader!

Now followed a month of intensive, rigorous training. We were a very mixed group in our 'class': some took to the training programme easier than others, and we inevitably compared experiences in our evening free time. On my class was an old schoolmate of mine, Jim Hughes with his dog Foxie. Jim was also a piano-tuner, and a very able musician.

Always our dogs were with us apart from mealtimes. Towards the end of the month of training, a discipline exercise was undertaken. Each dog was dutifully lying by his owner, completely unattached by a lead, or constrained by a hand. The trainer came in with a tray of fancy cakes, which we were to have with a cup of tea. "I'm placing this tray of cakes on the floor in the middle of the room," he explained. "If you feel any movement from your dog, you are to constrain him." The tray went down. Not a dog moved! When the tray was taken up again, choruses of dog praising broke out – it was a significant moment.

With all that's involved in training from puppyhood, working with a trainer and then with the eventual blind owner, considerable expense is incurred. It is most unlikely that any blind person could meet that kind of bill. But in order to make ownership of the dog strictly legal, a nominal sum is charged. What each person pays for their dog is strictly confidential. This and other formalities were completed on the last day. My trainer, Mike Tucker, gave me some final words of instruction, at the end of which he congratulated me on becoming a 'unit'.

I re-commenced my work as a piano-tuner, introducing Donna as a partner in the firm! All my customers, without exception, took to her. She was gentle, obedient, and always willing to work even in the foulest weather. I developed a habit with her that never failed to impress my customers. Having finished the tuning of a piano, Donna would get up, having lain by the piano for sometimes well over an hour. She would take the tuning tool from my hand, carry it proudly round the room two or three times, and then come back to me, dropping the tool right by my case.

She was really obsequious in her loyalty and affection. When we went to the park, for instance, I would release her for a free run, but she would just run circles around me. But she had an affection for Margaret, too. We were on holiday in Guernsey, and Margaret decided to have a swim in the sea. As she was beginning to swim out from the beach, Donna suddenly left me, took to the water, getting the other side of Margaret, trying to push her back to shore. O yes, Donna had made a big impact on our lives.

As a Christian, I had an interesting problem. There is in the Bible that which talks about 'The fruit of the Spirit' – "love, joy, peace, patience, kindness, goodness, faithfulness, gentleness, and self-control."

Quite simply my problem was, how could a dog exhibit "The fruit of the Spirit?" I thought about this a great deal, even mentioning it to others. Then it suddenly occurred to me – when we, as God's children, exhibit this 'fruit', we are what God wants us to be. It's all summed up in the word 'obedience', as the old hymn has it:

Trust and obey,
For there's no other way
To be happy in Jesus,
But to trust and obey.

Later on as I began to work full-time in evangelism, I would demonstrate to school children the peril of disobedience and the pleasure of obedience. I would imagine Donna saying one day: "I'm going to do my own thing today! I'm going to take a day off from obeying my master. Instead of waiting patiently at the kerb, I'll go just when I want to go." I pointed out that that could mean injury or even death for both of us. That was the ultimate peril of disobedience. But then I would give Donna an instruction, which she obeyed immediately, upon which I praised her, and patted her, and she displayed her pleasure with a fiercely wagging tail in uninhibited pleasure. The point was never lost on my audience.

Sometimes I would use Donna, and my second dog Andy in Gospel meetings. The trainer had been their pack-leader once. I came along to challenge his leadership as far as the dogs were concerned, and it's an attested fact that, early in the new relationship the dogs test the credibility of their new leader. I remember it happening with both my dogs – I had to assert my leadership to leave no doubts in the canine mind.

Satan is pack-leader of this world. Originally God was pack-leader of all that He had created, but Satan had made his bid, and humankind went over to him. Jesus came to win us back through His death and by His resurrection. He is still operating by His Holy Spirit to bring people back to the original pack where they can experience the pleasure of obedience to Him. What a wonderful analogy this is!

At about this time in the mid-60s, I acquired two regular contracts that I felt were quite prestigious. One was with the B.B.C. in Birmingham, looking after two Bosendorfer grands. I would go into the orchestra studio once, and sometimes, twice a week, getting to know the folk there. The B.B.C. had acquired this building whilst the Pebblemill studios were being built which would house both radio and television. The building acquired was none other than the Carpenter Road School where I had been as a young adolescent. The studio was where we used to perform our gymnastics! Donna would always accompany me, and we were invited to stay on for a recorded concert by the Midland Light Orchestra under its conductor, Gilbert Vinter. Mr Vinter took a real liking to Donna, who lay motionless throughout the recording. I felt so very proud of her!

The other contract was with Rackham's, the House of Fraser store (before mentioned) in Corporation Street, Birmingham. This meant going in once a week – usually on Fridays – and tuning pianos in stock under the direction of the piano salesman. I reckon this was Donna's most boring day. She had to lie, tethered to the desk in the heat of the store, only getting a break at lunch–time. As well as the pianos and organs on this top floor, there were also two restaurants, 'The Lilac Tree', and 'The Gay Tray'! When people saw Donna, they were instinctively drawn to her, and sometimes they would bring out of the restaurant titbits of food. This was strictly against the rules, and so anxious did I become, that the advertising department moved in on my behalf. They constructed a large notice, which read: 'PLEASE DO NOT FEED THE DOG'. This attracted a reporter from the Birmingham Evening Mail, who did a feature on Donna and her work with me. (It was a good advert for the store, too!)

At the end of Friday afternoons, Donna was so keen to get home that – rightly or wrongly – I tended to let her set the pace as we made for Moor Street station to get the train to Acocks Green where we were living. This meant finding the crossing that would take us down to the underpass and up the other side. We went at a fair rate, so much so that I can't help thinking that people not only stopped to see this whirlwind of man and dog, but actually felt it safer to get out of the way! This all typified the absolute freedom into which Donna had brought me. It was exhilarating to be able to move at such a pace perfectly safely. She even seemed to know which platform the train would be leaving from!

The Guide dogs for the blind association undertook regular aftercare visits during which the trainer would see how we were working as a unit. The dog's health was checked, including weight. After the visit, a letter would come from the Centre, making suggestions or giving directions where it was thought necessary. I was quite thrilled, because all the letters I received were of a congratulatory nature. Both Donna and I were in excellent condition!

Chapter Twenty

Our First Baby

EARLY IN JANUARY 1965, we had a phone call which caused us considerable excitement. The call came from Rev. Ben Peake who was general secretary of the Movement for World Evangelisation. M.W.E. was founded in 1931 for the purpose of spreading the gospel of Christ in every level of society through evangelistic crusades and Bible teaching in many parts of the world. They were also the well known organisers in England of the highly successful annual holiday convention at Filey in Yorkshire. Thousands of people would flock to this small East coast town from all over the United Kingdom. The staff at the holiday camp used to refer to this particular week in September as 'Holy Week'!

But our first visit to Filey was still five years in the future. Ben Peake told me that they had a team touring Portugal, conducting meetings as well as being involved in personal work. He mentioned two evangelists whom I had already worked with – Don Summers and Frank Farley. The soloist on the tour was Peter Smith from Guernsey, who was known to both Margaret and me.

There was also Dave Foster – a name not known to us then. He was described as a chalk artist, whose speciality was to draw instant pictures with board and chalk to the accompaniment of appropriate music.

Ben went on to say that their musician wasn't able to complete the tour: that they were looking for another suitable pianist. He wondered if I would be in a position to join them.

It was agreed that Margaret and I would travel together on this exciting venture. We joined the team at the University town of Coimbra. The first thing we noticed was that people would start coming an hour before the meeting was due to begin. The second thing was that meetings didn't often begin before nine o'clock in the evening! We were going to have to get used to late night activities. The third thing we observed was the keenness of the people. They loved our music; were entranced by Dave's chalk artistry, and were patient listeners to the preached Word of God, which had to be done through translation.

Margaret, Tim, Chris and Peter

The whole tour was hectic, but fun. We travelled to many parts of Portugal, taking large and small meetings. As just mentioned, all the speaking was done through interpreters, and this required some practice. It is only when someone is translating one's every word that one begins to realise how many colloquialisms and vernacular sayings one uses. Even the titles of Peter's songs were translated, and the problem was noticeable when he sang the Negro Spiritual 'Swing low, sweet chariot'.

The translator couldn't handle it and was totally nonplussed. Deciding on an alternative he announced: 'Swing low, sweet donkey cart!'

During our final week in Portugal, Margaret and I were detached from the rest of the team so as to include Faro in the tour. It was now early March, and Margaret noticed the apparent deadness of the fig trees in Faro. She was assured, however, that leaves would soon come, and then the fruit. That brought home to us the significance of Israel having become a nation again after apparent extinction.

We had a five-hour train journey back from Faro to Lisbon, where we were met by our kind host and hostess and taken to their club for Sunday lunch.

On the whole, I had not eaten very well in Portugal – I just couldn't come to terms with the food. However, the dessert on this occasion was delicious! It was fresh pineapple floating in Madeira wine. I hadn't had anything like this before: I demolished it with relish. My hostess, seeing how much I had enjoyed it, asked if I would like some more. It was irresistible. I had to say, "Yes, please," and another generous helping of the delicious confection was placed before me.

As I eventually got up from the table, I was visibly swaying, and had to lean on Margaret for support. "Take it easy," she advised me, "and whatever you do, don't start singing!"

Our kind benefactors took us in their car to see the sights of Lisbon. I saw nothing, of course, for I had slumped into the back seat and was sound asleep!

In all of thirty years since that tour, we have never returned to Portugal although the people there had left a lasting impression on us.

During our first night back home, we had a job to settle even to sleep. We got up and made a cup of coffee, going over and over the events of the last three weeks. It had been a wonderful time, as well as an introduction to the Movement for World Evangelisation, which was to play such a significant part in our lives in years to come.

After the national excitement of England winning the World Cup in 1966, we had our own excitement in 1967. It was then that we discovered that we were expecting our first baby. We were absolutely thrilled, and were somehow quite sure that it would be a boy. We started thinking about names – boys' names – and since we favoured something Biblical, we decided on 'Timothy'. Then we felt it would be nice, (even diplomatic) if his second name was something Scottish, since all Margaret's relatives on her mother's side were Scottish. So we hit upon 'Fraser", and so 'Timothy Fraser' was duly born on 8th May 1968.

I shall never forget the wonderful experience of hearing his first cry, and holding our baby in my arms – it was magic!

We were quite besotted by him, as I suppose most new parents are about their firstborn, and we cooed and fussed accordingly.

I must confess that I didn't feel 'called' to the practical side of caring for Tim. I preferred to leave that kind of thing to my wife who, after all, was a professional nurse! But a few months after he was born, Margaret hinted that she particularly wanted to go to the missionary meeting at our church. In fact, she hinted for the entire week, until I quipped that one has to be 'hintelligent' to pick up hints!

I agreed that Margaret should go to the meeting. "But what about the baby?" she queried.

"What about the baby?" I parried: "Just leave his milk in case he gets hungry or thirsty – or whatever it is they get at this age! He'll be fine."

With a few more assurances and reassurances, Margaret left me 'holding the baby!'

All was well for half an hour. Then I heard a cry from the pram in the dining-room. I dropped everything – (which was a pity, really, because I was drying the dishes!) I went to the pram, picked up Tim in my arms, saying, "Daddy's here, never fear!" We started to process round the room, but this seemed to make no difference – Timothy Fraser continued to cry. As an Uncle to seemingly countless nephews and nieces, I knew the answer: and said to Tim: "You're hungry, or thirsty, or whatever it is you get at this age", and I applied the bottle of milk. But that didn't do the trick, so once again, we processed, and this time I patted appropriate parts of his anatomy, assuring myself that he had flatulence. But it was all to no avail. In my growing frustration, I remembered a song, which went:

Art thou troubled?
Sweet music shall calm thee ...

So I took him to the front room where the piano was; placed him in his carry cot, and proceeded to play to him some Chopin. It seemed to do the trick for all of one minute – it was part of Chopin's Funeral March sonata! But during that minute, Tim summoned all the remaining energies of his tiny frame, and raised a cry which was destined to reach mummy who was all of four miles away!

I snatched him from his carry cot. "Timothy Fraser," I said, "the neighbours will think I'm into infanticide!" We retreated into the lounge at the back of the house. At this point, another thought struck me. Beyond our garden was the back garden of the Ivanhoe nursing home. What if I could rent him out for a while to the professionals? But then, should Margaret happen to come home a bit early, that would take some explaining!

Suddenly, it occurred to me that it must be getting darker. Of course! That could be the trouble. Tim was scared! Even for a little baby, what was happening seemed totally unnatural. Why didn't I think of it before? I went over to the light switched, and as soon as I switched on the light, wonder of wonders! – Tim looked around, stopped crying, and peace reigned!

I had been trying to soothe him; feed him, scold him, love him –but what he desperately needed was light.

By now, he had become so dehydrated that he took all of his milk, winded successfully, and went fast asleep.

When Margaret came home and asked how the evening had gone, I said, "absolutely fine!"

Margaret looked at Tim: "He looks a bit flushed." I thought to myself, he's all right – what about me! But then I recounted the story. I have been doing so ever since: because I recognised in the experience the great truth that men and women, boys and girls everywhere, who are distressed by the results of sin in their lives, can find themselves transformed by the light of the glorious gospel of Christ. He, himself, said "I am the light of the world. He who follows me will not walk in darkness, but shall have the light of life."

Chapter Twenty-One

Open Doors

BY THIS TIME, Margaret had given up her work as a district nurse so as to dedicate herself to looking after Timothy Fraser. Only the advent of our baby would have made her give up her much loved vocation. She had made many friends through her work – everyone seemed to love her!

This all meant, of course, that we relied exclusively on my work as a piano-tuner. The connection had built up well, and I was still involved in looking after the pianos in the big Birmingham store.

Not only was I paid to tune the pianos, but Roy, the salesman, would ask me to play to prospective buyers.

One day a couple who I immediately recognised came from Northern Ireland asked me: "Can you play 'To God be the glory?'" I immediately started to play

The old hymn with suitable embellishments on the baby grand I'd just tuned. My efforts bore fruit: Mr. & Mrs Nesbitt not only bought the piano, but also treated me to a lunch in the restaurant!

Roy was quite interested in my brand of gospel music, and on another occasion a young man came to the piano department because he had heard what he recognised to be 'Christian' music. We soon got into conversation, discovering that we were both Christians, and thus I met for the first time, David Pope!

Dave (as I soon came to know him) was studying behavioural science and psychology at Aston University. My day in Rackhams was usually a Friday, and from that time on, we would have lunch together – usually soup and a sandwich.

Over lunch one day, I noticed that Dave was more animated and excited than usual.

"What's on your mind, Dave," I asked.

"Well, it's amazing...I can't get over it! I was with the young people in our church last night, and – I don't quite know how it happened – but I started singing worship songs. They joined in, and we had a wonderful time of worship."

"That's great!" I encouraged. "You may well have discovered a gift that God is going to use. Go for it, man, and may God bless you!"

All this time, the work at Shirley Evangelical Church was going well. I was now co-pastor with Geoff Bowater, and we had developed a wonderful understanding between us. Geoff knew me as few people did. He sensed a restiveness in me: what he later called "The restlessness of an evangelist's heart".

"I'm quite persuaded," he said to me one day, "That we're going to lose you to a wider ministry." In 1969, I was receiving Christian literature from a centre in Sussex known as "The Torch Trust for the Blind". The people there were dedicated to the vision of reaching blind people, not just in this country, but overseas as well.

The more I read about them, the more restless I became. I began to pray: "Should I be involved, Lord? Is there something I should be doing to help reach my fellow-blind people?"

Looking back now, it seems so obvious that the Grand Designer was at work. For, just about this time, another phone call, four years after the first call, came from Rev. Ben Peake. I was initially surprised by his call, but my surprise was to grow at what he proposed.

"We would like you to consider the possibility of becoming a staff member of the Movement for World Evangelisation! I want you to tell me how you feel about that, and – can we meet at the Swiss Centre restaurant, Leicester Square next week?"

I was completely taken aback, and yet felt a surge of excitement as I boarded the train for Euston; got a taxi to the restaurant where Ben was waiting for me.

The conversation that day was far more important than the food! Ben asked me as to how I felt about my future ministry. When I shared with him my concern, which had been generated by the work of Torch Trust, he, too, got excited. "You could combine your work with Torch with the outreach work of the Movement." From that meeting, I knew that things were never going to be quite the same again.

I shared all this with Margaret, of course, but also with Geoff and Dave Pope over another Friday lunch. It was then that Dave began to wonder whether he should be praying about the possibility of full-time service for God. His church in Gornal also prayed with him, and one lady was heard to pray: "Lord, we pray as you'll bless him, and, Lord, put him to good use!"

Two more events were to take place that year, which were to mark out my future path.

The first of these occurred in October 1969. I had been invited to take part in the Torch Thanksgiving day celebrations held each year at that time in Three Bridges Evangelical Church near Crawley in Sussex.

I joined the minibus of young blind people from Birmingham, feeling at one with them right away. It was such a carefree, happy journey, and that spirit continued through the weekend. We stayed at Torch House, Hurstpierpoint, and it was almost like stepping into another world, and yet there was a familiarity about it, after all, these were 'my' people – we understood each other as blind people. We were not all without sight, however. There were sighted staff and other helpers too. Torch House had a family atmosphere, especially as people referred to Ron & Stella Heath – founders of the Trust – as 'Mum' and 'Dad'. Unfortunately, Margaret wasn't with me for that weekend. We didn't feel at that point that we could impose a lively seventeen-month old toddler on people we didn't yet know.

Only a matter of a fortnight later came the second important event. This was a meeting of the M.W.E. Council in Hildenborough, Kent. Some of the staff evangelists were there too, and – Dave Pope! Yes, he, too, had been invited to be looked over by Council! Once again, the fellowship was warm and friendly. Questions were asked of Dave and me as to how we thought we might fit in as staff members. What did we feel our role to be? Would we be happy to be away from home for weeks at a time? (Dave found that one easy – he was a bachelor, and still is!)

Six months after that weekend we were both staff evangelists with the Movement.

I had shared my vision with the Council for reaching my fellow-blind people with the Good News of the gospel. The way this could perhaps be done was through the formation of Saturday afternoon fellowship groups, which would integrate blind and sighted people in the context of an informal presentation of the gospel, followed by tea. The first of these groups was formed in January 1970 in Birmingham – my 'Jerusalem'. The next was Leicester, and from then on, groups began to form all over the country, the more so when I was released from my piano-tuning business in May. It was the beginning of what for me would be seven years of visiting Social Services in the mornings, Clubs for the blind in the afternoons, and deputation meetings in churches in the evenings.

At that time, the vision was very much mine. It was a pioneer work, much as Shirley Evangelical Church had been. The vision wasn't shared by the Torch committee, and I didn't have the grace to ask them – I simply got on with what I felt to be God's directing in my life. Later on, however, Ron & Stella saw and graciously acknowledged the potential of these groups, not only taking the spoken message to hundreds of blind people all over the country, but also being a channel, too, for the produced literature and cassettes.

The emergence of more and more local radio stations proved very valuable to us in those days. It was easy to get access into a studio for interviews, and I relished every opportunity. The Radio Four programme for the visually impaired known as "In Touch" featured the Torch work by actually interviewing staff at Torch

House, the late David Scott Blackhall being the interviewer.

In the spring of 1970 we rejoiced in the prospect of a second baby. Tim was almost two years old, and it seemed to be perfect timing.

As a staff member of M.W.E. it was incumbent upon me to be at the Filey Holiday Crusade in September. Not only were Margaret & Tim with me, but also Margaret's parents from Guernsey. They came so as to be able to help with babysitting in those cold chalets! It was a sacrifice of love because it also freed Margaret to be with me at team prayer-meetings and briefings.

The Filey team with Peter in the back row.
Front row: Stephen Olford, Lindsay Clegg, John West (Chairman MWE) and George Duncan.

When we arrived at the camp, we were given our packs, which included assignments for the week, and the Filey songbook. We got directions as to which chalets were ours, and as we made our way to our accommodation, there was a general air of bustle: people greeting each other loudly and enthusiastically: cases being carried into chalets from cars, which were then driven away and parked for the remainder of the week on the sea front. The atmosphere was amazing – infectious!

I was in awe of the privilege that I was enjoying. To sit down for an evening meal with international Convention speakers, ministers and evangelists like Rev David Watson, George Duncan, Sidlow Baxter, Stephen Olford, Ron Dunn from the States, and many others, not forgetting Linsey Glegg, the man to whom God had given the vision for this annual expression of fellowship around God's Word. Even now, wherever I go in the United Kingdom, I am sure to be gripped by the hand, and asked: "Remember Filey?" Even people who were children then enthuse about it to me now.

Filey also helped to raise the profile, not only of the work of Torch, but also that of the Disabled Christian Fellowship. A lounge was set apart for these groups so that people could come and meet us, and thus be drawn into the increasing family circle. M.W.E. delegated Joe Wiggins, a Council member to be with both groups, thus representing the Movement's concern to be of maximum help. They were great days, and I wish I could write more. Sadly, those days are gone. Filey has never been replaced; it was unique in giving expression to the wider ministry of presenting the gospel, not only in word, but also in music: choirs, smaller groups and soloists. I believe the church and this country are the poorer without Filey.

By now, warm fellowship and firm friendships had developed between me and the other staff evangelists with whom I was regularly working – John Blanchard, Peter Anderson, Tom Butler, and Eric Clarke, the soloist and song-leader. We as a team were getting invitations for evangelistic efforts in many different areas. One of these invitations came to John from Ballymoney in Northern Ireland. Trinity Presbyterian Church were anxious to put on a week of what was known as coffee-bar evangelism.

John approached me with the idea of joining him for this venture. "When is it for?" I asked. "Next January," replied John. I demurred somewhat: after all, our baby was due in mid–January.

Margaret and I discussed the matter, and in her usual open-hearted way, she agreed that I should go. But I was still full of mixed feelings. I would want to be at Margaret's side when the baby was born, just as I had been when Timothy Fraser arrived. The baby might come early, and I would feel that I had failed in not being around.

Things were made somewhat easier when Margaret's parents announced that they would come over to be on hand to look after Tim, and generally hold things together. So I agreed to go with John for my first visit to Ulster.

We were met at Aldergrove airport by the minister Derek Poots, who then drove us to Ballymoney. John took the front passenger seat and chatted to Derek all the way. I sat quietly in the back seat, wondering how everything would go. Would I be accepted? Thinking about the tensions that regularly made lurid news headlines: and wondering how Margaret was faring at home.

But what I couldn't possibly have realised then was that this visit to Northern Ireland was a watershed in my ministry. Nothing would ever be the same for me again. Ulster was written on my heart!

As soon as we arrived in Ballymoney, having our first meal with Derek & Mildred Poots and their family, I felt a oneness which was only enhanced as I came into contact with more and more people. Their humour, their out-and-out friendliness just warmed the heart – in short, I cannot speak highly enough of the generous nature of Northern Irish people.

At that time, I stayed with Henry and Isobel Woodrow and their two small boys, Hughie and John. The meetings went really well, and it was many years later that Rev Derek Poots introduced me to his "Right–hand elder", as he put it. Jack Hayes said to me: "It was during the coffee-bar mission in 1971 that I trusted the Lord Jesus Christ as my Saviour". "And now," interjected Derek, "I wouldn't like to be without this man's fellowship and help."

My next visit that same year included Wellington Street Presbyterian Church, Ballymena. The minister, David Alderdyce had a phenomenal sense of humour: he would reel off joke after joke. When he welcomed and introduced me to his church he said: "I'm glad to welcome Peter Jackson to our church. Every time I meet a fellow like him it reminds me of a budgie with no teeth – he was born to succeed!"

If this was the first joke I ever heard in Northern Ireland, it certainly wasn't the last. I reckon I have heard more jokes and stories in Ireland than anywhere else. During each visit I acquire more to add to my already considerable store.

I was told of an Irishman whose favourite book was a dictionary: "Because it explains the meaning of the words as you go along!"

It was in Ulster that I was told about a doctor talking to his patient. "I've got some bad news for you, and some dreadful news. The bad news is that you've only twenty-four hours to live!" "What's the dreadful news then," asked the anxious patient. "I should have told you yesterday!"

Scarcely a week after my return from a triumphant first visit to Northern Ireland, Margaret gave birth to Christopher Paul Raymond on 19th January.

There was the beginning of a protracted postal strike the next day, how glad we were, therefore, to have had our 'male' safely delivered in time!

At this time I still had my piano-tuning business that provided extra income, and with another mouth to feed, that was useful.

One of my customers who lived in Solihull was a Mrs Blow. She was both German and masculine. She had two sons that were both doing military training at Sandhurst – she was formidable! One day she asked: "How many children haf you?" "Two," I replied. "Dat iss goot! Never haf sree," she almost commanded. "Why not," I asked, puzzled. "Because, if you haf sree, when you stay at an hotel, who is going to eat zee udder haf of de grapefruit?"

I remember being assigned an after-sales tuning for a Mrs Pearson who also lived in Solihull. Usually I was the one who sought out opportunities to witness to my faith. However, this time, the tables were turned on me!

As soon as I walked into the house, I knew something was different. Mrs Pearson did not show me to the piano – instead, she showed me to an armchair. She asked me if I would like a cup of tea, and although I didn't at that moment, experience had taught me that refusal could often be taken as an insult to well-meant hospitality. I submitted compliantly.

The tea arrived on a tray together with a rather large plate of cakes – all at 9.15 in the morning!

While I was fully occupied with the contents of the tray, Mrs Pearson began to make what I felt to be a prepared and rehearsed speech for my benefit. She told me that her husband had recently died, but that I was not to feel in any way sorry for her. "You see," she said, "The Lord has promised to be a husband to the widow, and since I have known Him as my Saviour for many years, I can trust Him..."

Several fancy cakes and three cups of tea later, she was still telling me that the Lord Jesus would take care of me too, if I would let Him!

Here was a lady doing her Christian duty, testifying to all she could about her faith in God. She was carrying out her personal evangelism campaign! In her ardent zeal she completely discounted the possibility that I might be a Christian too. When she eventually paused for breath, I grabbed the chance to say:

"That's wonderful...let's have a word of prayer." I thanked God for her willingness to tell others about His saving power. I prayed that He would continue to take care of her, filling her and her home with His joy and peace.

When I had finished, she gasped:

"You didn't tell me you were a Christian!"

"You didn't give me the chance!" I laughed.

Yet another lady in Solihull started to tell me about her involvement with the local choir.

"We're doing 'Messiah'," she said. "I really love the chorus 'For unto us a child is born', but I don't understand what it means when it says 'Wonderful Counsellor', and about the government being upon His shoulder."

Having made sure that she really did want to know – bearing in mind that my job was to tune her piano, not to be a Bible teacher – I was able to explain that one day Jesus will return, and reign supreme in a new heaven and a new earth. Then I pointed out that for her, personally, it meant that she could place the government of her life on Jesus' shoulders. He could live His life through hers if she would allow Him, and she would then discover for herself how He could be the "Wonderful Counsellor, the Mighty God and Prince of peace" in her own life.

Some time later, her husband, a headmaster, wrote to me to thank me for being such a help to his wife. I never met them again, because they moved to the Banbury area.

Donna and I didn't often have much trouble in locating the homes of new customers. But one day we were in a middle-class area of Edgbaston with large houses and long drives to the front doors. In such circumstances, one could always use one's tongue to ask for a number, but no one walked around here – they were all in cars. There was nothing for it but to ring a doorbell and inquire as to the number of the house. On this particular occasion, I obviously hadn't learned to choose the words of my inquiry carefully enough.

I rang the bell, standing outside an imposing door. The lady of the house opened the door, and I blurted out: "Are you eighty-seven?" The door was slammed in my face, and I resolved to re-phrase my question in future!

By now, my diary was filling up both with M.W.E. bookings, and opportunities to realise my vision for Torch fellowship groups. This involved going to a place where there was interest in forming a prayer cell in preparation for setting up a group. Once that was established, plans were put in motion for me to return in order to contact the local Social Services so as to introduce myself and my aims. I told of my keenness to integrate blind and sighted people with a view to introducing them to the Christian faith.

The reaction I got was very mixed: sometimes it was really helpful; other times blatantly hostile. There were two schools of thought. One was that blind folk might feel patronised; the other that the blind themselves might exploit their disability. Some even thought that I was exploiting my own handicap in order to press home the Christian message. If this were true, then it was from the highest motives! But I must say that I have tried to be very careful of this danger.

It is certainly true that I like nothing better than to speak to my fellow-blind people about the gospel. I have discovered personally how Christ can bring meaning to the emptiest of lives, and have experienced the life-changing difference the living God can make. In this, I did indeed hope that I could identify with other blind people and, through the example of my own life, influence theirs.

But my interest was not confined to any one group of people: I coveted all people for the kingdom, wanting to bring Christ to anyone who was prepared to listen in whatever walk of life.

For the most part, Social Services were helpful. In the afternoons I would visit clubs for the blind, also visiting some who had recently become blind. Such folk had my ready sympathy, for it's one thing to grow up and be educated and trained for life as a blind person, but quite another to have to cope with blindness in later life.

I recall a good friend of mine, Stanley Miller who had been his firm's rep. He would drive for hundreds of miles, holding down a good job. He and Kathy, his wife, lived in Glasgow with their three children. But Stanley had contracted diabetes, which eventually took toll of his sight. Naturally he lost his job; couldn't drive a car any more, and lost literacy. But Stanley had a strong Christian faith, and set himself to learn Braille, and by that means, and by listening to cassettes, successfully studied for the Baptist ministry in Scotland. Other blind people might have given up and shut up shop, gone into their shell of isolation, but not Stanley! I take off my proverbial hat to him, and all those like him.

I once visited a newly blind man in Devon. I asked him and his wife how they were coping. Fortunately, this man had maintained his sense of humour. I suggested to him that – since he was not able to learn to read Braille, he might consider a Talking Book, which could be supplied, through his local social worker. "Talking Book," says he, "What do I want with a Talking Book – I married one, didn't I?"

I believe that it's not the questions that life throws at us, but the answers we give to those questions that make us or break us. I've often asked myself, does my faith depend on the shifting sands of circumstances, or the solid rock of the truth of God's word?

Having undertaken such an afternoon of visits, it was then a question of alerting the churches to the needs of disabled people. I would often read from Luke's gospel, chapter 14, where Jesus tells a parable of a supper to which all and sundry were invited. Lame excuses were made, so the king sent his servants to get more people to his supper. Still there was room, so this time, the king instructed his servants to bring in the lame, the blind, and the generally disadvantaged of society. From this I would point out that those who could come won't come, and those who ordinarily were not able to come must be given a chance.

Then Jesus said a wonderful thing! "If you do this, you will be blessed".

From these meetings came the workers who would form the backbone of fellowship groups in many towns and cities throughout the United Kingdom.

It was all very exciting and exhilarating. More and more prayer cells were forming fellowship groups, and at the same time, my work with the Movement was increasing with mounting opportunities for missions and house parties. In 1972, the M.W.E. team were leading a crusade in Guildford. Eric Clarke and I stayed with a Mr & Mrs Godden. Charles Godden was second-in-command at the Inland Revenue – a busy man who knew what an all-encompassing job could do to a man. He was interested in all that I was doing and, one morning at the breakfast table he asked: "What's your programme today?"

"Well, this morning I have a school Assembly and a team meeting. This afternoon we have a Ladies' Fellowship, and this evening we have the meeting in the auditorium at church."

Charles Godden then quoted to me these words from Psalm 103: "He knoweth our frame; He remembereth that we are dust …" And then he added: "it's we who forget!" That was a word in season for me. I began to realise that I really couldn't keep this up. In any case, the Movement were paying me a salary to do their work, and yet I was drawn inexorably to the work of Torch Trust.

The Movement were more than happy to finance my work with Torch, even though my feeling was that I was serving two masters.

My admiration for their generosity and kindness knew no bounds, yet I felt that I should dedicate and direct my energies into this vital work of reaching those who were physically and spiritually blind.

After much consideration and conversation with the Torch committee, I went to my M.W.E. friends assuring them that although I was extremely grateful for the support and freedom they had given me to continue my work with both themselves and Torch, I felt now that I was not being fair to them. My time was increasingly devoted to the work of Torch, and yet I was being paid by the Movement. I felt that I ought to be in full-time work with Torch who had suggested that I considered becoming their regional adviser.

The reaction I got from the Movement was kind, and indeed gratifying. They pleaded with me to reconsider. They honestly felt that I was making a mistake, and that they had no complaints about my shared work-load. They very much wanted me to stay on their staff.

The decision was a difficult one to make, but I felt it was right to leave, and reluctantly, they agreed to release me.

So in the summer of 1972 after another Mission – this time in Jersey – and a house party in Switzerland, I joined the staff of the Torch Trust for the Blind as Regional Adviser.

Chapter Twenty-Two

Even Higher Profile

MY WORK SCHEDULE did not let up in the slightest. I remember taking a train journey to Edinburgh, getting off at Newcastle to have a working lunch with a cell group there, and resuming my journey to Edinburgh. There was the time when I attended the Torch committee in Sussex, and next morning taking a plane from Gatwick to Edinburgh so that I could address a coffee morning at Charlotte Chapel.

Leaving the Movement meant a significant drop in salary, and with two children to look after, plus a mortgage repayment each month, our resources were often stretched to the limit. But our heavenly Father knew all about this.

On one occasion, I was staying in the home of the Misses Fraser in Tunbridge Wells. Elsie had held a post in the National Westminster bank and had got to know of the work of Torch when Ron Heath had spoken at the bank's Christian fellowship. We were now forming a fellowship group, and one morning, coming down to breakfast, and having said grace, Elsie and her sister Hilda stood either side of me. Elsie was the spokesman: "We believe that God is telling us to pay off your mortgage," she said.

I was stunned, not knowing what to say, and before I could think what to answer, she continued:

"Please ask your bank to let us know what your mortgage is, and we'll settle it!"

And that was the end of the matter. Nothing I could say would change their minds – they knew that God had spoken, and all I could do at that moment was to get on with my cornflakes!

Margaret and I will always be grateful to these Godly ladies who made a major contribution to our daily lives through their incredible generosity, because they were open to God's leading in the most surprising ways.

By now, Mr & Mrs Heath had begun to travel with me, visiting fellowship groups and telling the Torch family story at deputation meetings in churches all over the country. They came to Tunbridge Wells, staying with me at the Misses Fraser's home.

We had just arrived, and "luncheon was nearly ready," announced Elsie Fraser. Then she turned to me who was sitting on the sofa and asked: "Would you mind playing my Broadwood piano?" I got up, and she led me to the instrument, and as I took up my position on the piano-stool in full view of Ron & Stella, Miss Fraser took my right hand, and planted my index finger on a note, saying: "There's middle C!" Ron & Stella could hardly believe what was happening. How we've laughed about that incident! Fancy feeling that she had to show me, who had been playing pianos, tuning and repairing pianos for years, middle C!

I was now taking in more and more of the United Kingdom, including increasing visits to Northern Ireland. It was at the conclusion of the first meeting of the Belfast Torch Fellowship that a lady approached me:

"I wonder if you will remember me," she said, rather hesitantly.

I was at a loss, until she revealed that she used to be Gwen Brown, but was now Gwen Kennedy. This was Gwen who had been at Bockleton Court thirty-two years ago! The same Gwen who had played duets with Mr. Myers at Condover Hall where I had tuned the pianos. I was simply amazed! Gwen had married Alec Kennedy, a local man, and was mum to Mary and Ruth. Now we had met again, and I know I can say that our friendship has been a strength and encouragement to us both – especially to me.

And so the Belfast Torch Fellowship was formed in February 1971, to be followed by Glengormley, and Lisburn. And it was in Lisburn that one of the M.W.E. Council members had his business and residence. We had met Harold and Meta Patterson at Filey, and when I first became their guest, I didn't realise what a wonderful friendship would develop with them and their family. Since then, I have felt one of the family, and they have been responsible for my ministry in Ulster. They have been a tower of strength to me when it seemed that my ministry was on the line. There are just no words adequate enough to express what I feel about them and their contribution to my life.

These were dark days in Northern Ireland, yet I kept getting invitations from the folk there, and they were genuinely thrilled that we had no fear about coming over. Ron, Stella and I took many deputation meetings in churches; meeting social services, speaking to students at Belfast Bible College, never so much as hearing a bomb or a gun fired in anger.

Added to my schedule by now was the recording of gospel music with Word records. I was constantly amazed as to how well these were received, and it proved to be an extension of my ministry into many homes throughout the country.

In 1972 I was invited to take part in a programme for Radio 2 called 'The Gospel Road', which was hosted by Cliff Richard. Cindy Kent, Garth Hewitt and Adrian Snell were also on the programme – people who are still making a meaningful contribution to the witness of the gospel at this time.

The programme seemed to go well. Cliff interviewed me about my life and work, illustrated by excerpts of piano-playing. He was great to work with.

Before the recording we had quite a lot of fun. I would perform some technical acrobats on the piano, and Cliff would exclaim, "How do you do that!" I retorted, "How do you sing like that!"

I well remember having a fearsome cold at the time. Cliff sympathised, and produced a practical remedy: he handed me a packet of throat sweets. "Try these," he said, handing them to me, insisting that I kept the packet.

Later, when I indulged in a bit of name-dropping to a crowd of teenage girls, their reaction was to ask whether I still had the packet. Somewhat mystified, I simply told them that I'd thrown away the empty packet. They were horrified! "You should have kept it with his autograph on it," they said, nearly in tears.

But I wasn't the only member of the Jackson family to meet Cliff Richard. My oldest nephew Harry (known as 'Al) was a vocalist with the pop group known as 'The Applejacks'. They actually got into the top ten with their single 'Tell Me When'. The group continued to do well for a time, getting openings on radio, television and holiday cruises. Al told me that it was a hectic lifestyle; although the pop scene was intoxicating for many rising young stars, it held all kinds of dangers both moral and physical for the unsuspecting youngsters. My nephew saw what was happening, and after a brief success, became disillusioned with the pop scene, and got out.

For the most part, Margaret was at home looking after the boys, although we all went to a Christian Golfers' week held in the West of Ireland. Each evening, after dinner and presentations to the winners, I was responsible for music and the epilogue.

I woke up on the first morning there with the words "What doest thou here, Elijah?" The previous evening I had been personally introduced to some illustrious people: ministers, businessmen, professors, doctors, and – dear Lindsey Glegg of Filey. I felt totally inadequate – out of my depth, and can only hope that I was able to bring some blessing. In retrospect, it can't have been too much of a disaster since I was asked to do the same at another such week in Scotland.

But, as I say, Margaret had the less prominent part to play, staying at home whilst I continued my busy schedule. I was travelling widely, of course, and it was travelling 'heavy' – not light! I just couldn't waste hours of time sitting in trains doing nothing. So in addition to my case, I carried a portable typewriter with which I could transform each carriage into a mobile office. I carried on my back a Uher reel-to-reel tape recorder. By now I was fully conversant with local radio, and often made recordings, which I would send on ahead of my intended visit to an area for broadcasting.

Donna had now retired, and in any case, my hands were just too full for a guide-dog. On one memorable occasion I was travelling to Hurstpierpoint for a Torch committee. I arrived at Hassocks station from where I was to telephone Torch House, and they would send a car for me. The train was much longer than the platform, so when I alighted from the train, my case in my right hand, type-writer in left hand, recording machine on my back, I proceeded to walk towards the platform proper. However, I was unaware of the effect the weight of a heavy case was having on my equilibrium – as I walked, I was gradually veering towards the railway line! It was a late autumn evening; no-one could see me, and sure enough, with a dreadful shock, I crashed onto the line, together with all my heavy luggage.

The station master was alerted by the sound of my fall. He looked down at me with horror: "What the B hell are you doing down there?" he shouted in alarm. "For God's sake give me your hand and hurry up, the London-Brighton express is due any minute!"

I handed up my typewriter, recording machine, struggled with my case, and made it! I was conscious of a searing, crippling pain in my left ankle, otherwise I was mercifully undamaged. Incidentally, the express never came. There was a partial rail strike that day!

As well as the Torch committee, I had engagements in the Brighton area that week, and so I never gave a thought to going to hospital for an x-ray on my ankle. I just endured the pain, giving it the cold water treatment, and in a matter of a week, it healed. But that was a narrow escape, and a warning not to be too blasé in my travels.

With the care for the disabled on our national railways, such a thing would be most unlikely to happen again. Travelling is much safer nowadays. In the days of the single carriages, one couldn't be sure even which side of the train was the platform. Now, on the inter-city trains, one hears the click, as the automatic doors are unlocked, so one can step out of the train with confidence. I am so grateful today for all the assistance I get from caring staff.

One day I was to take meetings at a church near Sheffield to be guest with a couple I had known since childhood. It was lovely to be with them after so long a time, and as I was drinking a cup of coffee, the lady came downstairs and said: "I've put all your clothes away in the wardrobe and chest of drawers." "Oh no," I thought, "our system has broken down!"

You see, on our occasional shopping expeditions for my clothes, I know immediately when Margaret has decided something is right for me. If she looks at an article and says, "That's quite nice", I know we won't be buying it. But if she says, "That's nice", then that's the one we'll buy!

Our next problem was how to arrange my clothes in the case so that I would know what went with what. This was achieved by buying a case with a large compartment in the lid. Into this Margaret puts the accessories, which go with suit A, and the rest go in the body of the case together with suit B.

This system had worked very well for many years, now it had

crashed! When I got home after this particular visit, Margaret knew immediately that something was wrong about me! "What on earth's happened?" she said as she looked at my mismatched clothes.

Now Margaret ensures that I have colours that blend, so that if I should inadvertently mix things, there's no real harm done.

House parties were very much part of the work of the Movement for World evangelisation: Torch was no exception. Torch House at Hurstpierpoint would be packed with blind and sighted people at Easter, summer and Christmas. Sarah came to a young people's house party in the summer fully equipped. Included in her luggage was a pair of dancing shoes, which she expected to be using most evenings. On the evening of her arrival she came downstairs ready to begin a week of frenzied footwork, but was somewhat confused by the sound she heard. It was not the sound of a three-piece combo beating out a quick-step, but the sound of enthusiastic voices singing spiritual songs! Her heart sank.

"Good grief!" she complained to a friend later, "They're singing

I once was lost but now I'm found,

Was blind, but now I see

– and they're all as blind as bats!"

But it was not too long before she was joining in as enthusiastically as the rest – as a child of God!

Another girl, Frances, was fed up with all the talk about what was involved in becoming a Christian.

"What's all the fuss about?" she asked. "Surely being a Christian simply means that you're good and kind, and you try not to do anybody any harm."

"Would you like to know what the founder of Christianity said about it?" I asked her.

"Yes, I would," she replied. We went into the sun lounge together, still with our supper drinks, and I began to explain what Jesus said about himself in the Bible. "He says 'I am the way, the truth and the life, no-one comes to the Father except through me'." We talked about what this meant for a while. Then I suggested that she prayed, asking that God would show her how to become a Christian on his terms.

Frances happened to sit opposite to me at the breakfast-table next morning. "Good morning, Frances," I greeted her, "How are you this morning?" The reply I got filled me with joy: "I am a Christian," she said. "I asked God to make me one on his terms!"

Dougal was a character! He had some vision, and was a resident at Torch house. He provided us all with enduring memories of times spent in his company. But he'd had a sad life, having been abandoned on a doorstep as a baby, and taken into Barnado's homes. He had carried that rejection with him through life.

Though he had been accepted into the Torch family, he still lived with a subconscious fear that he would be rejected again if he stepped out of line. So he was a Christian. He learned all the right words to say, and joined in all the singing enthusiastically, giving every sign that he belonged.

Once, when we were all out on a country walk, Dougal fell behind. "Keep up, Dougal!" we all called, knowing that it would be safer if we all kept together. "I'm all right!" yelled back Dougal, "I'm not completely blind! I can manage."

We got back in good time for tea. Dougal came in towards the end of the meal: we slow hand-clapped him! "What happened?" we inquired. "Did you get lost?" It was quite evident how much sight Dougal actually had by his explanation. "I fell over a cow!" he said sheepishly!

One Sunday evening we all piled into a minibus and several cars to go to Three Bridges Evangelical church where I was due to preach. I spoke about what it meant to ask Jesus into our lives, not only to be resident, but president. Not only to be the guest, but the host, based on Revelation chapter 3, verse 20.

When we'd got back from the service, Dougal came to me and said venomously: "I hate you!" "Oh dear," I replied, "Why do you hate me?" "Because you have blown my cover," he responded accurately, but malevolently.

Dougal did not appear next morning for breakfast, which was most unusual – he was fond of his food! We all went into the lovely chapel and started singing heartily the words of a gospel chorus:

He sought me, he sought me,
when I was wandering far away.
He found me, he found me –
Oh, what a wonderful day!

We were totally unconscious of the fact that our singing travelled right up the stairs and into Dougal's room. As we were singing, God broke through into Dougal's life! He began to cry, asking God to forgive him and make him a real member of his family.

At coffee time that morning, he came to me and said: "I hated you yesterday, but I love you today!"

Blind people used to come from far and wide to share in these wonderful times. Here, as in meetings in other places, I was often asked to give my testimony and tell how I had come to know Jesus as my Saviour and Lord.

I would illustrate my development as a blind child and hopeful musician by playing some of my early pieces. I would describe how my ambitions changed from show business to evangelism. Then, as now, I would demonstrate the various styles of playing I went through, from my childhood attempts on the enforced classics of school days, and the contrasting dance music idiom of my home in the holidays.

Then I would tell how it all changed when I discovered that God loved me – and always had – and was waiting to show me a new way of living.

I would explain that there is no need to be afraid that we might not come up to God's expectations. God is never disillusioned with me because he never had any illusions in the first place! I pointed out that Jesus offers new life to anyone who is willing to admit defeat and surrender to him.

During the war, Ann Shelton used to sing with the Ambrose orchestra a song about a girl who was wooing a soldier. The name of the song sums up beautifully what this surrender is all about. The song is called "Lay down your arms and surrender to mine!" We're all born into this world as rebels against God by our very nature. God comes to us in the person of his Son, inviting us into his family through the merits of the death and resurrection of Jesus. When we admit to being conquered by him, he makes us more than conquerors! So we could adapt the words of that song by saying from God's point of view: "Lay down your arms of rebellion, and surrender to my arms of reconciliation!"

I try to explain that I consider my being blind a gift from God for special service in his kingdom. It is part of the essential me – something without which I could not be the kind of person I am. I don't regret being me.

I've forgotten the last person I ever saw. It might have been my mum, or the nurse or surgeon in theatre. And certainly I would like to have seen the girl I married! It would be great to see my children and grandchildren, and the exquisite view from our bungalow in Wales, with the varied cloud formations over the mountains and valley. But, written across my eyes are three vital words: 'Reserved for Christ!'

A chorus comes to mind that Miss Richardson, my first teacher taught us:

Wash me, and I shall be whiter than snow.
Cleanse me from sin and its power overthrow.
Come, Holy Spirit, and then I shall know
That the King in his beauty I'll see.

B.B.C. Radio Four became interested in my testimony, and I took part in the Sunday programme with Clive Jacobs. Local radio gave me lots of air time to propagate my ideas of integrating blind people with sighted folk by means of the gospel. The 'In Touch' programme came to Torch House to do a documentary on the work: it was exciting to get such media coverage.

Even the prestigious 'Woman's Hour' on national radio became interested in the work of Torch. They heard that we had a ladies choir made up of staff and residents.

The choir usually sang in three-part harmony, and we got over the problem of not being able to read printed music by playing each person's part on cassette. It was a very successful way of learning, because each person heard their own part independently of anyone else's, so when the choir got together, everyone sang just what they'd learned.

"Woman's Hour" found this intriguing, and presented the choir as an item in their programme.

In 1974 the 'World Congress on Evangelism' was held in Lausanne, Switzerland. It was sponsored by the Billy Graham Evangelistic Association, drawing thousands of delegates from different countries and cultural backgrounds. I went to the Congress, accompanied by Roger Mundy who was later to join Wycliff Translators as a geography teacher in their school in Papua New Guinea.

It was a tremendous occasion, and I remember meeting an American lady who was standing in awe of all the crowds of people swarming around. She turned to Roger and me and said: "My! I was just thinking: if the Lord came now, this place would be mighty empty!"

We met George Beverley-Shea, Cliff Barrows, and I tuned the Steinway piano for Ted Smith, the pianist. Then, too, I had the immense privilege of playing the piano quietly during Communion. This was the second time I had played in a Billy Graham meeting, the first being in the Friends' meeting House, Euston Road, London. He was addressing over a thousand ministers and church-workers.

However, I never did meet him.

The one thing that troubled me greatly was that, with all the 'papers' that were presented and discussed at the World Congress, no mention was made of reaching disabled people with the gospel. I tried in vain to put our point of view across as representatives of Torch Trust for the Blind to no avail – it wasn't part of the programme or plenary session. Whether subsequent congresses have addressed this subject, I don't know, but it made me sad, and not a little angry. Roger with his calm, quiet manner, tried to soothe me, and I respect him greatly for that.

We stayed in a hotel, getting the bus to the Congress each day. On our return to the hotel one day, Roger remarked to me that there was a piano in the bar. I started to play it, but it was grossly out of tune. We were, by now, on excellent terms with the manager. I said to him: "Your piano is out of tune!" "I know," he replied, "We can't get a piano-tuner round here. The nearest one is either in Montreux or even Geneva.

It's normal procedure for me to carry basic tuning tools with me, because I find so many pianos below standard. I said to the manager, "Would you like me to tune it for you?" "You mean, you can tune it?" he asked with incredulity in his voice. I assured him that I could and would. "If you tune it for me, you can bring four of your friends and have as much Fondue as you want!"

I tuned the piano, and Roger and I invited four other people to a grand feast!

The theme of the Congress was: 'Let the earth hear his voice'; but I returned, disappointed that no more disabled people would 'hear his voice' as a result of the first World Congress on Evangelism.

Now the Lord has raised up Joni Eareckson Tada with her 'Through the roof' Trust for such a time as this, and maybe the church will begin to sit up and take notice.

Chapter Twenty-Three

Hallaton Hall

As the work of 'Torch' expanded with more and more people being reached worldwide by the tape, Braille books and large print ministry, and with fellowship groups opening up all over the country, the headquarters at Hurstpierpoint became too small. There were so many people to be accommodated, for as well as the domestic and production staff, there were blind people who just wanted to visit 'Torch House' on a short term basis, others for longer. Special weekends were set aside for tape readers, Braille and large print transcribers. Then there were the house parties.

At Easter, summer for the younger folk, and Christmas. Soon applications outstripped accommodation, and it was clear that new premises would have to be found if the work was to continue to expand.

With mounting excitement the search began. A house of the right size and price was, of course, going to be difficult to find. But eventually Hallaton Hall in Leicestershire seemed to be just right. It stood in its own seclusion, having been a Convent school, and was surrounded by a high wall. The protracted move was made in 1974 – there was so much that had to be transported all the way from

Sussex to Leicestershire. I was as sure as anyone else that this was the right move: so much were we convinced that we began to make plans to move from Birmingham to Hallaton village so as to be near the new Torch House.

Things began well that year. The first house party with its increased accommodation was Easter, 1974. Helen Roseveare, famous author and Congo missionary was our guest speaker. It was a brilliant weekend, and Helen summed it up by saying, "This place gets under your skin, doesn't it!" My ministry that weekend was the 23rd Psalm – eminently suitable for our new, rural setting.

The dawn chorus was beautiful in Hallaton. It was a veritable bird sanctuary. There was a huge lawn that seemed to be owned by the large cedar tree, which provided welcome shade especially in the hot summer of 1976.

We had moved to premises in Market Harborough in September of the previous year: a big decision on our part, and a wrench from all that we had known so well over many years.

In 1976 Torch held its first international conference. It was all very exciting: delegates came from Israel, Parkistan, Australia, Japan, as well as European countries. I remember particularly Joseph and Mary from East Jerusalem; Peter and Pearl Sumner from Australia, and many more. Torch now had become global!

Yet this all contrasted with the uneasy feeling that was growing in my spirit in several ways.

For instance, Hallaton was definitely off the beaten track – miles from the town of Market Harborough, and even more miles from the nearest city, Leicester. There was something like three buses a week to Leicester, and virtually no public means of getting to Market Harborough. My vision was for integration: this was isolation. Blind people were totally dependent on sighted folk to get them anywhere. At that time, the Anglican Church did not cater for us as evangelicals, and the Congregational chapel seemed, somehow, unsuitable.

On Sunday mornings, therefore, a communion service was held which began to be known as a 'Torch communion'. In the evenings, cars and the minibus would leave Torch House, and therefore leave Hallaton village for churches in Leicester, Market Harborough, and even as far as Thrapston, Northampton. I was increasingly unhappy about this situation, and suspicion in the village was growing about what we were!

Something else, too, was beginning to happen about which I find it difficult to write.

The problem arises when the autobiographer has to deal with some things that are intensely subjective. Also, he wants to spare the feelings of people who were involved in what took place. I have to report this honestly yet with sensitivity, for it was to lead to a revolution in my own ministry.

Since the move to Hallaton in 1974, a new aspect of the work started to develop. It grew out of a genuine desire to help some of the blind people – mainly girls – who had been traumatised in their childhood. It began in a small enough way with one or two folk being delivered from evil spirits and released into a new fellowship with God. However, more and more people began to express their need for this type of deliverance ministry.

I began to be involved, too, although I was never totally convinced about the steady increase of its prevalence. At first, I supposed that this could be part of the work, but I was not entirely sure that God would lead in a direction which was in danger of diverting us from the original vision.

Then there developed a further phenomenon, that of prophetic revelations. This is a highly emotive subject within the modern Christian church. There are certain tests and constraints given to the church in the Word of God to prevent excesses in the use of the gift of prophecy. However, it must be remembered that Torch didn't belong to a local expression of the body of Christ, and this doubtless led to some excesses. Outside the discipline and security of a loving church it is virtually impossible to test the credence of the prophecy – or, indeed, of the prophet. Any Christian who is sincerely seeking for God's leading and blessing would certainly listen to someone who purported to have a message from the Lord. Outside of the church, people are very vulnerable, and I am suspicious of any 'revelations' independent of the body of Christ – His church.

Unfortunately, many of the prophecies supposedly received at this time were made against me and my aims for the work. But they were not aimed at me exclusively: others who were suspected of not 'toeing the line' were also targets. But I had, therefore, in all honesty, to look at what I was doing and saying, and pray earnestly that God would reveal to me any way in which I was stepping out of His will.

On Easter Sunday morning, 1977, Margaret and I listened to a cassette that had been given to me the night before from the leadership. It consisted of prophecies that had been written down, and which censured every aspect of my ministry. There were also prophecies relating to the future development of Torch, none of which has been fulfilled. Now I was in an untenable position, for I was not prepared to accept this as being from the Lord, even though the first person singular was used!

I trust that throughout my Christian life I have always been open to change if it should be necessary to avoid stagnation, and to be continually led by the Spirit of God in all I have tried to do. I confess that I was no paragon of virtue at this time of pressure. My actions were dominated by desperation, because my whole ministry to my fellow-blind people was about to finish.

The end came destructively and crushingly. Where I had behaved foolishly, I requested forgiveness, but although God forgives, people find it hard to forgive. Forgiveness must always be a two-way operation, so that nobody feels inferior or superior. We must forgive each other, not so much for one another's sake, but for Christ's sake who forgave us willingly and completely. Why haven't we Christians learned this beautiful thing? In the absence of the world's persecution, we persecute one another.

Not only was I persuaded that my work with Torch was finished, I also was convinced that my ministry was too. One of the names for Satan is 'The Deceiver', and we were all subject to his deception at this time. When he sows these seeds of distrust, nobody trusts anyone. Although, as is always the case in troubles such as this, the supposed offences are augmented way beyond actual events, I felt that I would never regain credibility, and worse still, that God's work was damaged beyond repair. There were times when even Margaret did not know what to believe, and our marriage came under threat.

To compound the sadness of that year of the Queen's Silver Jubilee, a family tragedy took place. My sister Marjorie was ill with terminal cancer, with not long to live. She was to be fifty-eight on 11th November, and my sister Lily thought it a good idea for the family to gather round Marjorie on her last birthday. We all agreed. However, in early November, Lily herself suffered two coronary failures, the second of which proved fatal. We were attending her funeral on Marjorie's birthday!

Barely six months later, we were at Marjorie's funeral at St Johns Church, Harborne. (The church that my first teacher, Miss Richardson, attended.) The minister, Rev. Tom Walker, was a good friend of ours and, during the service he said: "I know this is a sad time for you all. But I am glad to tell you that there is a silver lining even in these heavy clouds of grief. About a month before Marjorie died, one of my curates went to visit her. During the visit, she came to put her trust in Jesus for salvation. Now we know that she is in His presence!"

Margaret and I were thrilled with the news: and on our way out of the church, Rev Tom Walker said to us as we shook hands: "I knew that would bless you!" But for mum, it must have been all very harrowing. Not only had she lost a partner, but now two of her daughters. But as I try to bring it all to mind, she seemed to take it all quite stoically, and of course, Uncle Bert was a great support to her.

But what a year it had been! I had lost two of my sisters, and I was totally devastated. All my bookings were cancelled, and with a heavy heart I wrote to my great friends in Northern Ireland to tell them that I would not be able to visit them any more because I was no longer in a position to represent Torch.

I felt completely isolated. I had no financial backing from anyone, and since my work with Torch had not been conducive to joining a local church fellowship, I could not even enlist the support of a church family. My ministry was finished, and I would never be able to work for God again.

I shared my problems with some of my good minister friends, but they could only commiserate with me – they didn't feel that they could become involved. I was at rock bottom, but 'the rock' was God's word. Psalm 62 ministered to my situation eloquently.

My soul finds rest in God alone;
my salvation comes from him.
He alone is my rock and my salvation;
he is my fortress,
I will never be shaken….
Find rest, O my soul, in God alone;
my hope comes from him.
He alone is my rock and my salvation;
He is my fortress, I will not be shaken.
my salvation and honour depend on God;
He is my mighty rock, my refuge.

Now, of course, I had the additional problem of providing an income for my family. Timothy Fraser was nine years old; Chris was six. Margaret had sacrificed her nursing in order to look after the boys, so there was nothing for it but to return to piano–tuning, but it would take some considerable time to build up a business. What would we do until we were self-sufficient? My despair knew no bounds.

It was the people of Northern Ireland that came to our rescue, especially Mr & Mrs Harold & Meta Patterson. Soon after receiving my despondent letter, they contacted me. They were anguished to hear what had happened, but instead of joining in the condemnation, they went out of their way to assure me that my ministry was far from over where they were concerned. They proved it by arranging opportunities for ministry in the Province, thus providing much needed income and encouragement.

I can never adequately express my gratitude to the folk of Northern Ireland for their help. They gave me more than practical assistance – they restored in me a new hope for the future, and the realisation that God had not finished with me, but was taking me on to something new. I began to discover that past failings are no hindrance to future blessing. Not only did ministry opportunities begin to flow in, but the business at home began to take off.

I received an unusual phone call one day advising me to ring the education office in Leicester. "Don't mention this call," the person said mysteriously. "Just name your tuning prices, that's all." As a result of that strange call, I was given the South Leicestershire contract for schools – I was established!

My independent work as an evangelist and gospel pianist blossomed, with bookings in many places including Northern

Ireland. However, as my work in the regions for Torch was now finished; I was now spending more time at home. This gave Margaret and me time to rebuild our relationship, and it seemed a precious seal from God when Margaret began to expect our third child. Bethanie Claire was born on 20th May 1978 to the great delight of us all.

Yet even in our new joy, there was always a deep feeling of sadness about what had happened between Torch and me, and by this time – some two years later – there was another complication. Margaret and I were told of allegations that had been made with respect to improprieties on my part with two young women at Torch. I knew before God that I was entirely innocent of these allegations, but the rumours spread like wildfire, and I was in no position to refute them. Once again, I appealed to two friends of mine who were in the ministry to try and sort things out. However, the girls stuck to their story, and there was nothing I could do.

I had written many letters up to this time, trying to restore fellowship between us, not willing to come to terms with the anomaly of being out of fellowship and yet 'in Christ', but with these rumours circulating, it seemed to be a situation without hope. I can all too readily recall that desperately sad feeling even as I write in retrospect. Some folk may not easily understand why I have written all this down. They will regard this as being counter-productive; raking over the past; being negative. But I've had to write frankly, putting on record my feelings and failings as honestly as I can in the interests of truth and integrity. And, how else could I show that God's promise was true: "Never will I leave you; never will I abandon you!" He commands light to shine out of darkness. He restores the years that the locusts have eaten. Not only does he walk in the valley with us, he takes us through the valley!

As I write this some twenty-four years after all this happened, I can rejoice in the knowledge that our fellowship has been completely restored; the misunderstandings cleared up, the past buried. We are to learn from the past, not to live in it.

By this time we had also become firm friends with some folk we met through the Filey conventions. Don and Barbara Smith lived in Ammanford, South Wales, and we began to go there for holidays. Barbara taught piano to a good many children, and even during these holidays, I would do some tuning for her. They belonged at that time to a very small fellowship that had no church building, but simply consisted of a few people meeting together in a back room of the local pensioners' hall. They had a thriving Sunday-school. When we were there, I was invited to help with the children, and to give Bible studies to this embryo church. We thoroughly enjoyed our times of 'holiday' in the completely new surroundings of the hills and valleys of Wales.

In 1980, we received a telephone call, which eventually would lead to a new beginning for us all. The call was from our friends in South Wales. They told us that their little fellowship was growing, and that they were now meeting in the St. Johns Ambulance Hall in Margaret Street, Ammanford. But that wasn't all they had to tell us!

"We would like you to come and head up the work for us," they said. "Would you think about it, and pray, and consider moving here to help us?"

We did think and pray, and we didn't take very long to come to the conclusion that this was probably God's way of giving us all a new start after the sadness of the break with Torch.

We agreed to move, but there would be the initial problem of selling our house in Market Harborough before being able to purchase a property in Ammanford. We went on the market, confident of the fact that we were moving with the Lord's approval, and therefore He would see to it that the house sold reasonably quickly. It was going to take all of two years!

By this time, I had been with Andy, my new guide dog for some three years. During 1981, Andy and I took part in a very special occasion. It was the golden jubilee year of the Guide Dogs for the Blind Association. A special service was held in Westminster Abbey. I felt very honoured to be one of those chosen to have tea in the Royal Mews in the presence of Princess Alexandra, the Patroness of the Association. It was suggested that we had a sighted escort, and so thirteen-year-old Tim came with me.

Six hundred guide dogs with their owners and escorts assembled in the Abbey, the dogs settling down for the long wait as the service proceeded.

It was all very inspiring and uplifting, and we eagerly awaited the address from the specially invited guest, Lord Tonypandy, who was at that time George Thomas, speaker of the House of Commons. He looked down at all the dogs lying obediently and patiently at their owners' feet. Then, with his sonorous voice and Welsh accent he said, "I wish...I wish...I could get the same order in my place of work as we have here!"

At the conclusion of the service when the Benediction had been invoked, with one accord the entire company of dogs rose up...and shook! It sounded like a huge flock of birds taking off!

Now it was time to process along Birdcage Walk to the Royal Mews, so Tim, Andy and I proudly went along to be introduced to the Princess along with all the others. The Princess was very charming – a delightful lady – and she spoke very kindly to Tim who was absolutely thrilled.

Her equerry, however, was not quite so thrilled. Andy seemed inordinately interested in getting as close to the Princess as possible. The equerry told me very politely what was happening. I took control of the situation saying, "I'm very sorry, Andy has always been particular about the company he keeps!" The Princess laughed, and the interview was ended.

Chapter Twenty-Four

A Welcome in the Hillside

IT WAS NOW 1982, the year of the Falklands debacle. It was almost two years since we'd put our property on the market. We were concerned, too, that the bungalow we had set our hearts on would be sold to some other buyer. People came to view, but nobody got as far as committing themselves to buy. There were those who liked the property, but they had to sell, and so there was the inevitable 'chain'. Over and over again we wondered if we were in God's will or not.

We began to despair. What could have gone wrong? We decided that we would wait until the end of July. Then, if the house had not sold, that would be final. We would take it off the market, assuming that we had got the whole thing wrong; that God wanted us to remain in Market Harborough.

Our friends in the Ammanford Evangelical church prayed for the situation, and exhibited much more faith than we did. They weren't at all discouraged by the delay, being absolutely persuaded that everything was under God's control, and we needed just to wait on Him.

In mid-July, two sisters came to view the house with their father. They were local girls looking for a place to share. Margaret and I were not hopeful. It seemed very unlikely that two single sisters would want a four-bedroom house.

The girls' father stood with me on the patio whilst Margaret showed the sisters round.

"They'll buy it, you know," the man told me confidently ... "and it will be a cash sale – their firm will be buying it for them – something to do with tax ..." he went on conspiratorially.

We had the money within a week! Excitedly we rang the estate agent in Ammanford to inform him that we could now go ahead with the bungalow we had set our hearts on. "Oh," he said guardedly, "There is already someone else interested in that one now. I'm afraid it will have to go to the one who comes up with the cash first." We put the wheels in motion immediately, beating the other buyer by one day! The beautiful bungalow in Wales was ours!

The move was now scheduled for the end of September, – just two months – during which time I wrote one last, impassioned letter to the founders of Torch Trust. I pleaded with them to come and talk with us about these malicious rumours that had come to our ears. I reminded them that, if we weren't going to meet before we moved to Wales, our next likely meeting would be at the judgment seat of Christ. I so longed to walk in the light with them; to clear the air, and even to find out the supposed details of my misdemeanours. At last, they wrote. Yes, they would meet us in our home, on the Sunday afternoon before the move. We thought – this is real progress: we shall be able to resume good fellowship.

We managed, somehow, to get the children exported for the afternoon, and as soon as Ron & Stella came, we prayed together, asking for help and guidance from the Holy Spirit. Then I asked:

"Do explain to us what all these allegations are about." There was an awkward silence, and I could almost feel them looking to each other, then looking away. There was uneasiness in the very atmosphere. Then Mrs Heath ventured: "We really can't tell you – it's too awful to explain."

Then I said: "Do you really think that – having served God over so many years I would perjure myself before him by denying any involvement with these young women? If I had anything to confess, I would have done it long before now, and repented." More silence! And now I knew that there was no more progress to be made: they were fully persuaded about what they knew! We parted sadly, ... there was nothing more to be said; fellowship could not be established. It has made me unutterably sad to write this, and yet I feel I have to in order to be loyal to the facts of that appalling situation.

In retrospect, we feel that the explanation for all this lies in the practice of praying for the healing of memories. This went on in those days a good deal. Whilst in prayer, past situations would be prayed about, incidents that were painful were recalled and committed to God for his healing. I can see something helpful and beautiful in all of that: but there are dangers too. Where a person might struggle to bring a traumatic incident to mind, the 'Counsellor' might want to encourage memories through suggestions. Imagination could run riot, with more and more dramatic instances. Tears would flow, more assertions be made, and all in the name of the Lord, and for the high purpose of healing.

Whereas it has to be said that in some instances with wise and very careful counselling people have been greatly helped, there has also been irreparable damage caused. This has become recognized as false memory syndrome, and Margaret and I firmly believe that this is what happened in these cases. One of the girls was known to have all kinds of illusions with regard to past relationships, and we have been astounded that she was given so much credence by the Torch leadership. But whatever might be the true explanation of all this, Margaret knows that it did serious damage to me and my ministry, and to us both emotionally.

We moved to Wales with the confidence that we had done our utmost to resolve the situation, and that our hearts were clean before God. What we didn't know then was that it would be some twenty-four years before we felt totally accepted, and thoroughly welcomed back amongst our very dear friends at Torch Trust.

We moved on 28th September in lashing rain! It rained incessantly for two days, yet we knew that we had so much to look forward to – new surroundings, new people, and a new, young church longing for our support and input. Tim and Chris had very mixed feelings about leaving their friends in Leicestershire. It was an awkward age for both of them: Tim was fourteen, Chris eleven. But the one thing they both noticed having hardly been in Wales twenty-four hours was the friendliness of the Ammanford people. They were amazed that although they were completely unknown, people spoke to them with a warm smile, and this was very reassuring to us. Bethanie was only four years old, so the change had no threat for her.

Of course, I would need to have to set up a whole new piano-tuning business again, but I had not experienced too many problems in doing so before, and surely in 'the land of song' there ought to be plenty of pianos to keep in order. Barbara, being a music teacher was a great help, and she put me in touch with another local teacher, and things began to snowball.

My colleagues in the church fellowship were well versed with our problems, but also with the fact as to my independent work as an evangelist, knowing that when I came to join them I would still have a number of bookings to honour elsewhere. They also very graciously mentioned that they did not want to confine God's work by restricting my ministry entirely to themselves. So it was agreed that I would basically spend one weekend every month away, ministering in other churches. But, of course, there were times when I would be away for longer periods especially when visiting Northern Ireland, but I was careful to assure them that my trips away would not interfere too much with the work of the fellowship.

I soon settled in to what I now call my 'double life' – that of a piano-tuner on the one hand, and that of a gospel pianist and evangelist on the other. The former often serves to subsidize the latter, and that's a good thing. It means that I'm not wholly dependent on the giving of churches for my living. This can be a very real problem for those people working full-time in the ministry. So many demands are made on people's pockets and purses; churches have big maintenance bills to meet or building projects in hand, that supporting ministers of the gospel is not regarded as priority in many cases.

In these modern days there seems to have developed a whole new approach to the problem, especially by gospel rock musicians and their like. They now insist on a fee, rather than be subject to the variable, erratic giving of the churches. To meet this demand, churches have resorted to tickets for which people have to pay. Generally speaking, I'm not altogether happy with this near commercialisation aspect of presenting the gospel.

Quite recently, a group in the West country wrote, asking whether I would visit them, and would I please let them know what my expenses would be, and fee. This time I worked it all out – the time off work that I would lose in order to get there. The time off work in order to get back, plus the return train fare. It all seemed rather a big total to me, so I pared it down to £100. A sad letter came back, informing me that I was unaffordable! I vowed there and then that I would never work that way again. As far as I was concerned, that was a missed opportunity, and I'd do anything to hear from those people again, offering my services freely.

Money must never influence where I go. There's an expression around, which one would think should be in the Scriptures, but isn't, "God is no man's debtor". I wonder when that was first coined? But it's true. I have been to a church that can barely manage to meet my train fare: and I accept that willingly. But then, soon after, I will go to another church where they give so generously as to be positively extravagant! The great Provider himself, God my heavenly Father balances it all out. He knows our needs, and we are happy about that. But again, my situation is very different from others who are totally dependent on the generosity or otherwise of God's people.

One evangelist said to me once, rather sourly, "I think some Christians shop in a different supermarket to me." I agreed with him, for I've had the experience of visiting a church in the North-West of England for a few days, not only working in the church, but also in the schools of the area. In that particularly large church, there was plenty of obvious affluence. I was so busy doing what I love best of all that there was no opportunity to 'tent-make' – tune pianos. Yet what that church gave me led us to temporary insolvency compared with the average salary of its members. But then, God is their judge, not me. I just wish they wouldn't lead me into temptation!

To keep the record straight, I must add this too. Margaret and I can look back, remembering those who have been outstandingly generous to us just when we needed help. These are unforgettable to us, and we thank God for them.

If anything, my work in Northern Ireland was increasing. My good friends the Pattersons had become my 'Agents', organising my diary over there, arranging everything. The troubles were still very much to the fore during the 1980's, with much time and coverage being given to the atrocities committed, and relatively little time to what God was doing in the lives of individuals who were prepared to listen, and respond, to the message of salvation through Christ alone. There were those who were coming to the realisation that God was not the God of the Protestants, nor the God of the

Catholics, but the God of the sinner. We're all born rebels against God: Catholic rebels, protestant rebels; religious rebels overtly renegade rebels – but all rebels, just the same.

My visits to the Maze prison were always memorable. There was one time when I was asked for means of identification. I apologised: "I'm sorry, I was refused a driving licence!" But my friend Harold had the answer. "We've got a record of his in the car." The prison officer replied: "Aye, we're interested in people with records!" Harold gave him the record that had my picture on it, and the prison officer duly noted the title, "Just as I am." Said he: "That's just how we take 'em!" We all laughed, and were allowed in with my accordion. I toured the compounds, encouraging the men to sing some of the old hymns, still very much loved in Ulster. I was introduced to men who had become Christians since being admitted on terrorist charges.

On one occasion I was presented with a 'Gideon' Bible in a leather case made in the prison. I brought it back with me to Harold and Meta's, showing it to them with some pride. When they opened it up, they began to exclaim and laugh. "What's the matter," I asked with some concern. "Do you know what's written on the flyleaf," asked Meta. Well of course, I didn't. They read to me this inscription: "God bless you: From the members of the U.D.A., Long Kesh". (The U.D.A. being the Ulster Defence Association, which is an illegal organisation.)

One of my visits to Northern Ireland was scheduled in the week after a dreadful shooting in a church in Armagh. Several of the folk in our fellowship pleaded with me not to go. They felt that this was a new escalation of the violence, which would be focussed on churches. In fairness to Margaret and our church, I rang my friends in Ulster assuring them that I would still love to come over; but what did they think? They put the ball straight back into my court: "We want you to come, but you must make the decision." I was glad to go, with even more prayer support from many people.

My first assignment – would you believe – was to lead a house party, which included twelve ex-terrorists! It proved to be one of the highlights of my ministry: to witness men who would cheerfully have shot each other to pieces, now bonded by the love of Christ! This was something very special. One of the men used to belong to the Irish National Liberation Association. Liam had been on hunger strike in the Maze with Bobby Sands, but came off his protest just in time. Now, here we were, sitting together, eating a roast beef and Yorkshire pudding Sunday lunch. We had wonderful fellowship that weekend – quite unforgettable.

Another feature of my visits to Northern Ireland were the Filey reunions organised by my good friend Harold Patterson. Members of the M.W.E. Council would be at the dinner together with Bible teachers and Filey artists – Dave Pope, Bob Christie, and Ulster's own Eric Clarke. Bob was there with his thinning hair; Dave with his richly endowed head! On one occasion, Bob said to Dave in front of us all, "Lovely to see you again, Dave." Dave replied: "Lovely to see you, too, Bob." Bob then laid a hand on Dave's head: "The Lord hath given, ..." (Then, placing his hand on his own thinning scalp): "The Lord hath taken away": and then all of us joined in: "Blessed be the name of the Lord!"

These were rich times with humour and memories, and I always felt so privileged to be part of it all.

After one of these Filey reunions, I was due to speak at a church in Belfast. Our friend Edith Mc'Connell was to drive a group of us to the church – but Edith got lost in the Falls Road area of the city. She was distinctly nervous: it was just not the place to be lost in as a protestant! Mr Joe Wiggins, a Council member, was sitting in the back of the car. He said innocently in his rather poshly spoken way: "Shall I open the window to get a direction?" As rapidly as any machine–gun fires, Edith said: "Indeed you'll do no such thing, you'll get your head blown off!" We stifled our laughter – Edith was in dead earnest – she was really panicky. She knew the situation better than we did, after all.

In my evangelistic ministry, I have learned not to press for instant decisions. I'm sure there's a place for that in certain types of Gospel Crusades, but it's just not my experience. Yet God has often encouraged me in causing me to meet people he has blessed, sometimes years after they've been at one of my meetings. In Belfast one evening, a lady in her late twenties approached me with her two young children. She introduced herself:

"I've been wanting to meet you for such a long time! You came to our fifth form some thirteen years ago. I remember what you said that day, and I realise now that it was all part of the process that was to bring me to Christ." (And with another hand grip), she said: "Thank you very much!"

I recall meeting a lady in Bromsgrove Baptist church who was in her early forties telling me that she trusted the Lord Jesus Christ for forgiveness and salvation the night when I gave my testimony at a house party in North Wales. She said: "I was twenty-one then: I'm now forty-two!" And when this kind of thing happens, the prayer we learned at school comes to mind which include the words: "Teach us to serve thee as thou deservest; to fight and not to heed the wounds; to toil and not to seek for rest, to labour, and not to seek for any reward, save that of knowing that we do thy will." Yet God, in his love for us and understanding of us, gives these encouragements along the way. we know, too – in the words of the Queen of Sheba to King Solomon: "The half has never yet been told!"

In 1985 my Mum and Uncle Bert celebrated their Silver Wedding. It co-incided with mum's eightieth birthday. I rang up the Birmingham Evening Mail to see if there was any 'human interest' story in this. They jumped at it, and sent a reporter and photographer to my unsuspecting mother and stepfather. The result was an article and photographs about the woman that had celebrated two Silver Weddings with two brothers! I'm so glad I thought to do that because, the following year, Uncle Bert died, to be followed in 1988 by a fatal road accident in which my mother was involved. A carpet salesman from Wolverhampton was coming out into the bright sunlight from Aston Express Way, and at the same time, my mother was crossing the road with a friend. Mum took the full force of the van, never recovering consciousness. She was just eighty-three years old. Earlier that year – (in fact, in January) – Margaret's father died. In the previous autumn, we had seen a spacious property, which included a separate 'Granny' flat, and we suggested to Margaret's parents that all of us would move into Glanamman. We doubted very much whether they would agree: after all, Mr Ozanne had been in Guernsey all his life, and Mrs Ozanne since 1930.

But to our amazement, they agreed; sold up, and we were able to sell our small bungalow and move in to 'Nant Oer', which is Welsh for cold stream!

Harold and Meta Patterson outside Nairobi Cathedral

We believe, now, that Mr Ozanne had some premonition as to his going into the presence of his Lord and Saviour: he would never have agreed to move otherwise. He could wisely see that it would be better for Margaret's mum to be near us: but it was a very sad time for us all. On top of losing her husband, Margaret's mum had the upheaval of leaving her adopted island. It was so hard for her, but she's made of rugged Scottish fibre!

In 1989 my travels went even further afield. Harold & Meta Patterson's son Trevor had taken a teaching post for two years in a Christian school in Nairobi, Kenya. He had many contacts in the Nairobi churches, and the idea was that Margaret and I should go with Trevor's parents to do some ministry, but mainly to have a holiday with Trevor. It was all duly arranged; Harold & Meta so generously paid our air fares, and we paid for Bethanie to come out with us. (She was eleven at this time, and very excited to be going to East Africa.)

However, before going to Kenya, we had to make a terribly difficult decision with regard to dear Andy, my faithful companion.

He had been showing signs of advancing age, and about three weeks before we were due to fly, all but collapsed on the drive after I had taken him for a walk. His back legs had given way.

Margaret and I took him to the vet. who informed us with great sympathy and understanding that Andy's quality of life from now on would be very poor. She said: "He is in terminal decline. Difficult to know just when the end will come."

Would it be fair for us to make the boys responsible for Andy in that condition whilst we were away? Finally – after much thought and deliberation, we made the decision. As I had done with Donna, so I had to do with Andy – lift him on to the table, which to me resembled a sacrificial altar. "I will never replace you," I said to him, and never have!

Bethanie, too, like all of us, was upset at Andy's departure. But at least we felt that this coming adventure would, in some way, help to alleviate the recent anguish.

On the outward flight, Beth was taken on to the flight deck by one of the stewardesses. She peered down at the twinkling lights far, far below.

"What's that village down there?" she asked the crew.

"That 'village' is Cairo," they laughed.

Later she was telling someone about the experience. "I saw the lights of a little village called Cairo way below us ..."

"What?" said her companion: "That's the biggest city in North Africa!"

It's inevitable that I have to carry basic tuning tools with me wherever I go. I was to play during two morning services at the cathedral in Nairobi. On the Saturday afternoon, I was shown the Broadwood grand and, sure enough, it needed my attention. In all, I tuned three grands and three uprights, one of the grands being in a Pentecostal church where I was to play and speak at a prayer-meeting.

The piano, when played, rattled and vibrated alarmingly. It didn't take me long to realise what was happening – there were sundry objects on the soundboard beneath the strings, some nuts and a rather handsome silver pen which the Pastor gratefully put into his pocket! (There was no knowing how long it had been there, nor whose it was!) The average congregation of this particular church was five thousand! We had a wonderful time there, meeting so many lovely people including the Pastor's wife who had a special ministry in making and decorating wedding cakes for the girls who got married in the church. There were so many young people – really keen to be involved in the presentation of the gospel: and keen enough to have all-night prayer-meetings. It was a truly wonderful experience to be in that church – quite unforgettable!

During our second week in Kenya, we travelled out into the bush country to visit Ron & Maggie Briggs and their three children, Susie, Philip, & Naomi. They were missionaries from Northern Ireland, and lived primitively among the Masai people, miles from anywhere. On our way to them we were stopped by fearsome looking Masai warriors armed with spears! Preconceived ideas about cannibalistic tribesmen flashed into our minds. For a moment or two we were filled with apprehension as the men asked Trevor where we were going. (Fortunately, Trevor had a useful smattering of Swahili.) "Bwana Briggs," said Trevor. "Ah, Bwana Briggs!" they shouted happily, waving us on with smiles.

This little family had won the hearts and respect of everyone around them. Ronnie had become proficient in the Swahili language; was a hard worker, and Maggie a real home-maker in spite of the primitive conditions. The only water supply they had had to be brought in by tractor.

The place was so dusty – dust getting everywhere, even changing the colour of one's hair! We declared that we would never again grumble at rain. Much of this dust was volcanic; we were in the region of Mount Kilimanjiro.

One afternoon, we decided to have a picnic by the river. Ronnie said to me: "Tell me what you think these are." I sat down, and he placed my feet in what seemed to me to be trenches. "I've really no idea," I said. "They are elephants' footprints!" replied Ronnie. "This is their route down to the river when they come for a drink." I realised then and there that, as a blind person, I really had very little idea as to the enormous size and weight of an elephant. Dare I say it – this was an eye-opener!

Beth enjoyed the sights of Kenya – the monkeys, zebras, ostriches, and many other animals in the wild. But there was an experience she had with the Masai women which was not so good.

She was, in our opinion, dressed sensibly in trousers in order to get around more comfortably in the bush. (That was our first mistake.) It was important, too, that she wore a cap to keep the overhead sun off her head. Our second mistake was that Beth was carrying little Naomi on her back.

Suddenly, Beth came across a group of Masai women who, on seeing what they assumed to be a girl dressed in boys' clothes, hurled abuse at her! She tried to cover up her hair with the cap to make herself look more like a boy, but it was a hopeless task. The fact that she had a child on her back declared her to be a girl, absolutely and finally in the minds of the Masai women. Beth could do no more than to run back home as fast as possible.

After staying with Ronnie and Maggie and the three children for almost a week, we set off for the final week of our holiday which was to be just South of Mombasa – right on the shores of the Indian ocean.

The weather in Nairobi had been distinctly cool that August. It was obvious to us that Nairobi is somewhere in the region of 8,000 feet above sea level, and that August is their winter. But when we reached the Mombasa area, the weather was completely different. It was like a hot summer's day in Britain. We had a houseboy to look after all our needs; we totally relaxed in the sunshine, drinking passion fruit juice by the gallon! Beth found girls of her own age to play with, both in and out of the warm sea.

That week went by like a dream! It's an obvious truism to say that "All good things come to an end", but we had enjoyed such richness of fellowship, relaxation and renewal, and all through the generosity of our good friends, Harold & Meta.

By now, Tim had completed his studies at the Welsh college of Technology in Abertridwr; had commenced his own business in West Wales, and was soon to be married to Alyth, a local girl of Scottish descent. Chris also was destined to be a piano tuner-technician, and was on a three-year course at Newark in Nottinghamshire. Margaret had started nursing again part-time "to keep," as she says "My hand in".

Meanwhile, our church was growing from strength to strength. We had called a young man, Kevin Adams, to be our minister, and he was to prove of immense value to us. We soon became too big for the St John's ambulance hall, and moved into much larger premises. Things were continuing to go very well.

Chapter Twenty-Five

To This Present Day

THAT'S JUST ABOUT BROUGHT US to the end of the previous edition of this book. So much has happened since the last page of that book, and I feel that I should sum up the last twelve years.

The autobiographer has a problem that the biographer doesn't have. The biographer has parameters – from birth to death. The autobiographer has no such defined parameters. 'Heaven in sight' is a kind of sequel to this book. Having had Helena to ghost write, 'One day I'll see you', I had a problem – I kept on living!

Having now virtually rewritten this book, my problem persists: where do I finish? Will there be yet another book? There is so much more that I could have written even in this book, but I don't want to presume upon my potential readers. I can't and won't assume that they want to hear about every detail of my existence. I believe some long and involved autobiographies assume too much. Yet I must add just a little more.

In the mid '90s our church experienced a purging. The means

was that which became known as the 'Toronto blessing'. Some twenty or so folk left us, which was about a third of our congre–gation. Included in those that left were our very dear friends, the founders of the church, Don & Barbara. They, with the others, had become dissatisfied with our style of worship. Unfortunately, as often happens, there was bitterness and acrimony; barbed criticisms, and letters that would have been better unwritten. To lose such wonderful friends for us was painful, reminding us of the pain we had experienced in the mid '70's.

Yet now, looking back, we can see that it was a purging for further growth. Since that time, under Kevin's sound ministry of the Word of God, our church has expanded significantly, and we now expect to move again, this time into a restored chapel on the main street in Ammanford. Through that particular valley we've now reached an even higher plateau than before.

In 1995, 'Keynote Ministries' was born. The following year, the church 'separated' Margaret and me to the work of our ministry. They laid on a lunch for the whole church; presented us with gifts, and read out letters from churches where I had ministered over the years – letters of kind comment and commendation. It was a beautiful thing that our church did. This happened when I was sixty-five!

That was the year when we became grandparents to Tim & Alyth's twin sons, Alistair & Callum. Six months later, we were grandparents again to Beth's daughter Rebecca – known as Becky.

By the time we crossed the millennium threshold into the twenty-first century, I was travelling more extensively than ever.

Since my experience with the American soldiers during the war, and in view of the debt I felt I owed to their gospel music, which liberated me into becoming a gospel pianist, I had always wanted to go to the States. It had been suggested on many occasions, but nothing had materialised as yet. But in the year 2000, a pastor Alan Robinson from Northern Ireland with whom I had often worked, but who was now in Pennsylvania, invited Margaret and me to spend ten days of part holiday, part ministry in three churches.

To me, this was not only the fulfilment of an almost life time ambition, but it was a kind of pilgrimage. We were received so warmly by everybody. There seemed so much enthusiasm everywhere, and we were delighted to be there. I remember saying to the church in Carlisle, USA: "We live in Wales, which is known as the land of song. But now we feel a tremendous gratitude to be in the land of gospel song!" It was an unforgettable trip, and there are plans already laid for a return visit.

The title 'One day I'll see you' was Helena's inspiration. But, will that be true of you, my reader? It will if we have laid down those arms of rebellion spoken about earlier. And I often wonder what it will really be like when my eyes behold my Saviour.

Just one more incident before I travel on past the back cover!

In the early 1970s I was tuning the piano of a Mrs Dwyer in Solihull. She told me that her son worked as a house surgeon at Selly Oak hospital, Birmingham. I commented that that was where I lost my appendix when I was a lad of eleven, and that I had always wanted to meet the surgeon who had virtually saved my life. "Who was the surgeon?" Mrs Dwyer asked. "A name I could hardly ever forget," I replied. "Mr Gore..." "Oh, Jimmy Gore," she exclaimed. "I believe he is still there. I'll find out, and see if something can be arranged."

True to her word she rang me up some weeks later. "Can you get to the hospital next Saturday morning at eleven o'clock to meet Mr Gore?" "I'll be there," I said. "Thank you so much."

As I waited for him to come into the lounge, my excitement was palpable. Then he came; we clasped hands, and I said: "You won't remember me, but you operated on me when I was dangerously ill some thirty years ago. I've always wanted to meet you so that I could thank you, and let you know that I am living a full life in the service of God."

Then, surprisingly, he said to me: "I do remember you. We didn't operate on all that many blind children: yes, I remember you very well."

It was a moment and meeting I shall never forget. I was told afterwards that there were tears in his eyes; there were in mine too. Yet that meeting pales into insignificance compared with the moment when I shall meet my Saviour.

I said to a man only the other day who professed himself to be an atheist: "Supposing you're right, and at the end of this life there's nothing: there will be no winners. But supposing I am right and you are wrong: surely you will be the loser." It has to be a matter of faith – of trusting God who came in the person of Jesus. If faith is a risk, then I prefer to risk being right.

Just before Jesus suffered for us on the cross, he said to his friends: "Now is your time of grief, but I will see you again and you will rejoice, and no one will take away your joy."

I've surely forgotten the last person I ever saw. It might have been my mum or my Dad. It might have been the nurse that wheeled me to theatre, or the eye surgeon that was to perform the final operation on my eyes. But the next person I shall see will be the Lord Jesus Christ in his radiant glory!

The Jackson family

I know, beyond a shadow of doubt, that this will be my experience. Pondering on this glorious thought one day recently, I wrote the following song, from which I'll quote one verse:

Dear Saviour mine, I long to see you,
To fall in worship at your pierced feet.
To hear your voice that welcomes me to glory,
And join with saints around your throne.
Until that day, my blessed Saviour,
Help me to live according to your Word:
That I may feel no sense of shame or sorrow
When I shall see you face to face.

EPILOGUE

You see, I am loath to leave you. I have had your attention (divided or otherwise) for so long a time. And when one thinks that one has finished a book, there are things that one wishes one could have said, or perhaps said differently: so here is one more attempt. (Dare I presume upon your continued patience?)

I fear that I have not given enough space to the restoring power of the grace of God in respect of my work with the Torch Trust for the blind. There had been a serious breach of fellowship that seemed to be terminal. Yet, Twenty-four years later, fellowship has been restored; wounds have been healed, and I am at perfect liberty to be working with Torch, seeking to integrate blind and sighted people by means of the gospel. How wonderful this is to me!

Forgiving can sometimes be like a pill which is at first bitter, but whose centre is sweet, always leaving a pleasant taste in the mouth. And, from my reading of Scripture, it seems to me that forgiveness is never a one-way exercise. We are constantly exhorted to "Forgive one another". Whenever there's breach of fellowship, forgiveness has to operate on both sides. The building of the bridge of reconciliation has to begin at the same time, and from both ends. O that Christians could learn this lesson! Much of the church's internal persecution would cease, with the result that many more 'disembodied' believers would be brought back into the fellowship of the church.

Visible signs of our restored unity occurred in 2001 when I was invited to take my place on the Torch Regional Outreach

Committee. There was no formal proposal or seconding: I was kind of 'assumed' back on Committee as if I hadn't been away at all. And when I was given the privilege of playing and speaking at the Torch open-day, it was like coming home!

The original vision that God had given me had never dimmed, and it's a joy to be able to include work amongst my fellow-blind people within the wider ministry. If anything, the need is even greater than it was, thirty or so years ago. People are growing older, and in spite of medical progress, visual impairment is still a great problem to an aging population. Then, too, the church in its worship has become more visual with modern computer technology. This tends to isolate visually impaired people from aspects of worship. Recently, I was in a church where even the announcements were displayed on an overhead screen. Generally speaking, churches are making no provision for blind people. Here is an extract from an email from a blind lady in Canada – just to show how international this problem is.

"...In some sense, I find the more Biblical a church is, the less help they are willing to give the disabled. Of course there are exceptions, but there tends to be an openness, an acceptance of people lacking in our high and mighty churches who have 'The Word'. We need to be careful we not only preach, teach, and study the Word, but that it is lived out in the very practical meeting of the needs of others."

The idea of Torch Fellowship Groups is in no way to patronise visually impaired people. We are in this together – blind and sighted people. I have known blind folk find use for their natural gifts in the setting of a Fellowship Group, which may not have been possible in a church. But we need that bond of fellowship and friendship with the local churches, for we are inter-dependent.

So now, I am gloriously busy in the work of the gospel, not only in the United Kingdom, but overseas as well. How long will I continue? (My Margaret often asks that question.) I have gone on record as saying: "I'll go on proclaiming the gospel either till I drop, or I'm lifted!"